Endorsements

"Thanks to your advice, I've been able to stall my foreclosure indefinitely."

M. F. , Wilson, WI

"A year ago my wife and I were facing financial ruin. Thanks to your advice, I was able to discount my mortgage over $9,000."

J. B., K. C., MO.

"I am bankrupt and out of work for over ten months, yet in sixty days, I made $30,000 with your techniques."

S.B. , Greenville, MI

"Using your advice, I filed bankruptcy over two years ago but never finalized it. It doesn't show on my credit nor do creditors contact me anymore. Thanks."

P.S., St. Louis, MO.

"I settled a $14,000 judgment for $1,234 and had it completely removed from my credit reports thanks to you."

G. V. , New York

"You saved me $500,000 in less than one hour with your asset protection program. Thanks."

D. G., New York

"I stalled a foreclosure three years, eliminated all payments and virtually lived 'rent free' with your advice."

A. L., Los Angeles

"Two weeks ago I was broke with bad credit and judgments against me. I now have a monthly income of $27,575 because of you. Thanks."

S. S., Snowcamp, N.C.

"I am a janitor making $1000 per month. Following your advice, I tripled my income in thirty days with no-money-down."

A. P., Pueblo, CO.

Formulas for Wealth

How to Create a Fortune in Real Estate

Richard C. Powelson, Ph.D.

Skyward Publishing
Dallas, Texas

Publisher: Skyward Publishing, Inc
              Dallas, Texas
              Marketing: 813 Michael
              Kennett, MO 63857
              Phone (573) 717-1040
              Fax (413) 702-5141
              E-Mail: skyward@sheltonbbs.com
              Website: www.skywardpublishing.com

Library of Congress Cataloging-in-Publication Data

Powelson, Richard C., 1929-
    Formulas for wealth / Richard C. Powelson.
       p. cm.
    ISBN 1-881554-08-2
    1. Real estate investment--United States. 2. Real estate investment--United States--Finance. 3. Real property--United States--Purchasing. 4. Real estate business--United States. I. Title.

HD255 .P69 2001
332.63'24--dc21   00-052239
                                              CIP

Contents

A Message from Richard C. Powelson, Ph. D.   7

Myths and Facts   13

PART I: BUYING NO-MONEY-DOWN   19
1. No-Money-Down   20
2. What No-Money-Down Means   26
3. Getting Started   29

PART II: REAL ESTATE: YOUR BLUEPRINT
         FOR SUCCESS   39
4. Realtors and What You Need to Know   40
5. Rules for Buying No-Money-Down   47
6. How to Pick the Right Realtor   55
7. Elephants Don't Bite   64
8. How to Become a Winner in Real Estate   71
9. Weasel Clauses and Special Clauses   112

PART III: FINANCING: THE KEY TO REAL
          ESTATE SUCCESS   123
10. Make Financing Work for You   124
11. The Creation of Wealth Formula   128
12. Introduction to Financing   134
13. Creative Financing   145
14. Creative Ideas for Notes and Loans   163
15. Becoming Wealthy Using Notes   171

PART IV: MORE ABOUT LOANS, NOTES, AND
          OTHER CREATIVE IDEAS   177
16. Managing Payments   178
17. Managing Your Transactions   195
18. More Ways to Grow Rich   208
19. Other Techniques   214
20. Lease-Options   231

PART V: BONDS: THE GREATEST FINANCING
          TOOL OF ALL   255
21. Creative Use of Bonds   256
22. Problems and Solutions   266
23. Benefits of Using Bonds   274
24. Other Uses for Bonds   282
25. Build Cash Flow   292
26. Using Bonds to Buy or Sell   297
27. Everyone Wins   305
28. Try One of These Ideas   312
29. Tax Implications   318
30. A Final Note about Bonds   324
31. Creative Ways to Become a Millionaire   330

A Message From
Richard C. Powelson, Ph.D.

In your hands are proven methods for always getting what you want, secrets so powerful that this information will allow anyone with the belief, desire, and proper attitude to become financially independent. When you learn to use them, you absolutely cannot fail. You will look back and wonder why no one ever taught you this information in high school, at college, or at the university. This information is, in fact, so practical that it could, if used properly, make most jobs obsolete.

It is true that we are all interested in becoming financially independent and being able to do whatever we want in life. Most of us are interested in making money, and all of us would like to be our own boss. Wouldn't it be nice to have the option of going to your boss and saying, "Boss, I quit." Your boss would probably say something like, "How can you quit? Look at the economy. Others are laying off workers or forcing them into early retirement." If he's curious about your new change in mindset, he might even ask you to share with him the secret so he can quit, too. You can smile with confidence and reply, "I upped my income. Up yours."

Believe in Yourself

Sadly, however, the majority of the population feels financial independence is out of their reach. Those who do believe are told that it won't work, or they are made to believe that they can't make it on their own. They are reminded of the old adage: To make money, it is necessary to first have money or just be lucky. Unless one is lucky enough to win a large amount of money in the lottery, marry into money, or inherit it, most are taught that it is best to just accept their fate in life. Sure, if a person has money, that individual might get lucky in the stock market, but how many actually have enough money to gamble on this happening?

People in America are taught by verbal comments and by role models that the best way to make money is to get a job, work from nine to five, and save. Upon retirement, this savings and social security are supposed to amply take care of them for the rest of their lives.

But let's examine the real facts. Ninety-five percent can't afford to retire at age sixty-five. With the cost of living increasing at a rapid rate, most couples today need two jobs just to survive, let alone get ahead, so saving money is out of the question. The money earned on the job is readily eaten up in taxes, and few have real job security, even if working for the government.

Most Americans have two dreams: to own their own home and to go into business for themselves so they won't be dependent upon others for survival. The problem with buying a home is that 50% of all Americans can't qualify for a conventional loan and 70% have a blip on their credit reports from time to time. Going into business is also risky since 90% of all businesses fail within a few months. To top it off, if a person even considers the possibility of owning a business, there are all those folks around who continually remind that person that he or she can't succeed in running a business.

People soon believe that they aren't smart enough or intelligent enough to make it on their own. The only way to succeed or be financially secure, according to the majority of those in society, is to get a job.

Perhaps you work for a boss, as most Americans do today. What happens, through no fault of your own, if you lose your job? When you lose your job, you may find yourself without good credit, without money, and without a job.

Jared experienced this exact situation, and having no place else to turn, he opted to give real estate and my methods a try. His dad was very negative, however, so Jared, on his own, bought and sold real estate and made over $60,000 cash in just three months. He deposited it into his checking account and, since he was very proud of his accomplishment, he showed his new savings to his dad. His dad replied, "I don't care what you did. It still doesn't work. Get a real job!" This was the response, in spite of Jared's success.

When you try my methods, some of you will experience exactly the same response from family members and friends. Just say, "I agree, but making all of this money is just too much fun to give up." Then forge ahead, just as Jared is doing, and make your thousands or millions.

What you are about to read is not taught in high school, college, or in real life, yet it is so practical that anybody can do it. In fact, real estate agents are not taught what you are about to read. I know because I have often taught them how to pass the standard exam. However, if you learn the invaluable lessons here, you cannot fail to make your hopes and dreams come true. And, as you will later discover, it's not going to be difficult or require long training on your part. With as little as two hours per week spent on this course, you can easily accomplish your goals.

The only person or thing that will hold you back is you. If you're not careful, you can become your own worst enemy. You don't need a job, money, or even good credit to accomplish and get what you want in life. All you need do is learn the information and just imitate one or more of the techniques. I can't force you to do it, but for those who believe, this information will lead toward success and help you achieve your dreams.

Have a Written Agenda

Definite plans produce definite results. Indefinite thinking typically produces no results. Unless written, plans can become lost in the shuffle and excitement of daily activities and responsibilities. Without written goals or plans, memories may become hazy. Written goals serve as a reference or reminder of your needs, wants, and desires. Having a written goal, you know where you are going and where you are growing. In plain words, you tend to gain from life the exact rewards you expect to achieve and receive.

Our mind is creative, and conditions, environment, and all experiences in life are the result of our habitual or predominant mental attitude. The attitude of our mind depends entirely upon what we think. Therefore, the secret of all achievement and all possessions depends wholly upon our method of thinking.

Those who succeed in life realize that perception becomes reality. This is true because we must *be* before we can *do*, only to the extent that we *are*, and what we *are* depends upon what we *think*. It is our attitude toward life that determines our experiences. If we expect nothing, we shall have nothing. If we demand much, we shall receive much in return.

It is important to remember to avoid mental patterns of poverty or failure. The saying, "The rich get richer and the poor, get poorer," is oh, so true. Most of the rich think positively on a daily basis, although they may not be aware of it. They live their lives surrounded by riches and the evidence of riches is continually filling their consciousness; they regularly attract more and greater riches, which are ever refueling their consciousness with an image of wealth; they thus attract more and greater riches to themselves. The mind actually attracts what it thinks about during the day.

Those who have less wealth constantly think of what they need and are forever talking about it. Without their being aware of it, their minds are filled daily with *need* images. They are often the very people who readily complain, and if something doesn't work the first or second time they try it, they give up, saying, "It won't work," when, in fact, it would or could have worked had they put more time and more effort into making it work.

Their more successful counterparts, on the other hand, with a proper attitude would find a way to make things work and would keep trying until something did work.

Remember that we tend to become what we imagine ourselves to be. Do you want to be more successful? Are you currently being paid what you think you're worth? Do you want to be more productive? Would you like solutions to problems? Do you want to be more decisive and positive instead of being loaded down with doubt, worry, fear and being told you can't do it or that it won't work?

If so, avoid mention of any old habits or conditions you wish to discard or eliminate. Forget competing and start *thinking creatively*. And always remember that what you speak about, you must think about. What you think about, you must bring about.

Be a Critic

From beginning to end, I want you to be a critic. If any time while reading this book you say to yourself, "I can't do this, or it won't work for me," just stop reading this book, and put it away. To read on would be a waste of your time because what I write does work and has worked for many.

Keep in mind that the only thing separating you from the many who succeed is your own thought processes, the attitude you hold in your mind. If you do wish to proceed, I want you to put aside all negative thoughts and concentrate on what is within the pages of this book. It can and will change your life.

This information has helped more people achieve their goals than any other information on the market today. Only when a person wants, needs, accepts, and sincerely appreciates help, and above all else, puts forth enough effort to help himself or herself, can that person truly turn life around and start climbing the ladder that leads to success.

This information was designed strictly for people who understand that if you want to make more money in one day than most people make in one month or one year, you must take advice from one who has already done it. I have. I know it works.

You have two opportunities that can change your financial life today: 1) read my words, every word and 2) act on them. Both are your choices and your choices alone.

To succeed, it is not what you say or know, it is what you do that counts. That's a true statement for all of us. Galileo was quoted as saying, "You can't teach a person anything; you only help him discover it for himself." That's what this information is about—helping you discover for yourself what you are going to do with the rest of your life.

You Can Achieve Your Goals

How long it takes for you to achieve your goals is totally dependent upon you. Some people use this information to make $5,000 their very first week while others take six months or longer to start making money. I had one student who waited two years before starting, and he only used the information to purchase his home.

He walked out of the closing with $9,000 cash in his pocket, and all he did was follow my instructions.

Mark Twain was quoted as saying, "Inherently, each of us has the substance within to achieve whatever our goals and dreams define. What is missing from each of us is the training, education, knowledge, and insight to utilize what we already have."

The attitude of your mind necessarily depends on what you think. Therefore, the secret of all achievement and all possession depends upon our method of thinking. Our future is entirely within our own control. It has been said that the best way to predict the future is to create it yourself. I'd like to be a part of that creating of your future. If you have the desire, there is nothing that can't be accomplished.

Good Luck!

Myths and Facts:
Buying and Selling Real Estate with No Money Down

MYTH: There is no such thing as a no-money-down sale or purchase in today's economy.
FACT: No-money-down transactions take place every day. The only reason realtors say they don't is because they don't know how to do it themselves.

MYTH: Some lenders will tell you they will not make a loan without the buyer putting up some sort of cash down payment.
FACT: Many lenders will allow the buyer to use something other than money as a down payment, allowing the buyer to buy using none of his or her money.

MYTH: Sellers always get the maximum amount when selling.
FACT: 80% of all sellers don't sell for what they could get using alternative methods of financing.

MYTH: Buyers tend to buy and pay what the property is worth.
FACT: 80% of all buyers pay too much when buying.

MYTH: Most Americans can qualify for a conventional loan.
FACT: Over 50% of all Americans can't qualify for a conventional loan.

MYTH: The majority of Americans have good credit.
FACT: Over 70% of all Americans have a blip on their credit reports from time to time.

MYTH: There aren't enough real estate agents to work with.
FACT: There is one agent for every 345 Americans.

MYTH: All agents are created equal.
FACT: They are created equal by passing a qualifying test, but very few are creative or successful. They are not taught how to solve problems or be creative in buying or selling. I know. I taught them how to pass that test.

MYTH: You must have good credit, a job, and money down to buy real estate.
FACT: You don't need money down, a job, or good credit to buy. You just have to know how to do it.

MYTH: You must use a conventional lender to buy real estate.
FACT: More sales are made bypassing conventional lenders than made through them.

MYTH: You cannot assume a non-assumable loan.
FACT: You *can* assume a non-assumable loan, but you have to know how to do it.

MYTH: If I can't sell for my mortgage balance, my credit will be ruined.
FACT: You can sell for even less than your mortgage balance and not have your credit affected.

MYTH: There is no way to turn a negative cash flow into a positive one.
FACT: You can turn any negative cash flow into a positive one by knowing how.

MYTH: You can't sell for no-money-down and still get all cash.
FACT: You can sell for no-money-down and still get all cash.

MYTH: The agent asks, "If you buy for no-money-down, how will I get my commission?"

FACT: You can buy for no-money-down and the agent can get his or her commission in cash.

MYTH: Buyers can't get paid when buying real estate.
FACT: Under the right set of circumstances, buyers can buy for no-money-down and walk out of closing with cash. In fact, you can make a living buying real estate, getting paid every time. I have students who have become millionaires buying real estate yet can't qualify for a bank loan. One student made 3.5 million in 45 days buying for no-money-down.

MYTH: You need to live in a big city to be successful investing in real estate.
FACT: You need to know how to invest to be successful. I have one student who is a millionaire and has close to a $200,000 per year positive cash flow in a town of 12,000 population. He buys using none of his money and gets paid every time he buys.

MYTH: I'm too old. I'm too young. I don't have any education. I can't do it.
FACT: Age and education make little difference. If one has the proper desire and belief, anybody can do it. I've helped 14- and 80-year-olds buy real estate using none of their money and not having to qualify for a conventional loan.

MYTH: This particular no-money-down technique won't work on a particular purchase, so no-money-down doesn't work.
FACT: There is no single technique that will work *every* time, but there *is* one that will. You just have to find and use it to be successful.

MYTH: Some say, "You can't do it—you're wasting your time. Forget it and get a job."
FACT: If you have the desire and belief, there is nothing you can't accomplish. The critics just don't know how to do it.

MYTH: You have to be licensed to buy and sell real estate.
FACT: You don't need to be licensed. In fact, many times a license is a hindrance.

MYTH: Again, all agents are created equal, so it doesn't make any difference which agent you use.

FACT: You can literally get an agent to work for you free just by picking the right one.

MYTH: Agents are open to new creative ways to buy and sell.

FACT: Agents are reluctant to change and won't accept or understand anything out of the ordinary, so many times they refuse to submit an offer.

MYTH: Agents don't have to submit your offer.

FACT: By law, agents must submit every offer regardless of what it is. If they don't, you can report them to the real estate commission and have their licenses suspended or revoked.

MYTH: The agents will buy the bargains themselves, so I won't get any good deals.

FACT: Some agents will, but the huge majority won't. They are not taught how to buy but rather how to sell and list.

MYTH: It's impossible to buy for no-money-down and never make a mortgage payment.

FACT: I have 10 ways you can buy for no-money-down and never make a mortgage payment.

MYTH: There is a Due-on-Sale Clause; therefore, the existing financing plays no part and you don't need to know that before making an offer.

FACT: You can buy regardless of the fact that there is a Due-on-Sale Clause, and the loan will not be called. You must know the existing financing to help you in making an offer.

MYTH: It's not important why the seller is selling. In fact, it's none of your business.

FACT: Always ask the reason a seller is selling. You may be able to solve the person's problem without giving cash.

MYTH: The seller won't help with seller financing. Why is that important anyway?
FACT: Over half of all sales are made with some sort of seller financing.

MYTH: Lenders feel that if a buyer has a cash down payment, it will cut the possibilities of having the loan go bad and having to foreclose.
FACT: There is no correlation between what the buyer puts down for a down payment and the number of foreclosures. I've seen people pay all cash and *lose* their homes because they can't pay the taxes. In addition, if the market value of the property falls to less than the mortgage balance, common in many areas, the lender will foreclose regardless of the down payment made initially. Foreclosure rates are higher now than they have been for years.

MYTH: Once a foreclosure starts, there is no way to stop it.
FACT: You can stop and, in some cases, even prevent the lender from foreclosing.

MYTH: Once a foreclosure takes place, both the lender and the owner lose.
FACT: True, if done the conventional way. However, it is possible to eliminate all foreclosures and at the same time insure both the lender and the borrower of no loss.

MYTH: 80% of all real estate failures are due to a lack of financing.
FACT: 80% of all real estate failures are due to a lack of knowledge of financing.

MYTH: You can't buy real estate when you have bad credit.
FACT: You can buy properties regardless of your credit. In fact, I'll give you 11 ways to do it.

MYTH: Agents have an open mind when it comes to selling your property.
FACT: Most agents have a closed mind when selling and are reluctant to try anything they don't understand. As an example, selling

under a lease-option is an excellent if not the best way to sell, yet agents are reluctant to do this because they don't get a commission until the closing happens.

MYTH: Agents are very knowledgeable in how to buy and sell their own homes.
FACT: It's easy to sell or buy for somebody else, but when it comes to actually doing it themselves, they have the same nervous feelings you have. I had two students ask me how to buy and sell their own homes. One worked for HUD and the other for FHA. Two other agents called and asked me to define equity.

MYTH: I won't know if I'm successful after buying until I see what happens to the market place.
FACT: You make your profit when you buy—you realize that profit when you sell.

MYTH: I don't know what questions to ask, so I can't succeed.
FACT: The questions are in this book—just copy and ask them.

MYTH: I'm not smart enough.
FACT: All you need is common sense. Apply that and you'll be successful.

QUESTION: What real estate should I buy if I'm investing in it?
ANSWER: All real estate is good in good times, but you need to buy something that is good all the time, so buy something people have to have--a place to live.

QUESTION: If I concentrate on what people have to have such as a single-family home, are there enough opportunities?
ANSWER: 12,000 people move every minute! What does that tell you?

QUESTION: What do I do first?
ANSWER: Read this book. If you are interested in further information or help, please do not hesitate to call or write.

PART I

BUYING
NO-MONEY-DOWN

1

No-Money-Down

I'm often asked, "Can you still buy real estate for no-money-down?" Perhaps you're questioning this yourself. Maybe you've heard comments such as "It can't be done" or "It's illegal." Lenders, at times, won't allow no-money-down offers and others will say no-money-down no longer works. Yet, if done correctly, not only is it possible to buy and sell for no-money-down but it is possible to pocket cash with this type deal. Then why do some lenders say that it can't be done? Because they don't know how to do it.

Before we go any further, let me explain what I mean by no-money-down. No-money-down doesn't necessarily mean that the seller doesn't get some cash, or even all cash, and the real estate agent doesn't get a cash commission. It just means that the buyer is buying without using personal money. If done correctly, everyone wins. There are no losers. A person can even offer to pay all cash yet buy without using personal funds and make $25,000 or more with each transaction.

You Don't Need Good Credit

You don't need good credit, a job, or even cash to make this offer. In this book you will find methods so powerful that you can actually use real estate as a business while working out of your home. A telephone and fax machine can make you $250,000 a year, and if you don't like getting up early every morning and getting dressed to leave for the office, you can do this work in the privacy of your home while dressed in your finest underwear.

You'd be amazed at how many sales are being lost because the agent doesn't understand the power of a no-money-down sale. Given the right set of circumstances, almost any property can be bought and sold for no-money-down. I know one agent who sold sixteen properties over a two-month period, all with no-money-down, and another who actually got out of the real estate broker business because other agents didn't understand his methods. He now makes over $500,000 a year and owns nothing other than his own home. His story is included in this book.

A Few Questions

Let me ask you a few pertinent questions. Do you own something that is worth less today than you paid for it? Have real estate values gone down in your area? Are you having a problem renting out something you own for the mortgage payment? Maybe you have bad credit, no job, have no money, and can't qualify for a loan. Would you like to learn how to get a lender to say *yes* after already saying *no?*

Everyone Wins

In all honesty, if lenders would adopt my methods and follow my advice, it would be *impossible* for them ever to make bad loans. Think about this—the buyer buys for no-money-down—the seller sells for no-money-down, and the lender makes the loan without risk. In this scenario, the best thing that could happen to a lender is that the buyer defaults. In that case, the lender doubles invested money and never experiences a loss.

If the buyer performs as agreed, the loan gets paid off, and the buyer gets back all mortgage money. How would you like to take out a thirty-year loan for $100,000, pay it off, write off interest and other expenses over that time frame, and then have the U.S. Government write you a check for $100,000 as a reward for paying back the loan? How many loans do you think would go into default if the borrowers knew that if they paid off a loan, they would, as a bonus, get all invested money back?

Even if a house purchased for $100,000 dropped in value to $80,000, the borrower would end up with a free and clear $80,000 home plus $100,000 cash in the bank. Who cares if values drop?

And, what if the value actually went up as has happened in the past? Think of the profits that can be made from just investing in one single-family home. As an investor, you can literally buy just six houses for no-money-down and become a millionaire in a few short years.

Yes, you can be that investor. In fact, if you are renting, you are buying for someone else. Your rent makes someone's mortgage payment.

If you are seriously looking to go into business for yourself, why not consider investing in something that everyone needs and is buying? Why not invest in your future? You deserve a good life, too.

Worried about the Competition

As a new investor, you might worry that there is too much competition. Forget the competition. There really is nothing to worry about there. The average agent is not your competitor since most won't get involved in no-money-down transactions. They are trained to sell, not buy. They are told that in order to make money, they must make commissions. Commissions come from selling and listing.

I remember many years ago when I got started in real estate with my dad. He had his own real estate and insurance agency and had three salespeople. Multiple Listing Service was nonexistence then, and all listings were "open" listings, and agents did not share information. In fact, I remember several agents who actually crossed the street to avoid the possibility of carrying on a conversation with another agent. In those days, women didn't sell real estate either. I dare say that women today make the majority of sales.

Many agents, then, didn't even have to pass an exam and could get a license by just writing and asking for one. I passed the Broker exam when I graduated from college, but most agents didn't bother to take exams.

If you had gray hair back then, which I now have, you had credibility. If you were young, owners and buyers tended to not trust you.

And dress code has also changed.Have you ever noticed how all bankers dress alike, as do attorneys and doctors? Well, real estate people were no exception. Instead of suits, however, the standard dress for real estate agents was loud sport clothing. Agents drove only Fords or Chevrolets for the most part because they didn't want to appear too successful for fear they wouldn't get a client's business.

Being young and aggressive, I decided that in order to succeed I had to do something different. I've operated all my life with this philosophy. I find out what everybody else is doing and then do something different. I said to myself that if agents in general wore sports clothes, I was going to wear three-piece suits. If they drove Fords and Chevys, I was going to drive a Cadillac.

A Gold Cadillac

I'll never forget it. I bought a used gold Cadillac, and was it ever pretty! There was no other car in town like it. I drove that car around town for two weeks to be sure everybody saw it. Would you believe that I received not one but several phone calls from other agents in town telling me that I couldn't drive a Cadillac and wear a suit and be successful selling real estate. When I asked why, they all said because I looked "too successful" and nobody wanted to do business with somebody who was too successful. I even joined a country club, and you should have heard the criticism I received. I replied by saying that I felt that people actually preferred to do business with successful people, not the other way around.

Times have sure changed. What do real estate agents drive now? A Cadillac, Mercedes, Lincoln, or other such cars. If nothing else, I lay claim to helping the real estate industry change its dressing and driving habits. So, the next time you see an agent driving an expensive car or wearing expensive clothing, please think of me.

I'm sure you are wondering how successful I was using this approach? I sold forty-seven houses that year, which was a lot at that time, and bought thirty-five, all for no-money-down, I might add. I made more money buying the thirty-five than I did selling the forty-seven.

Well, back to my story about agents not buying property. My dad also owned 10% interest in a travel agency that allowed him and my mother to travel around the world for very little. He was a history teacher who never made or had a lot of money, but this small ownership allowed them to look at places and things dad had been teaching about for years. Since I was the only other Powelson around, I was in charge when he was gone.

When Opportunity Knocks, Open the Door

During one of their many trips, I was in the office one day when a lady came in wanting to sell some acreage she had just north of town fronting on a major thoroughfare and next to what was to become a tollway to Chicago. The land was zoned for residential use only, but if it could be re-zoned commercial, the value would go up dramatically. I immediately saw an opportunity that if I could personally buy the land instead of listing it and selling it to somebody else, I could make much more than by just selling it. So, being naive, I literally said to the woman that if she'd take X amount of dollars, I'd buy it myself, never believing that she'd even consider my *low* offer.

Much to my surprise, she called the next day and said she'd take my offer. Then, I panicked. I had no money and had yet to learn how to come up with money or borrow it. So I applied the ultimate no-money-down technique. Since I had access to my dad's checking account, I just wrote a check for the land. Even in those days, before no-money-down was even heard of, I purchased some land using none of my own money.

Eventually my parents returned home, and I had to tell my dad about the transaction. Needless to say, he wasn't very happy. I will never forget his words: "Son, you don't *buy* real estate; you *sell* it. Even my dad didn't believe in investing himself but only looked at real estate as a way to make a living.

I said, "Dad, this is a super opportunity, and we can make a lot more money than we could if I just sold the land." I should mention that the title was taken in my dad's name. I felt that only fair since I used his money to buy. I will never forget his response: "We'd better make money!" The way he said it bothered me for a spell but not for long. I lucked out. We were approached about selling the land, which I had just purchased using my dad's money, and the offer was 1,000 times more than I had paid. Needless to say, my dad looked upon me with a bit more respect. In fact, the purchasers stated that they needed more land, and if we could get our neighbors to sell, we could make several commissions as well.

I'm sure you can guess that my dad's faith in me was renewed. He was able to do what he liked best, sell for commissions. However, there was one drawback. Because the purchaser wanted to remain anonymous, we had to promise not to reveal the purchaser's name to prospective sellers. I wish I could say that I negotiated all this, but my dad played the prominent role. I just got him to this point. It was up to him to convince our neighbors to go along, which they did. Eventually, everything closed smoothly, and we ended up with a huge profit and several more commissions to boot.

Interested in knowing who the buyer was? Ever heard of McDonald's? It was one of their first few purchases. If you ever have the opportunity to drive up Lake Street between Aurora, IL and N. Aurora, look for a McDonald's just as you are about to enter the tollway (at least at that time) to Chicago. For a short time, I was the owner of that land.

Needless to say, my dad was now elated that he had been out of the country and that I had taken it upon myself to buy that land—which would never have happened if he had been in town. My bonus was enough to pay off my existing mortgage on my home.

However, before you begin patting me on the back, let me complete the story. McDonald's was so satisfied and happy with our performance that they offered me the opportunity to have that McDonald's restaurant for a small investment of just $10,000! Me—sell hamburgers? Never? I passed it up and have been regretting it ever since. I could have done both very easily. Since I'm now becoming a member of that older, wiser generation, I, like so many others in this age group, don't regret what I did but what I didn't do. This is something I regret.

2

What No-Money-Down Means

It is essential that you understand the no-money-down techniques as outlined in this section. Refer to these techniques as often as is necessary. Once you grasp the concept of no-money-down, the rest is easy. Again, a no-money-down offer simply means that the buyer is buying using none of his or her personal money. Someone else is supplying the money. This could be the seller, a lender, a partner, an investor, or other entity. Nor does it mean that the seller doesn't receive some cash or that the real estate agent doesn't receive a cash commission. Buying for no-money-down is perfectly legal and, if done correctly, is a "win/win" situation for everyone involved.

If people tell you that you can't do it, just remember that the reason they tell you this is that they don't know how to do it themselves. If an agent tells you that you can't buy real estate for no-money-down anymore, ask that agent if he or she has ever sold a home with VA financing.

Start with the Concept

To give you a better understanding of the concepts used here, let me start with an easy example. Let's take a property with a value of $100,000. This could be any priced property, so don't get hung up with the $100,000 figure. Just get a handle on the concept. This property can have an existing loan on it, or no loan at all, but most properties have some sort of loan already on them. If this is the case, the loan can either be taken over by a new buyer, or it must be paid off when the title is transferred. If it can be assumed, this can be done "with qualifying" or "without qualifying."

When you read an ad or an agent tells you that a loan is assumable "without qualifying," that simply means that anyone can take over the loan regardless of personal circumstances. A person can have bad credit and no job or income and still take over the payments on that existing loan. Most of these loans are older FHA or VA loans.

If the ad reads assumable with qualifying, the person taking over the existing loan must qualify and be accepted to do so by the existing lender. In this case, credit and income will play a part as to whether the person will be able to take over the loan or not.

If a loan is not assumable, the purchaser or investor can't take over the existing loan, and if you are the investor or buyer, you must find new financing. If new financing is required, a lender will qualify both you and the property for a loan. If the property is an income property, the lender will also take into account the net income of that property in qualifying you.

For example purposes only, let's say that the $100,000 property has an existing loan balance of $60,000. This means that this property has a $40,000 equity. Equity is the difference between what the property is worth and what you owe, not necessarily what you paid. If we are going to buy this property for no-money-down, we need to solve the $40,000 difference between what is presently owed and the sales price. Since we want to buy for no-money-down, somebody else will have to provide us with that $40,000. You will find numerous solutions to this problem in the book, but let's quickly go over a few options.

- The buyer can take over the existing $60,000 loan with the seller taking back a note and mortgage for $40,000 secured by his or her property. The buyer makes payments to the seller on this note.

- The buyer can take over the existing $60,000 loan and give the seller a $40,000 note secured by something the buyer owns.

- The seller can sell on either a Wraparound or Contract of Sale. In this case, the seller remains responsible for the $60,000 loan but now has a note and mortgage from the buyer for $100,000.

- The buyer can refinance the existing loan to $80,000. This $80,000 goes to the seller at closing. The seller pays the balance on the existing $60,000 loan and keeps $20,000 in cash. In addition, the seller takes back a note for $20,000 (the difference between $80,000 and $100,000). This note is secured by a mortgage on either the buyer's property or something the buyer owns.

- The seller could refinance to $80,000 and sell on a Wraparound or Contract for Sale or with the buyer assuming the loan and the seller taking back a note for $20,000.

In each scenario, the seller is willing to be flexible and work with the buyer. But what happens if the seller insists on all cash? If the seller insists on all cash, the buyer should purchase at a discount. There are many examples of how to do that included in this book. Or, if the buyer qualifies for a VA loan, it's possible to obtain a new $100,000 loan, giving the seller all cash. Again, the buyer buys without using personal money. If the buyer is purchasing a home to live in, the buyer might also obtain an equity loan after closing. Lenders will loan up to 100% of value or what the person has paid.

Buying and Selling for No-Money-Down Is Easy

Every problem and every possibility is covered in this book. Given the right set of circumstances and the co-operation of both the seller and agent, buying and selling for no-money-down is quite easy.

If your desire is to become financially independent, it is important that you learn how to use no-money-down techniques when buying and selling real estate. Then you can create your own stepladder to success.

3

Getting Started

First, ask yourself these questions: Are you as healthy as you want to be? What would you do if you had more time? Do you want a different occupation or wish to be better positioned in your present career? Do you want to be more successful? Are you currently being paid what you're worth? How much money would you like to earn? Are you looking for a business opportunity that can't fail? Do you want to buy or sell your own home? Are you inspired and enthusiastic? Are you interested in stopping a habit? Do you want to become more productive? Do you want to solve a problem? Do you want to overcome discouragement, frustration, anxiety, stress, or negative thinking? Do you want to become more decisive and positive? If you answered yes to any or all of these questions, you are ready to proceed.

Be Creative

You have to be creative in your thinking. I like to use the example of a father dying. He had three sons, and before he died he asked each of them to put $1,000 in his grave when he was buried. His first son was a doctor, and he put $1,000 in cash in the grave. His second son was an attorney, and he, too, counted out $1,000 to put it in the grave.

His third son was one of my seminar graduates. He wrote out a check for $3,000 and took out $2,000 in change. The third son broke the pattern. He was creative. Find out what everybody else is doing, and do something else.

Apply Common Sense

Secondly, apply common sense to everything you do. A few years ago, I had an attorney listen to me for two days. The following Sunday night he came up to me and said, "I learned more from you in two days than I did in four years of law school—more common sense information that I can apply for both myself and my clients." He went on to say that he "passed the bar exam a year ago" and that "twenty-seven people flunked the test and twenty-two of the twenty-seven were in the top five percent of the class. They had the best grades and the best jobs waiting for them. All they had to do was pass the exam. Yet, they didn't."

He asked me if I knew why, and I answered, "No," and that it didn't "make any sense to me." He explained, "They didn't pass the exam because the questions on that exam were not the same as the questions in the textbook, and they didn't know what to do. Since I didn't know what to expect on the exam, I just went out the night before, had a couple of beers, and relaxed. When I opened the exam, I was stunned to see that it was far different from anything we had studied or we thought would be in the exam. I just applied common sense, and I passed the exam." My third recommendation, then, is apply common sense.

Learn from the Women

You can take a lesson from women because most of them have much more common sense than men do. Most men have been taught by male role models to answer questions with direct answers. Women, on the other hand, seldom give a direct answer. I challenge all of you men reading this book to ask your girlfriend or wife a question and see if she gives you a direct answer. Most won't.

I will ask my wife a question, and she responds with "Why are you asking?" She went out to dinner the other night with female friends, and I asked her where she ate. She replied, "What difference does it make?" Women invariably will answer a question with a question. Women will not give an answer until they know why a person has asked a question. Most of the time, men don't even give it a thought and quickly answer whatever question is asked with a direct reply. Let me give you a quick example as it applies to real estate.

Tell What You Want Them to Know

In order to qualify for a loan, most lenders will want to see if you make enough money and have good credit before committing to a loan. They might ask for verification of income over the past couple of years by asking you either to provide them with a 1040 or some 1099s. Mortgage brokers or companies can use this information to "shop" your loan application to several lenders. I don't like every Tom, Dick and Harry knowing about my personal situation, so when asked for this information, I reply, "I don't want to waste your time. How much do I have to make to get the loan?" Or, "How much do I need in the way of a down payment?" I also ask, "If I have the down payment and the income, do I also have to have good credit?" The idea here is that you never commit yourself to anything until you find out what they want.

A Lesson to Learn

I have one student who has over a half million dollars of credit with credit cards. He no longer works, so he can't qualify for a loan, and his credit can be terrible, but it doesn't matter. Whenever he wants or needs money, he goes to the bank with credit cards in hand and gets a cash advance. He doesn't have to qualify for this advance or prove how he is going to pay the money back. He uses this money to buy bargains. He likes cars and trucks that he can buy for cash at a discount and sell at a profit. At one of my seminars, he told the following story.

This student said that he once had attended an auction where he knew that a flat bed trailer was to be auctioned off. He had no idea what the trailer was worth, but he knew it had some value to someone. So, he got a $20,000 cash advance on his credit cards and attended the auction. He ended up being the successful bidder at $13,000. He took the trailer home and parked it in front of his house.

Later that day a man knocked on his door and asked him if that was his flat bed. My student said that it was. "What are you going to do with it?" the man asked.

My student replied that he intended to sell it.

"How much do you want?" was the man's reply.

What would you say? You want to make a profit but you have no idea what the item is worth. If you say $25,000, it might be too low—and if you ask $100,000, it might be too high. So, answer a question by asking a question.

Instead of offering a price, my student asked the buyer how much he was willing to pay. My student had a difficult time controlling himself when the buyer stated that he could "have a cashier's check" the next day in the "amount of $80,000!" Obviously, if this person will pay $80,000, it's probably worth more, but don't get greedy. $67,000 isn't a bad profit for a couple of days work.

The Ultimate American Dream

For most Americans, the ultimate dream is to be financially independent and be able to do as one wishes to do without depending on others. Most would welcome the opportunity to make more money and be the boss. Those who are lucky enough to be born into a financially secure family business have very few worries. However, most are not so lucky, and many are continually seeking a way to quit their present job and are looking for avenues that will allow them to go into business for themselves.

Within the pages of this book, you have the tools at your disposal to make that dream come true. These techniques are so powerful that when the opportunity knocks, you will have the knowledge and power to successfully open that door and step into a new career, one you will be in charge of, and one you can control. The principles in this book are not fiction but are a sound compilation of what I've learned from being in this business for over thirty-five years. Each example, full of actual experiences and facts, will help you move forward and reach your goals.

Don't Compete—Create!

My favorite saying is: "Don't compete—create!" There is no problem or situation that can't be solved or overcome. The only thing keeping you from getting what you want out of life is *you*! It never ceases to amaze me why one person uses information, such as is found in this book, to become financially independent while another reads it and takes no action. The only reason for achieving less than success is that perhaps the person who doesn't make it either doesn't believe that these techniques will work or isn't willing to spend the necessary two hours or so every week to make the plan work.

It's unfortunate that most Americans spend more time planning a vacation, a shopping trip, or going fishing or hunting than they do buying their own home. Maybe that's why national statistics indicate that 80% of those buying pay too much for their homes and that 80% of those selling don't get enough when they sell. Yet, buying a home is the largest purchase a person will ever make.

Freebies Don't Work

I personally guarantee that what you are about to read works, but I can't guarantee that it will work for you. Sadly, many Americans are basically, well shall I say, lazy. Sure, if someone offers something for free most will take it, but few will act on what is so easily received.

I have been giving seminars nationally for over thirty years. However, as a test, I decided to give away my materials to all who asked. I then compared the results of those who received free materials to those who paid for the same materials. Guess who came out on top? Those who took the time and money to invest in their future came out the winners. Those who received my materials free never even gave the techniques a try.

What lesson can we learn here? If people are willing to invest in themselves, they have a chance of winning. If they are unwilling to invest, they have absolutely no chance.

Attitude Counts

Just remember that it is individual attitudes toward life that largely determine experiences. If a person expects nothing, that person shall have nothing. If a person demands much, that person shall receive the greater portion.

I hope all of you demand a lot!

Why Buy Real Estate for No-Money-Down?

- The obvious—you don't have cash for a down payment.

- You have cash, but you don't want to tie it up. Use your cash only for bargains. I'll discuss dozens of those situations.

- You want to maximize your profits per dollar invested by controlling as much property as possible with the least possible cash. Why use $50,000 to buy one property when that same amount of money might get you five to ten properties. This is called leverage.

- The more you owe the more in deductions you get for taxes. If you owe $50,000, you can only deduct interest on that amount, but if you owe $100,000, you've increased your tax deductions.

- You want the income and benefits of owning property with the least possible investment.

Why Sell for No-Money-Down?

Remember what I said earlier. Just because you sell with no-money-down techniques, it doesn't mean you don't get some cash—or in many cases, all cash.

- Selling for no-money-down means you get your price.

- Obviously, more people qualify to buy for no-money-down than for a conventional loan where they must come up with a down payment. This means your chances of selling have gone from zero to 100%.

- If the deal is handled correctly, both the buyer and seller win.

- There are more than 100 ways to sell real estate. Selling for cash is just one. No-money-down offers an alternative method of achieving your goal.

- You can even offer to buy for cash when you have no money, turn around and sell for no-money-down, and you can put cash in your pocket at the same time.

Should I Ever Pay All Cash?

There are two times when you might consider paying all cash. The first is when you are contemplating retirement or perhaps have already retired and either can't afford payments or don't want to have any. The second is when you find a property that you can buy at a wholesale price but in order to do so you need to come up with cash.

For example, sometimes you will find a $100,000 market value property that is selling for $70,000 to $80,000 cash. Many times sellers need money fast and are willing to discount a property just to get that cash. Instead of hoping to get a higher price, they opt to take the cash offer and quick closing without contingencies. Banks with foreclosure properties for sale and builders who need to free up credit lines with banks are excellent places to find such deals.

An Interesting Point

You don't need any cash yourself to make many good transactions. If done correctly, you can purchase using none of your money. Depending on where you live, you can actually make $250,000 to $500,000 a year buying properties for cash.

Be on the look out. Find a property that you can buy for cash at a discount, such as the $100,000 property that you can buy for $70,000 to $80,000. Make a cash offer. As soon as the contract has been signed, turn right around and advertise that same property to somebody else for $100,000, no-money-down.

However, the person you sell to must have good credit and qualify for a mortgage. That person obtains a new $70,000 to $90,000 loan, and you carry back a note and mortgage for the downpayment, which is the difference between what the person borrows and the $100,000 price.

Just be sure your buyer borrows enough to allow you to pay cash. If the person borrows more, that money is yours at closing, and you get a note for the difference. Secure that note by recording a mortgage against the property you are selling.

Many lenders will allow the seller to take back a note and mortgage for the down payment because it gives the lenders two people to look to if the buyer defaults. These progressive lenders know that the seller isn't going to lose his or her equity so if the borrower defaults, the seller will more than likely step in and take over the mortgage.

Besides, if the borrower has good credit and qualifies to make the payments, the possibility of default is slim, at best. If the lender insists on the buyer having a cash downpayment, either look for another lender or solve that problem with information you'll read in this book. Every problem has a solution, and you'll find many solutions throughout this book.

If your buyer borrows $90,000 and you buy for $70,000, you will get $20,000 cash at closing plus a note and mortgage for $10,000. If the person borrows just $70,000, you will take back a note and mortgage for $30,000.

Structure the terms of this note with something your buyer can live with. Keep the note for income, trade it as cash for something else, or sell it at a discount.

Jared's Story

Recently, Jared paid $130,000 cash for a property that had a market value of $165,000. He then sold it for $165,000, no-money-down. His buyer qualified and obtained a new $130,000 first mortgage. Jared took back a note and mortgage for $35,000 secured by this same property. He then sold this $35,000 note and mortgage for $25,000 cash to an investor.

Jared knew how to play the real estate game. If you find that it is necessary, as is sometimes the case, to close quickly, meaning there isn't enough time to find another buyer, either borrow the money on a short-term basis, using your own money or get a partner or investor.

Actual example: There is a $37,000 bank foreclosure that the holder will sell for $20,000 cash, provided the buyer closes quickly. The buyer doesn't want to tie up $20,000 so the person finds an investor to put up the $20,000 on a short-term basis for a 20% return, or $4,000.

The buyer then sells this property for $37,000 with his or her buyer obtaining an FHA owner occupied loan or 3% down. After closing, the person, who happens to be a student of mine, pays the investor $24,000 and pockets the balance. My student also pays all closing costs and gives his buyer some credits which allowed that buyer to buy for no-money-down.

Kevin's Approach

Another student of mine, Kevin, uses this technique but applies a slightly different approach. He has removed all risk from his purchases by eliminating the need for him to find another buyer before closing or getting an investor. This idea works extremely well with foreclosures and builder-owned properties. It might also work for you if you find a seller who doesn't know how to sell at market value.

This one particular builder who Kevin knew had a $250,000 home that he wished to sell and would take $200,000 cash. Knowledge is power, and Kevin applied his knowledge to make a nifty $25,000 without any risk.

He said to the builder: "If you are willing to sell for $200,000 cash, I will pay you $200,000 cash, but what if I am able to get you more than $200,000. Would you split anything over this amount with me?" What does the builder have to lose? He is guaranteed $200,000 but also could end up with more money. Whatever he gets is gravy. The builder, of course, replied, "Yes."

Kevin then said: "I am entitled to 50% of all money over $200,000, with you getting 50%, and I would like my 50% to be paid in cash at closing. Is this a problem?" What difference would it make to the builder? Whatever he gets is more than what he's already agreed to sell for, so he has no problem agreeing.

Kevin offers to sell for no-money-down, and his buyer qualifies and obtains a new $200,000 loan. In this case, the builder and Kevin take back a note and mortgage for $50,000 secured by a second. However, since Kevin's agreement is that he gets cash for his 50%, he walks out of the closing with $25,000, and the owner/builder takes the entire $50,000 note and mortgage.

The builder nets $25,000 more than he would by selling for cash. Kevin doesn't have to worry about finding a buyer or an investor immediately and eliminates all risk. Think about it.

Did Kevin need money, a job, or good credit to do this? Absolutely not. All Kevin needed was the knowledge of how to handle the transaction. That's all you need, too. Now that you have the knowledge, why don't you give it a try?

PART II

REAL ESTATE: YOUR BLUEPRINT FOR SUCCESS

4

Realtors and What You Need to Know

Maybe you're thinking that all licensed real estate agents are created equal. Nothing could be further from the truth. National statistics indicate that there is one agent for every 345 Americans. That, in itself, is scary. Common sense suggests that they can't all be equal in production or knowledge.

If you mistakenly pick the wrong agent, be prepared for lots of frustration and discouragement, plus losing many purchases that you could and should have made. Some agents act as if they are God, refusing to submit your offers, or they may say your offer is illegal if you are buying for no-money-down.

The Agent Must Submit Your Offer

First of all, it's the agent's responsibility to submit every offer, regardless of what it is. If an agent doesn't, you can have the person's license suspended or revoked. Secondly, if the agent questions your method of paying or financing, ask that person to check the Civil Rights Act 1868, Title VIII, which states that it is illegal for a real estate person to discriminate in "terms or conditions of financing."

I know of one agent who refused to submit an offer and had his license suspended for six months. Another didn't submit an offer because he didn't understand it. The seller later admitted that he would have taken the offer if he had known of its existence, especially in view of the fact that he sold for less than this offer. In this case, everybody lost. The agent lost a commission. The seller lost a sale and money, and my student also lost since he was the one who had it resold at a profit. The broker, responsible for his salesperson's actions, also lost and was sanctioned by the real estate commission.

As a former agent myself, I'm continually frustrated with noncreative, nonbelieving agents who refuse to listen to something out of the ordinary. This is due, in part, to the broker of the firm who makes them conform to company policies. These companies operate under this rule: Find a buyer who has great credit, a super job, a big down payment, and has no problem qualifying for a loan. These brokers are actually told to forget anything out of the ordinary.

Companies Operate a Numbers Game

Most real estate companies operate a numbers game. If enough associates produce something, the company will be successful. If somebody doesn't produce, the company finds someone who will. These companies don't worry that 50% of their perspective clients can't qualify for a loan. They concentrate on the 50% who can.

Such companies are also afraid that if an agent is too successful, the person might leave the firm and open a competing office. However, if you as an agent are reading this book, and if you will take the time to learn and adopt what you are about to read, you can easily triple your income in a very short time. Those agents who are using my information are the most successful agents in their area and are operating on their own.

I would love it if every agent applied what you are about to read; however, past experience tells me that they won't. I once volunteered to give a free seminar to agents of the ten largest firms in a certain city. Not one single firm wanted to listen or change its thinking or method of operation.

The business-as-usual attitude leaves little room for growth or change. When I first started selling real estate for a living, all agents represented the seller only. If you are dealing with an agent who works for the seller, pay close attention to my "rules when dealing with realtors." I have often thought to myself, Wouldn't it be great if the buyer also had representation—someone who had the buyer's best interest in mind?

Buyer's Agents

Some agencies agreed with my thinking and began advertising their companies as "Buyer's Agents." It took a while to catch on, but today there are plenty of firms who offer this alternative. I will say this several times. If you are a buyer, look for buyer representation via a buyer's agent. If you are an agent, I suggest you consider offering your services to buyers. Buyers are at a definite disadvantage when buying because most have little knowledge about what to buy nor do they know how to make the most profitable purchase.

National statistics indicate that 80% of those buying pay too much. Also, the rules change when you have your own Buyer's Agent. You must be honest and forthright with that person in every detail and make sure the person understands what you are attempting to do. If the person is a negative, nonbelieving, or noncreative person, look for someone else. Insist, if at all possible, that that person be present when one of your offers is submitted.

A Buyer's Agent Can Help

Let me give you an example of just one way a Buyer's Agent can help you. Even though I'm no longer active as an agent, I was asked by a good friend of mine in Kansas City to help him buy a home. He found the home he wanted but asked if I'd negotiate the purchase for him. In effect, I represented him as a Buyer's Agent. Like most people who are looking to buy their own home, he was emotional about this house and "had to have it." Money was not a problem with him, and he could write a check for whatever it cost to buy that home. My concern was that he'd pay too much for the home and later find that he couldn't resell it for what he paid. Since he is a retired MD, I'll refer to him as Doc.

Doc's Story

I said, "Doc, I will help you buy the home, but I need your cooperation in not expressing any opinions or making any statements that might hamper my negotiating." I might add I did this transaction as a favor to Doc and didn't charge him for my help. Since I had yet to see the home, Doc had the real estate agent pick the both of us up to take a look at it.

Before the agent arrived, I asked Doc to sit in the back so I could visit with the agent in the front. As we were approaching the neighborhood, I had the agent drive us through the area so I could see how well it was maintained and the prices of other homes in the area. There were "For Sale" and "Sold" signs in the area, so I was able to determine what buyers were paying.

The price range in this neighborhood was between $120,000 and $140,000 at that time. The asking price of the home that Doc wanted to buy was $123,500, so we were in the ballpark pricewise. Transportation was also close by, as was shopping, and the home was located close to a Catholic church and school. All of these things are important when buying, even though none of it may be important to the buyer. When it comes time to sell, these are things buyers are looking for when making an offer. If the owner had asked $140,000 or more, the property would have been overpriced and something Doc shouldn't buy. It's best to buy the "least expensive" property in the area. $123,000 was on the lower end of value for the neighborhood but still more than I thought Doc should pay.

Everyone Has a Reason to Buy

Everybody has a reason for wanting to buy a particular house and Doc was no exception. Since he had never been married (he is a bachelor whose only two companions are German Shepherd dogs), he wanted a home close to his country club, but more importantly, one that had a large fenced-in yard. This house provided both of these benefits, and Doc was ready to act.

After viewing the home, I agreed that it was perfect for Doc. Doc took me aside and said, "Should I offer $110,000 but tell the agent that I will go up to $115,000 if necessary?" (Note my rules when dealing with "seller" agents.)

I said, "Doc, don't say anything. Just let me negotiate for you."

We got back in the car, again with me in the front seat, and I mentioned to the agent that Doc was ready to make an offer. She turned to address Doc and asked him how much. I replied that Doc had asked me to negotiate for him and that I would be making the offer on his behalf. I told her that I wasn't earning a commission here and that I was just doing my friend a favor.

I then explained that when I sold real estate for a living, most properties were priced higher than the owner expected to get to allow for negotiations between buyer and seller. Buyers want to feel they are getting a good deal so are looking to pay less than the asking price. The norm was 10% when I sold properties, and I asked her if that were still the case. She replied that it was closer now to 5%.

I knew up front that I could at least negotiate for a 5% reduction in price or about $6,000 to $7,000 less than the asking price. This information alone brought the price down to what Doc would be willing to pay, $115,000. Still not enough in my opinion.

The Seller's Motivation

I asked the seller's motivation in selling. We want to concentrate on sellers who are motivated to sell, not just sell if they get their price and their terms. The agent replied that the owner was a widow who had recently fallen in love and was planning on getting married as soon as her house sold. She would then move in with her new husband. Is this motivation or not? You bet! Not only is she motivated to sell, but I suspected that the price she received wasn't as important to her as it might have been had she needed the money to buy something else. Before reading further, take a minute or so and ask yourself, based on information provided, how much you would offer? Try to be fair both ways, and don't make such a low offer that you insult the owner, for ridiculous offers are real deal killers.

Doc's Offer

Doc had no idea what I was going to offer, and I thought he was going to have a heart attack in the back seat when I said, "Doc wants to offer $107,500." Remember that Doc had told me he would pay $115,000.

I then continued, saying, "This offer is not negotiable. Doc won't go up in price. In fact, Doc has looked at two other homes with another agent and if the owner won't take this offer, we plan on making offers on those homes." I paused a moment and then added, "Now that I have told you what Doc will pay, let me tell you why the seller should take this offer." It's important to give the agent some ammunition in the way of information whenever you make an offer. "The reasons she should take this offer are many. First of all, even though it has three bedrooms (very small), it really is a one or two person house, not one for a family. Not every person or couple who doesn't have children would be willing to live in a neighborhood that is loaded with kids. Most couples of this nature are more prone to a quiet area. Secondly, in this day and age all offers are made "contingent" on financing or something else such as the sale of their own home. You never really know until the day of closing whether the sale will close or not. This home is "perfect" for Doc since he lives alone. Money is not a problem, and Doc won't need any financing. In fact, he can write the owner a check tomorrow morning for her home. He is flexible as to when he can move in, and he is even willing to buy some of her furniture if she wishes to sell."

Now, I had not discussed any of this with Doc beforehand. I also pointed out that if she countered or refused this offer she was, in fact, buying back her home for this amount in hopes of selling it at a profit. Because of this, I felt that the offer was very fair for both the owner and Doc. The offer was drawn, and the agent dropped us off at the country club where she had picked us up, saying she'd call once she had an answer.

Afterward Doc asked, "What do you think?"

"Don't worry, Doc. She'll take the offer."

"What if she doesn't?"

"We'll cross that bridge when necessary."

We didn't know whether she'd call me or Doc, so Doc called me almost hourly wanting to know if I had heard anything. I kept reassuring him not to worry and to get ready to move. Sure enough, the owner took the offer.

In effect, I saved Doc $7,500 by negotiating for him. This is what a Buyer's Agent can do for you. The right one can literally save you the amount of a commission which, in effect, means that the Buyer's Agent is actually working for you for free. The agent earns his or her commission by saving you money.

You will read this several times in this book, but it's worth repeating. You make your profit the day you buy real estate. You realize that profit when you sell. To buy right in the beginning can make you financially independent. To make a mistake could quickly bury you. The same applies to your agent. Pick the right agent, and you're on your way. Pick the wrong one and get ready to fail.

I prefer that agent to be a "Realtor."

5

Rules for Buying No-Money-Down

Let's presume you want to buy a house but you have little or no cash for a down payment. Do you walk into a realtor's office or a Sunday open house and say: "I want to buy a house for nothing down?" What do you think the realtor will say? As we've said, buying for no-money-down doesn't mean that the realtor doesn't get a cash commission, but most realtors just don't understand the process. Worse yet is when a realtor refuses to submit your offer, leaving you with no choice but to go around that person and submit it yourself.

Since you can seldom depend on a conventional realtor to do your work for you, it is necessary for you to plan your nothing-down acquisition so you know how to take advantage of an opportunity when it presents itself. Can you buy every house for nothing-down? No! You will recognize the situations where a no-money-down purchase is possible and where it isn't. You will also learn 50 or 60 different ways you can buy for no-money-down. If one technique isn't appropriate for your particular situation, find another one in this book that will work. Here are some of the rules you should consider before making that nothing-down offer.

- **Know the maximum monthly payment you can afford.** A good rule of thumb is to plan on spending no more than

33% of your gross family income on housing costs.

- **Know your home price range**. You should generally be looking at properties priced three to four times your gross income.

- **Don't expect your first home to be your dream home.** The important thing is to acquire your first home. Then start building equity. Later you will own that dream home.

- **Understand today's creative financing methods.** This book is filled with techniques showing you how to buy using none of your own money. Just be sure you, or the property, can support the monthly payment.

- **Work with a realtor who understands creative financing.** The majority of realtors think that clients must come up with a 20% down payment and borrow the balance from a lender. Find an enthusiastic agent who understands creative financing. If an agent has never heard of or has never done a nothing-down sale, that agent is not the right one for you.

- **Expect the seller to help finance your purchase.** I have a series of questions you should ask the realtor or seller. Pay close attention to them and use them. It's amazing how many times I've asked why a seller needed all cash, and the real estate agent simply did not know.

- **Don't be afraid to make an offer.** Once you find a home or other property you think is suitable for a nothing-down offer, don't hesitate to make a written purchase offer. I learned a long time ago that making verbal offers is a waste of time.

If you think an agent won't be enthusiastic about presenting your written nothing-down offer, and they usually aren't, include in your offer the following clause: *This offer to be presented to seller only in the presence of the buyer.* That means you get to go along with the agent and explain your offer. On the other hand, if your agent is enthusiastic about your offer, let that agent earn the sales commission and present the offer without you.

- **Don't expect every nothing-down offer to be accepted.** However, if you've done your homework correctly and picked the seller with the "right" motivation, you should have an excellent chance to get that purchase. Many times buyers want to buy the property they want on their terms, ignoring the fact that the property they want to buy for no-money-down doesn't fit what the seller wants. If that happens, look for another property.

- **If you are buying, consider using a Buyer's Agent.** As we've pointed out, the majority of real estate agents work for the seller. This immediately puts you at a disadvantage when buying. Since many people are weak in negotiating skills or know little about real estate, it is difficult to recognize a good purchase. If this is the case, consider using a Buyer's Agent.

A Good Buyer's Agent Is Creative

Since the Buyer's Agent represents the buyer and, as such, has the buyer's best interest at heart, it is wise to let that person negotiate for you. A recent report indicates that a Buyer's Agent will save you from 6% to 8% over what you'd pay for a home buying through the seller's agent. On a $100,000 sale that's $6,000 to $8,000. That agent will also be more creative since the person has your best interest in mind, and the person will also earn commission. These agents will submit lease-option and owner financing offers that many times prove to be quite difficult when dealing with a Seller's Agent.

Look for a realtor office which advertises that they are Buyer's Agents. Be truthful with them in every aspect, including how much money you have and what you are trying to accomplish. Turn that agent loose, and the agent will look for properties that fit what you can afford and will do much of your homework for you. You may not like every property the agent finds, but at least you won't be wasting your time and energy looking at properties you can't afford anyway.

Remember: When buying, use a Buyer's Agent.

The One True Negotiating Secret

Generally speaking, the worst person to negotiate for you is you. Why? Because if you are like most people, you tend to be emotional when buying something you want, instead of approaching it with logic. This idea is especially true when buying your own home. It's much easier to be logical when buying something for an investment. The negotiation then becomes a black-and-white picture. However, when it's your home we're talking about, other things come into play.

> *Regardless of how difficult it might be, try and apply the principal of "He who cares the least wins."*

When selling something, either for myself or on behalf of others, I play to your emotional side. I want you to feel that you must have this and will do anything to get it. It's also much easier to deal one-on-one rather than find yourself in a bidding war over who gets what you want. This concept is especially true with auctions.

The Emotional Frenzy

Did you ever notice the frenzy of bidding to buy something? Most of the time we end up paying more at auctions than we might otherwise pay just negotiating with the seller one-on-one. I recall attending a real estate auction in Breckenridge, Colorado a few years ago where some condominiums were being sold. I inspected them a day ahead of time and was furnished a price list of what they had been asking. Thinking I might get a bargain, I waited for the auction. Without exception, every condo went for more than I could have bought it a day earlier.

Why? Because the buyers got caught up in the frenzy of buying and bid much higher than normal. I've seen this happen many times. Don't get caught up in emotional buying.

Cleveland

I gave a seminar in Cleveland a few years ago where students of mine asked me if I'd negotiate a 20-million-dollar purchase they wanted to make. I told them I'd do it on one condition. They had to leave me alone and let me negotiate by myself.

One of the investors was an attorney. He insisted on being there when I negotiated because he wanted to protect the investors' interest. We argued for some time, but he wouldn't give in. I finally said, "Okay, but please don't say anything." He agreed with this request, but I'm sure you can guess what happened.

The Negotiation

For this transaction, I was negotiating with a very experienced owner from Florida, and the negotiations were intense. He knew the attorney was involved as a buyer, so even though I was talking to him, he was, in effect, directing his comments to the attorney. The more we negotiated, the more the attorney got caught up in the negotiations until he could take it no longer.

He actually stood up, threw his notes on the table, and said, "Okay, we'll pay your price." All my efforts were for naught. Needless to say, there were a few words between the investors after the meeting, and they ended up not buying the property after all.

Your Emotions Can Be Expensive

Regardless of how difficult it might be, try and apply the principle of "He who cares the least wins." As hard as it might be, try and divorce yourself from having to have whatever it is that you are trying to buy. The best way to do that is to have somebody else negotiate for you.

If dealing with a realtor, allow the realtor to do it, but if you are left to do it on your own, you might consider doing what I did when buying a home in Colorado Springs. This is when I sold my real estate, insurance, management and appraisal business in Illinois and decided to settle in Colorado Springs.

It's easy for me to avoid being emotional when negotiating for you, but I'm just like you when it comes to something I want to buy. The only difference is that I realize this and try to remove it from my negotiations. This has worked for me, and I've received several phone calls from others who used the same technique to buy their homes.

Act Uninterested

When working with realtors, try to avoid showing interest in one particular property. As soon as you do, the agent will want to sit down and negotiate an offer. I know— I was very good at it myself. Also, you must be most careful not to insult the other party completely. If this happens, you won't be able to buy the property at any price.

That's another reason to have somebody else negotiate for you. That person can cover him- or herself if the offer is too low by taking the seller's side when first submitting it. If it's a realtor, the person can explain that, by law, they have to submit every offer and can thus cover a low offer or an offer that might be upsetting to the seller.

The Colorado Springs Move

> *If you want to drive a realtor up the wall, pretend you don't care which house you buy.*

When we decided to move to Colorado Springs, I decided the best way to find what we wanted and where we should live was to use the services of a realtor. I had sold my real estate agency in Illinois and was planning on getting a license in Colorado later. Before doing so, however, I visited with the local Chamber of Commerce and a local bank. I told the banker that I was moving to town and would be opening a checking account in his bank. I asked him for his suggestions as to where I should buy.

I did the same with the Chamber of Commerce. If you are moving to a new community that you know nothing about, I strongly recommend you do the same thing. Both the banker and the Chamber of Commerce representative recommended the same area. It had the best schools, country clubs were in the area, and it was the fastest growing area of the city. So, we quickly decided that we would concentrate on looking only in that area.

We-Don't-Care-Attitude

Before looking, I told my wife to avoid expressing any interest in anything we looked at. I told her to just look, make mental notes, and we'd talk about it later that night. Don't give the realtor any impression that you like one place more than the other. After each inspection, the realtor asked how we liked the home and wanted to know if we'd be interested in making an offer.

She became frustrated over our seeming we-don't-care attitude. I remember telling the realtor that each house is just bricks and mortar, and we don't get emotional about buying anything. This drove her up the wall. She had never worked with homebuyers who didn't find something they wanted and became emotional when buying it.

The Offer

After looking at many homes, I finally informed her one evening that we were ready to make an offer. She was amazed since we had shown no interest in anything she had shown us. She asked which house we wanted to make an offer on, and I replied that we liked several but we'd make an offer on the home on Constellation Drive. She, of course, said all the right things, such as "It's a beautiful home, the schools are perfect for your children, and I know you'll be happy with this choice."

Three Offers

She then asked how much I wanted to offer. I told her, and she immediately replied that it was too low and the seller wouldn't even consider it. She asked if I'd "go up in price." (Remember—don't ever tell a realtor that you will go up. It's okay to go up later, but don't tell them that when submitting an offer.)

She said she would submit the offer but doubted that it would be accepted. She then got up to leave, but I asked her to please sit down because I wasn't finished yet. I told her that since she felt the owner wouldn't take my offer, I might as well make an offer on another house at the same time. I explained it would save time for both of us.

If you want to drive a realtor up the wall, pretend you don't care which house you buy for your family. Realtors are just not prepared for this. We finished the second offer, and she asked, "Are you through?" I said, "No, my wife likes another house, so we might as well make an offer on that one as well." In all, we made three offers on three different houses that night.

The Appointment

I then said to the realtor, "This is what I want you to do. Make an appointment tomorrow evening at 7 p.m. to submit the first offer, have another appointment at 8 to submit the second, and an appointment at 9 to submit the third. You said that the first offer wouldn't go through anyway, so we might as well get the other offers submitted the same evening. There is one stipulation, however. When you submit the first offer, please show her my other offers as well. In other words, let her know that if she doesn't take my offer, she stands to lose me as a potential buyer."

Can You Imagine the Seller's Response?

Put yourself in the place of the seller. When she immediately responded that the offer was too low and she wanted a counter offer, the realtor said, "Mr. and Mrs. Powelson don't really care which house they buy. As a matter of fact, I have an appointment to submit this next offer at 8 and another offer at 9. If you want to take a chance that they don't buy one of the other houses, okay. Otherwise, you're going to have to make up your mind now."

Guess which house I got? The only one I wanted, the first one. I would have gone up in price, but I took the emotional aspect out of my negotiating and, as a result, got the home I wanted. Remember to keep emotions at arm length, if at all possible.

One last thing. I'm sure you're wondering what would have happened had one of my other offers been accepted and the first one turned down. I always have a Weasel Clause in my offers that allows me to back out if need be. Note examples of those elsewhere in this book.

6

How to Pick the Right Realtor

First of all—what is a realtor, and how is the person different from any real estate salesperson or broker? A realtor's designation comes about because that person pays dues to become a member of the local, state, and national association of realtors. This is an organization dedicated to education and high moral and ethical conduct. I have served on the ethics committee. Because

> **By the time you finish reading and digesting this book, you will know more than 90% of those licensed to sell real estate.**

of these high expectations from the realtor group overall, you have additional protection and support in case of any disagreements between buyer, seller, and realtor. This is not the case when dealing with a person who is not a member of the Board of Realtors. For my credentials, I am a Past President of the Illinois Association of Realtors and a Past Director of the National Association of Realtors.

In addition, realtors are continually challenged to further their education and keep current of the latest changes in the real estate market by attending what is called the GRI program. This is an education program that runs from one to four years overall. I was on the committee that started such a program in Illinois, was a member of its first four-year class, and even taught a financing course.

MLS

Most realtors also belong to the Multiple Listing Service, referred to as MLS. This program was designed so that all listings could be shared with every member of the MLS, not only increasing the exposure of all properties listed for sale, but also allowing any realtor who is a member to show any property listed in that service. I was part of the organization of MLS in Illinois.

MLS has come a long way since it was first introduced to the real estate public. In the beginning, paper work was unbelievable, and to find out what properties were for sale by others, you either had to wait for the weekly MLS book to be delivered or call various offices about their listings. The books were bulky and thick, and looking through them took much time and energy.

Then computers arrived, making it far easier for realtors to find out what was for sale. Realtors can now punch in number of bedrooms, school districts, and prices merely by operating their computers.

When I started selling real estate, people actually wasted their time showing properties. They didn't qualify buyers, either for money or what they wanted to buy. I quickly changed that approach for myself and later taught a course teaching realtors how to use their time more productively.

Knowledge Comes after School

By the time you finish reading and digesting this book, you will know more than 90% of those licensed to sell real estate. Why? Because real estate people are not taught creativity. They are taught how to pass a test. I know because I taught them. Everybody who took training from a real estate school was assigned a certain number of questions to remember, and later the person was to give back these questions to the school. We took these questions and continually updated the changes so that our graduates knew what was coming. We taught them the questions and gave them the answers. Learning how to sell or list wasn't the primary concern.

Once a student passes the test and becomes a realtor, the public tends to think of the person as someone who is very knowledgeable in real estate. In reality, a licensed real estate agent may know very little about the ins-and-outs of buying or selling. Any further training occurs when one joins an office or from joining groups at the local, state, or national level, such as the GRI program.

If a new agent takes a job with a conventional realtor's office, the person won't get much help there either. Most realtor offices provide training of some sort but downplay anything out of the ordinary and thus stay away from creativity of any kind. The main exceptions are CCIMs or commercial brokers and exchangers. I did both and was an appraiser as well. The ordinary method of financing doesn't work or apply with most commercial and exchange properties, so they have to be creative.

Use Common Sense

If you must use a realtor, apply common sense. Let's first look at a realtor wanting to list your home or other property. He (or she) will promote the fact that he belongs to MLS and, therefore, will give you maximum exposure. Not only will you get the realtor, but you will also get every other office in the community as well working on your sale. Sounds good, but let's look at reality

A listing agent and a sales agent share in the commission. Many agents are good listing agents but poor salespeople while others are good at selling but poor at listing. Try and find an agent who does both successfully.

Never list your home with a relative or friend just because the individual has a license. List your home with someone who is successful in your neighborhood and price category. Some agents sell cheaper houses better while others concentrate on the more expensive properties. If you are selling something for $40,000 and list with an agent who specializes in $200,000 properties, you will not be successful. Likewise, if you are selling a $200,000 home, don't list with an agent who sells only the cheaper homes or properties.

Contact Three

I suggest you contact three realtors before listing your home. Don't tell them initially what you want but ask for their opinion as to what it will sell for. They will show you a table of comparables of what other properties in your neighborhood sold for and suggest a range for an asking price.

If one is too high or too low, discard it and seek another opinion. Use only realtors who display sold signs in your area or have a track record of sales in your neighborhood. Ask them what percentage of listings they sell themselves as opposed to others selling their listings. Ask them how long it usually takes to sell a home in your area. Given the fact that realtors split the commission if a different realtor sells than lists the property, a listing realtor should want to keep the entire commission and so should be dedicated to selling his or her listing personally if possible. I used to pride myself by declaring that our office sold over 90% of our own listings.

Know What an Agent Can Do for You

Ask the agent what he or she will do for you. This includes advertising, perhaps writing letters, holding open houses, etc. Realtors should guarantee you a certain amount of advertising. I also suggest no listing be longer than three months. Some realtors just list and hope somebody else will sell for them, and when the property doesn't sell, the realtor quickly sets up all kinds of showings just before the listing is due to expire in an effort to get you to re-list. Be sure and make it clear at the time of the listing that if the realtor doesn't perform as agreed, that you have the right to pull the listing during that three-month time frame. The shorter the listing, the more they should work at getting the property or house sold.

Ask Questions

If your house is shown a lot and doesn't sell, ask the realtor his or her opinion as to why you haven't received an offer. Chances are your price might be too high, or you are not offering the proper terms. Ask for suggestions as to what you can do to help sell it. If you are dissatisfied with your listing realtor, don't hesitate to change listing agents at the end of the listing period.

Real estate people are very reluctant to suggest you sell, or buy, on a lease-option, yet that is one of the best, if not the best, ways to sell in today's market. They will avoid suggesting this option since their commission is postponed until the sale actually closes. I purchased my last home under a lease-option. And, it's a great way to buy foreclosures from lenders who are familiar with this technique.

> **When buying, never tell the realtor you will go up in price.**

When listing, keep your asking price no more than 5% above what the realtor, or appraiser, says it will sell for. Everybody likes to dicker some, but if you ask too much, you won't get a sale. For example, if your home is worth $50,000 and you ask $64,000, you will discourage those who are looking in the $45,000 to $50,000 range. Also, many buyers feel something is wrong with a house if it has been listed for too long a period of time. I tend to look upon this as a plus as a buyer myself since the seller should now be more realistic and creative with an offer.

To Review

When listing, do so with a person who has been successful in your area and in your price range. Stay away from relatives or friends. Ask for suggestions as to what you can do to make your home show better and be open to alternative ways of financing, such as taking back a mortgage and still get all cash.

The Other End of the Spectrum

Now let's examine the other end of the spectrum, working with a realtor who wants to sell you something. Chances are you will contact that realtor yourself either because you answered an ad in the newspaper or drove by the property and noticed a sign. If you call about an ad or a sign, ask to speak to the listing agent. Real estate people have what is called "floor time." That simply means that they take all incoming calls and are entitled to refer to the person calling as their client.

The person answering the phone may be new to the office and probably won't know the details of the particular property you are calling about. If possible, try and speak to the person who actually listed the property. Common sense says that person knows more about that property and the seller's motivation in selling than anyone else.

If you are working with your own agent, ask that agent to find a property that suits your needs and in a price range you can afford. He or she, in effect, will represent you as a Buyer's Agent and hopefully work in your behalf. Remember—real estate people work for the seller. They have a fiduciary duty to the seller and, as such, convey your feelings and what you might say to the seller.

Later I will cover what to say and what not to say to real estate people in general. Again, common sense dictates that if you want to buy a commercial building, you deal with a commercial agent. If you want to buy a $200,000 home, you deal with a person who works in that price range. You also want to work with an agent who understands your offers and will be in attendance, if possible, when the offer is submitted. It's better to have someone on your side, as the buyer, explaining your offer and its benefits.

It's even better if you can be present when the offer is submitted to answer any questions the seller might have, although the listing agent probably won't allow this to happen.

Rules to Follow When Dealing with Realtors

1. **When buying, never tell the realtor you will go up in price.**

    As an example, if you offer $110,000 and tell the salesperson you will go to $115,000, I can guarantee that the seller will find out. The first question a seller asks the realtor when an offer is received is "Will the buyer go up?" The salesperson has a fiduciary responsibility to tell the seller that you will. You can always go up later; just don't tell the realtor you will.

2. **If buying, point out all the negatives of the house to the realtor, such as decoration, plumbing, lack of closets, bedrooms, and square footage, anything you notice.**

Give the salesperson some ammunition to use when the person talks to the seller and submits your offer.

3. **Point out to the realtor (or seller if you are dealing one-on-one) that if the seller refuses your offer, the person, in effect, is buying back his or her house for this refused price.**

I can't begin to tell you of the number of sales lost by both the realtor and seller when this is not addressed. Here is an actual example: offer $110,000—counter offer from seller for $113,000. The seller is actually risking $110,000 to make an additional $3,000. Sure, the buyer may go up, but if not, the seller loses a potential sale.

4. **Be careful in telling the realtor too much about your personal situation, especially how much money you have.**

This is especially true if you are trying to buy using none of your own money. If you tell a realtor you have no money, the person will drop you.I used to do it myself. I received a call not too long ago from a student who wanted to make a no-money-down offer to the seller, but the realtor wouldn't submit it because the buyer wasn't putting any of his own money into the offer. His response was the usual "How am I going to make a commission if you have no money? Besides, I'll tell the owner not to take the offer. No-money-down deals are illegal." The buyer asked me what to do. While I don't like making this suggestion, sometimes one has no choice. I told him to go directly to the owner with the offer, bypassing the realtor.

The owner took the offer and my student bought the house. The realtor ended up getting his commission (in cash, I might add) and all was well for all parties. Yet, if I hadn't told the buyer to go directly to the seller, the seller would have lost a sale. Real estate people have a tendency to pre-determine or tell the owner what to do instead of just submitting what they have and letting the seller make a decision. Remember, when I say a no-money-down offer, it doesn't necessarily mean that the seller doesn't get a down payment and the realtor a cash commission. It just means that the buyer buys using none of his or her own money.

5. **Ask the realtor what the present interest rates are, what it will take to qualify for a loan, and who is making loans on what you want to buy.**

If he or she doesn't know these answers or just says financing is up to the buyer, you are not dealing with a qualified, knowledgeable realtor. Many real estate people are what I call "order takers." They are thoroughly familiar with a seller's market, but when it's a buyer's market, they aren't always up to snuff on things such as this. I had dinner out the other night and met another couple. During our conversation, I discovered the wife was a realtor with seventeen years experience. Yet, she had no knowledge of what financing was available, nor had she ever heard of one of today's most powerful financing tools which allows buyers actually to finance 100% or more legally. Pay attention because I'll be explaining this little-known technique in detail later.

6. **My saying is "The dumber you act, the better your chance of success."**

This doesn't mean that you're dumb; just act that way. Realtors are reluctant to do business with those they think know more than they do or who submit offers they don't understand. I have a series of questions, which I'll unveil later, that you should ask every seller or realtor. If either asks you why you're asking questions, respond as follows: "I don't know, but I read someplace that I should."

7. **Keep emotions out of your offer. Be logical at all times.**

This won't be hard if you are buying an investment property since you are looking at a cash return on investment. As a realtor, I can convince you to go the extra mile and perhaps even pay more than you should. Which leads me to rule 8.

8.   Never buy the most expensive home in the area.

If all the homes in the area are in the $120,000 to $140,000 range and the home you like best is $170,000, don't buy it unless you are prepared to take a loss if and when you resell that home. In other words: "Don't fall in love." My saying is the following: "Love is zero in tennis; it's zero in real estate as well."

9.   Amenities, such as swimming pool, basement, recreation room, hot tub and the like may be nice, but you'll never recoup this expense when you resell.

In a warm area, a swimming pool might be important, but in a colder climate, it can actually be a hindrance.

10. Buy from motivated sellers only.

These are people who have to or want to sell, not someone who says, "I'll sell if somebody pays my price and my terms." I will be talking more about this later in the book, but a motivated seller is one who is getting divorced, has lost a job, has transferred, has creditors and the IRS after him or her, or perhaps has two properties and can't support both.

11. Most sellers are looking for one of two things—price or terms.

If a seller is concerned about price, such as $100,000, look to get your terms. This could be no-money-down or a small down payment with seller help in financing. If the seller wants a cash offer, offer less than the property is worth, such as $75,000. If the person wants both price and terms and is not flexible on either, simply look for another property.

7

Elephants Don't Bite

When I give live seminars, I usually start by asking these questions: "How many of you have been bitten by a mosquito?" Of course, everybody raises a hand. I follow it up with: "How many of you have been bitten by something but didn't know what it was?" Again, every hand goes up. I then ask: "How many of you have been stung by a bee?" Most people have at some time of their lives, so most people raise their hands. I finish up by asking: "How many people have been bitten by an elephant?" Nobody raises a hand because we all know that elephants don't bite!

What does this mean? The thought that I want to put into their minds and yours is this thought. "It's the little things that we do and the little things that create the big results!" You can apply this to anything in life, but let's concentrate on how to use it in real estate.

Closing Dates

Do you know you can change your closing date by as little as two days and eliminate a real estate commission, closing costs, moving expenses, and even a negative cash flow? In fact, you can delay a mortgage payment up to two months with this information. Nobody else teaches this little technique that I know of, but I have been doing it for over thirty years. It worked back then, it works now, and it will work for the next thirty years as well.

This one technique could save you hundreds and even thousands of dollars every time you buy or sell a house or property. Do you know that as a buyer you can walk out of almost every closing with cash in your pocket? It's perfectly legal, yet agents and lenders will tell you that you can't do it.

Little Things Can Produce Big Results

One quick example of how little things can produce big results happened to me several years ago. I sold a home that I owned in Colorado Springs, Colorado. My buyer was a Colonel in the Air Force, so he qualified for a VA, no-money-down loan. I was asking $60,000 for the home, and it was appraised by the VA for $60,000. The problem was that the Colonel could only qualify for a loan of $50,000. This meant he was $10,000 short of what I wanted. The real estate agent came to me and said, "I'm sorry, but the Colonel can't qualify for a loan higher than $50,000. Would you sell for $50,000?" My home was worth $60,000, the buyer was willing to pay $60,000, and the only thing preventing my sale was to solve this little $10,000 problem. He could have put a $10,000 down payment himself which would have solved the problem, but he didn't have the money.

Since I didn't want to lose him, I told the agent that I'd take a note for the $10,000. The agent quickly replied that VA didn't allow the seller to take back a note and mortgage secured by a second on the property being sold. I already knew this, and I had a solution, but I thought I'd first ask the agent if she had any ideas. She replied, "No. I guess we'll have to look for another buyer."

I told her that I was perfectly willing to wait one year for the $10,000, and I would be happy to take a note for that amount secured by his furniture. This solution had never entered her mind, and both she and I could have lost a sale if I hadn't suggested this little technique.

Many of my questions from students concern ways to solve a particular problem. Every problem has a solution. You just have to find it. Not long ago I received a phone call from another student who was about to purchase a property. He ran the offer by me, and after a few questions, I determined he would be making a $10,000 mistake by going through with his offer. When I showed him what was going to happen, he was most appreciative and immediately withdrew his offer.

Little Ways to Make and Save Money

There are lots of little ways to make and save money that most of us are not aware of or just don't use. A credit card is a good example. Ever buy something and boom— you are billed within a week or two? Yet, other times you can buy using that same credit card and that purchase doesn't show up on your bill for two months.

How would you like to guarantee that two months free use of your card? I might mention, however, that in order for this time to be free, you would have to pay off your card in full once billed.

The next time you get a credit card bill in the mail look at the due date shown on your statement. That is the date that is important. First, it tells you when you have to pay your bill in order to avoid a late charge. But, more importantly, it also tells you how to buy free use of that credit card using this information.

For example, I have a card that has a due date of the 23rd of the month. If I buy something and charge it on that card on October 22nd, I will be billed and have to pay that charge by November 23rd or one month later. However, if I wait until October 24th to buy that item, I won't be billed until December or two months later. Why? Because billing is computer generated with set, specific cut-off dates.

After that date, your charges go into the next cycle. Well, real estate works the same way. By picking a proper closing date, you can eliminate payments up to two months, plus pay other costs you might otherwise have. For example, I refinanced sixteen units I owned in Kansas City. I deliberately refinanced them on the 16th of that month. Since I refinanced that month, I didn't make a mortgage payment, and since I refinanced the sixteenth, I didn't have to make one the next month either.

I was able to keep all the rents for two months without making a mortgage payment. Is that powerful or not? You can do the same thing refinancing your own home—eliminate a payment for two months just by knowing when to refinance. Why don't real estate agents tell you this? Either because they don't know or, if they do, they don't tell you about it. Not only can the changing of a closing day put cash in your pocket, but it could also increase agent sales drastically by allowing more buyers to qualify. Let's examine closely how it works.

How to Pick a Proper Closing Date

First, from a buyer standpoint, let's say you are taking over an existing loan on the property. This simply means that you are going to be making the payments that the seller has been making on his or her loan. Set your closing date the third to the fifth of the month. Just remember to never close the first of the month.

Why close on the third to the fifth and not just the third or the fifth? Because the third or fifth might fall on a Sunday. By closing on either the third or the fifth, you can pick a Friday or a Monday.

First example: Let's say this is an income property of some sort. It could be a rental home, a duplex, a fourplex, an apartment complex, an office building, or even a shopping center. When are rents normally due? They are due on the first, of course. You prorate rents when closing, meaning that you are entitled to all the rents from the day of closing until the end of the month. Insist on these rents being cash to you at closing and not a credit on your purchase price.

We all know that some tenants don't pay on time, meaning that there are still rents to be collected after the closing. Who collects those uncollected rents? Many people think the buyer does because he or she is now the new owner. However, because the seller was the owner when the rents were due, it's that person's responsibility to collect. The person has to give you the cash at closing and worry about collecting later.

When I purchased 140 units several years ago, the seller, upon closing, had to pay me $10,000, in cash, the uncollected rent on the properties. Even though he argued that it was my responsibility, the closing agent reminded the seller that he was the owner when the rents were due and to "Please, write Mr. Powelson a check." I don't know about you, but an extra $10,000 here and there isn't bad at all.

Likewise, the mortgage payment is normally due on the first of the month and payable by the tenth or fifteenth, giving the borrower a grace period to make the payment. However, since you will be closing the third, it will also be the responsibility of the seller to make this payment as well.

Now here's where many realtors, closing agents, and attorneys falter. You can also prorate the mortgage payment. It's fair that since you, the new owner, get to keep 28 days of rent, you should also be liable for 28 days of the mortgage payment. Many say, "Well, you got the rents, so you have to make the mortgage payment, and it's a wash." On the surface this makes sense, but in reality, this thinking is flawed.

Your mortgage payment includes principal and interest. The principal portion reduces your mortgage balance while the interest is the fee or penalty you pay to borrow the money. The principal portion is paid current, meaning that if you make a January mortgage payment, you will see your mortgage balance come down slightly. However, interest is paid in arrears! While they do charge you interest, they can't actually charge you any until you use the money. This means that your January payment is the responsibility of the seller. Why is this important? Because for the first half of any loan, almost all of your payment is interest.

Example: You could take out a $100,000 loan today, to be amortized over thirty years. You can make every payment on time for the next fifteen years and still owe about $87,000. Your loan balance doesn't come down much at all until the last half of the loan. Since interest is the responsibility of the seller, you will pick up hundreds or even thousands of dollars in rent and just give back a few dollars for the principal proration.

The money you receive could be your down payment, pay your moving or closing expenses, or be used for whatever you desire.

If you are purchasing your own home, you literally end up moving in without having a mortgage payment until the following month. Common sense suggests that if you are the seller, you should try and close at the end of the month. With this method, the new buyer will be responsible for collecting the rents and making the payments.

New Financing

How about new financing? If you are the buyer and obtain a brand new loan from a lender, the rule changes a bit. Find out when your payment is due and when your grace period ends. This is quite easy because your billing or mortgage payment book will show there's a late charge due date. Most likely this will be the sixteenth of the month. This means your payment is due the first but payable by the fifteenth. If it's the eleventh, then your payment is due the first but payable by the tenth.

Using the more likely date of payable by the fifteenth, set your closing date for the sixteenth. By so doing, you eliminate a payment for the month you are moving in or when buying an investment property.

This is how I use it. I bought a rental house a few years ago that rented for $800 per month. The mortgage payment was $850 per month, so I had what is called a "negative cash flow" of $50 per month. I don't suggest you do this normally, but in my case I bought almost two years of no negative by changing the closing date. You might do likewise.

My closing was set for October 13th. I called the mortgage company and asked the lady when my first payment would be due. She stated it would be due the first of November. I said, "I travel a lot, and I'm wondering if it would be possible to postpone the closing until the 16th." She said that wouldn't be a problem. I then asked, "If we close the 16th, when would my first payment be due?" She said if I didn't close until October 16th, I wouldn't have to make a payment until December 1st to 15th. When would you rather have your first payment due, November 1st or December 15th? I quickly changed my closing date to the 16th.

I'm going to round the figures out to avoid confusion. The house was rented for $800, and the tenant had paid the seller $800 for the month of October. Rounded off, this meant that he was the owner for the first half of October, and I was the owner for the last half of the month. Therefore, he was entitled to keep $400, and he was to give me $400 for my share of the rent. I asked that the $400 be in cash.

November came around, and the tenant paid me $800 rent.

Since we closed the 16th of October, I didn't have to make a mortgage payment for November, so I put the additional money with the $400, giving me $1,200 in cash to help with the upcoming negatives. December came around, and I received $800 in rent, but now I was $50 short. However, because I kept the $1,200 aside, I actually eliminated a negative cash flow on that little rental house for upward of two years. In that time span, I raised the rent so there was no negative.

There was an interest proration for the last half of October, so I didn't actually get to keep all of the $1,200, but what I received was enough to eliminate my negative until I was able to raise the rents. And this was just a single-family home. Think how you can use this to your advantage with big income properties. This technique has been working for me for over thirty years and will continue to work for the next thirty years, yet nobody seems to make you aware of this fact.

8

How to Become a Winner in Real Estate

As mentioned before, I've been teaching people how to buy real estate safely, cautiously, and conservatively, with absolutely no risk, for some thirty years. It never ceases to amaze me how some will take my courses and advice and become millionaires or financially independent, while others will just simply file the information away and never use it. And yet, the amazing thing about real estate over all other endeavors is that we are all created equal regardless of personal circumstances. Unlike other occupations or investments, height and weight play no role, age makes no difference, and money and a formal education are not necessary. Why does a man with a sixth grade education, an eighty-year-old woman, an eighteen-year-young person become wealthy in a matter of a few short years while others never take that first step?

Experts tell us that success is largely dependent upon attitude. Winners perceive themselves as winners, plan winning strategies, and usually win. Before victory comes the plan. Vince Lombardi once said, "Practice doesn't make perfect—Perfect Practice Makes Perfect!"

The second step in becoming a winner is developing that plan. The plan should take into account your natural abilities, the obstacles you are likely to confront, and some calculation of the precise nature of the award you should receive in relation to the effort you expect to extend. A winner plans on ways to win. If planning to go fishing or hunting, or even take a vacation, would a person just throw fishing gear, hunting gear, or vacation clothes in the car and start out? No. Most would plan that outing before starting.

A winner will make every effort to maximize award and minimize effort. I don't care what endeavor you seek to accomplish, more often than not, the rules remain more or less the same--the winner masters the rules of the game.

Construct a Plan

A winner constructs a plan that conforms to the rules of the social games which characterize society, and the payoff is that a winner maximizes potential for gain in most if not all human interaction. The person does this by thinking and planning—acting in accord with logic rather than emotion. Winners evaluate systems carefully that have a direct bearing on personal income, their ability to preserve capital, and their ability to survive a series of tomorrows. Winners discover the true value of the payoff.

Winners accept the truth of change, don't follow the crowd, act in accord with logic rather than emotion, and understand the rules of the game. They maximize effort, plan ahead, think positively, and take advantage of their own natural abilities.

For many, winning does not come easy. There are those who have the same capabilities, the same opportunities, the same training and instruction, yet fail to succeed as winners. If there is one thing that separates a winner from a loser, it's the fear of failure. Rather than take the risk of failing, a loser will just sit back and not even try.

One has to give him or herself permission to be successful before becoming a winner. This book is designed for those who perceive themselves as winners. It is designed to show you how to create a plan of success, develop a plan, and how to master the rules that will guarantee your success.

New Rules for Accumulating Wealth

For generations, people have been brainwashed into thinking

that if they are sufficiently hardworking and frugal and sock money away in their savings accounts, they will eventually acquire wealth. It doesn't work that way, and simple mathematics explains why. If you, a solid citizen, earn $50,000 per year and, by some miracle, manage to save $5,000 of this amount, and if you earn interest at the rate of 6%, at the end of 30 years, you would have accumulated half a million dollars. But the reality of the matter is quite different. First, you have to pay taxes on your earnings. Then, you have to pay taxes on the interest from your savings.

> *No one, absolutely no one, can get rich by saving money out of personal earnings.*

No one, absolutely no one, can get rich by saving money out of personal earnings. Anyone who acquires real wealth does it either through luck or by the judicious use of other people's money. This is what we call leverage.

Leverage at Work

Here's an example of how it works. Say you buy a home for $100,000 and pay $20,000 down and borrow the rest at ten percent. If the home rises in value at the rate of 10% a year, at the end of five years, its compounded worth is $160,000. You have paid $40,000 in interest and still owe $80,000. But, you have cleared $40,000, thereby doubling your initial down payment. This is an example of leverage. It is the homebuyer's best friend.

A private residence in a good location is the bargain you should look for. You can buy it with valuable borrowed dollars, pay it off with increasingly cheaper inflated dollars, and watch its value skyrocket. You can make far more money with it than by simply saving your pennies. And, over the years, you can make far more money with it than you will have to pay in interest on your loan.

If homes are doubling in value every seven years, as they have in the past, then by paying for your home with 80% borrowed money, you will quintuple your investment in those seven years. In contrast, if you had paid all cash for that home, you would merely have doubled your money. And, if you use none of your own money to purchase a property, the numbers become unbelievable. Without any doubt, the key to making big money is to do it with other people's money.

Therefore, we start with Rule Number 1—use only other people's money or leverage.

How Safe Is Leverage?

In today's unstable financial climate, just how safe is leverage? The answer is that, provided it's handled correctly, you're safer with it than without it. Let's take an example—a property worth $50,000.

You are sitting with $30,000 in the bank and have the choice of financing the property with a $5,000 down payment or of putting up the entire $30,000 and borrowing $20,000. Some investors feel more comfortable using the $30,000 as a down payment rather than $5,000 because they feel nervous about the economy, especially when buying an income property.

Remember this point. Generally speaking, regardless of the economy, the less you put in the way of a down payment, the better off you will be. If the economy is good and real estate values are going up, buy six houses with $30,000, instead of just one. If the economy is bad and real estate values fall, you stand to lose only the amount of money you put down on a property.

Which is better, to lose $5,000 or $30,000? Besides, the lender might be more reluctant to foreclose if you have little or no equity while I can assure you that lenders will definitely foreclose if you have lots of equity. In either case, you are rewarded for putting down as little as possible and possibly penalized for coming up with a big down payment.

Rule 1: Your Greatest Leverage Is Options

Many people think that in order to make money in real estate, you must first own the property. This is not true. All you have to do is control that piece of real estate. Having an option eliminates negative cash flow while allowing you to completely control that property and at the same time do it with very little money and hardly any risk.

Here's How It Works

Let's say you find a property for sale at $300,000. It is priced under the market, and you can see that the value will go up drastically in the next three years. You don't have $300,000, nor do you have any way that you can come up with the $300,000 to buy the property. In addition, even if you could come up with the $300,000 to buy the property, because of the interest rates, there wouldn't be enough income to make the mortgage payment. Instead of buying, why not consider asking the seller to give you a three-year option to purchase at a set price. For this privilege, you will agree to paying the owner an option deposit of $10,000. You lock in a specific price and control the property for $10,000, not $300,000. You have no mortgage payments, no taxes or insurance payments, and you don't need good credit to accomplish this.

- ***Benefits to the seller:*** While the seller doesn't sell for cash now, the person gets the use of the option deposit tax-free. That's right—all option deposits are tax-free until the option is exercised or rejected. They are also getting *their* price. If you don't perform, they get to keep your money. You could even sweeten the pot by $10,000 every year to renew the option or perhaps increase the price each year. In the meantime, the seller still owns the property legally and can take the tax benefits and collect all income until the option is exercised.

- ***Benefits to you—the buyer:*** You now control a $300,000 property for $10,000. If the value doesn't increase as you think it might, you can always refuse to exercise your option and walk away from the property. You only lose $10,000 in this case, not $300,000. You have no mortgage payments to make and no headaches regarding property management.

Good News. The IRS has ruled that if you don't exercise your option and forfeit it to the seller, while you do lose the $10,000 deposit in cash, you can write it off your income tax, so you end up losing nothing.

Isn't this the ultimate in LEVERAGE?

Rule 2 – Buy Income Property

There are basically two kinds of real estate investments. There is that investment that produces no income for you and the one that produces an income. Generally, when we think of non-producing real estate, we're thinking of land. There are exceptions, of course, but basically this assumption is accurate. We either pay all cash for the land or put down a small payment and make monthly payments. When we pay all cash, we receive nothing in return except the hope that the land will increase in value. If we follow the second course, we experience a negative cash flow because the land produces no income but continues to absorb dollars.

On the other side of the coin, there are those properties that produce an income for us. They generate an income because they house tenants who pay rent. These investments take on various forms, but basically they include houses, apartments, mobile home courts, motels, nursing homes, shopping centers, office buildings, retail stores, and warehouses. I strongly recommend investing in income property over land, not only because of the income received from that type of property but because of certain tax advantages offered by income properties that land doesn't offer.

Any income property is a good investment in a stable and growing economy, but what if the economy is unpredictable or you want to invest in a "sure thing?"

People have to have a place to live, so why not invest in what people have to have? In a recession or a depression, office buildings may not be in demand. But homes and apartments, particularly those in a reasonably good location, will always be in demand. Which to choose—homes or apartments? That's a question only you can answer, and it depends upon your temperament. There are numerous opportunities in both areas.

In general, the single-family home is your safest and most conservative investment. It is easy to understand, easy to manage, easy to liquidate, and avoids many of the problems that might occur such as rent controls. In addition, they are very easy to finance. You generally buy single-family homes for appreciation and don't look for a large positive cash flow.

For those of you looking to go faster, then consider the apartment approach. Apartments are sold based on income, and all you have to do to increase the value of an apartment complex is to raise the income. Let's examine each in detail.

Single-Family Homes

Investors with limited funds are finding it increasingly difficult to make investments that will stay ahead of inflation and at the same time yield a fair return. Other investments such as stocks, bonds, mutual funds, savings accounts and even tax-free municipals fare even worse insofar as their average net yields are concerned. Investment in single-family residential rental properties offers an excellent alternative. Here are a few of the benefits you can expect from investing in single-family rental properties:

- Costs of construction are rising rapidly throughout the United States. Since 1967, the Commerce Department's construction cost index has increased by a whopping 115% as compared to an 81.5% increase in the price of goods and services. There is every indication that this trend will continue. Increasing new home construction costs will undoubtedly contribute to keeping up the prices of existing homes.

- "The Mortgage and Real Estate Executives Report" has reported a continuing demand for single-family homes. They base their report on two factors: a) the median age of first-time homeowners has fallen to age thirty-four. This is significant because the younger age group is a large portion of the total population. b) a significant number of single persons are opting for home ownership rather than renting.

- Houses can be readily financed. It is possible to get up to 100% financing on most single-family homes from institutional lenders, and sellers are also quite flexible in "helping" buyers with financing.

- Houses are one of the most liquid types of real estate. A house that is priced at a fair market value, or offered with the right terms, can usually be sold in a relatively short time.

- Renters tend to pay a higher rent for a single-family home than for an apartment with the same amount of space. This appears to be the case even though apartments often offer such amenities as swimming pools and tennis courts.

- Single-family homes are usually the last to fall under rent controls.

- While no property holding is entirely trouble free, there are many management benefits tied to single-family rentals. You don't have to provide all kinds of non-income producing extras, such as pools, tennis courts, and barbecue grills. Nor do you have to worry about utilities since the renter assumes responsibility for them. In addition, tenants are not in a position to talk to each other about rental rates, lease terms, services and maintenance. Consequently, you don't have to contend with tenant committees, rent strikes, claims of favoritism or bias, and the possibility of bad tenant reaction when an occasional undesirable renter has to be evicted.

- You can accumulate a large portfolio of real estate properties in financially manageable increments. If you choose to withdraw some of your equity after building it up, you can refinance or sell one or two houses. It isn't necessary to encumber or liquidate your entire investment. This type of flexibility can give you some significant tax benefits.

- When it is time to take your profit, liquidating a few properties at a time can minimize taxes. When selling, if you wish, you can use the installment sale and convert your equity into long-term purchases for passive income.

- Another advantage is found in spreading your properties in several locations as a hedge against unforeseen neighborhood changes. This way you are protected against being badly damaged by such minus factors as downzoning or having an undesirable project built alongside your "all-eggs-in-one-basket" property.

Some Negative Factors

No investment is ever made without some element of risk, however slight. Banks have failed and cities have defaulted on their bonds. Here are a few of the potentially negative factors which you may face as an investor in single-family rentals.

- There is no absolute guarantee that the value of your property will increase during the projected holding period. Unpredictable circumstances can cause property values to stagnate or erode for extended periods of time.

- In the event of a vacancy, the property is 100% vacant. For whatever time it takes to find a new tenant, you'll be faced with ongoing mortgage payments and other costs.

- Single-family rentals require some management time and attention. Rents must be collected, repairs made, and regular inspections carried out. When a vacancy occurs, the property must be prepared for the new tenant—and the new tenant must be located.

- There is always the possibility of financial loss from tenant damage and from non-payment of rent. And sometimes it takes an excruciatingly long time to go through the process of evicting a deadbeat from the premises.

- It is impossible to predict how long it will take to sell a property and at what price it will be marketed.

To sum things up, you should weigh the potential negative aspects of investing in single-family rental property against the high rates of after-tax return which are usually generated by this type of rental. However, if you select solid property in a desirable location, your chances of coming out ahead are good to excellent.

How about Apartments?

With land rising steadily in price and the cost of building and maintaining a single-family home going up, there continues to be a steady market for rental apartments. Apartments will always be in demand. Singles usually rent as do young married couples. Other renters include those with young children who are in a transient situation or cannot afford to buy a home, older people who are retired or are returning from the suburbs to city centers, and perennial "cliff dwellers" who never buy houses. It is unlikely that apartment houses will ever go out of style. The owner always has the option of converting units into condominiums or co-ops.

So, how does the beginning investor get started in an apartment venture? Like the rental house, the duplex, triplex, or small apartment house can all be excellent real estate investments. One's risks are minimal in this type of ownership. If you wish, you can absorb your own rental costs by taking up residence in the building. And, if you're in a position to do so, you can offset management and maintenance costs by taking over these duties yourself.

With today's high occupancy rates, the demand for apartment units makes vacancies easy to fill. An occasional empty apartment, being only one of several or of a number of units in a complex, won't hurt your pocketbook to the degree that an unrented single-family home or commercial property would.

What are the best buys in the multiple unit rental fields? If you take the time and trouble to look around, you can usually find old or abused apartment buildings that you can buy, remodel, and refinance. Or, look for apartments that have the potential of being converted to condos at some future date. Also, look for properties with attractive financing that can be assumed or where the existing rents are quite low and offer the potential of being raised. I strongly suggest that you look only at properties where the tenants pay the utilities.

Still not sure which direction you should take—houses or apartments? Then ask yourself these questions.

- Are there more single-family houses than apartments?

- Are there more single-family homes for sale than apartments?

- Do more opportunities exist in single-family homes or in apartments?

- If you guess wrong on location—are you better off with one or two homes in that area or an apartment complex?

- If you have to manage people, are you better off having them separate or together?

- If rent controls come into play, are they more likely to be applied to single-family homes or apartments?

- If you need cash quickly and have to sell to get it, are you better off selling one of your single-family homes or an entire apartment complex?

- Are there more buyers for single-family homes or an apartment complex?

- Are the tenants a bit higher quality in single-family homes or in apartments?

- Do you have to do more homework when buying a single-family home or an apartment building?

- Is it easier to finance a single-family home or an apartment project?

- If there is a fire on the property, the street is blocked off from traffic, or you have to replace a furnace or roof, are you better off with a single-family dwelling of an apartment complex?

Guide to Buying Apartment Buildings

- ***Buy only sound properties.*** This statement applies to buildings that are financially and structurally sound. Consider the neighborhood, design of building, survey and reputation of the property.

- *Have a plan to increase income*. My suggestion is small rent raises every few months unless the rents were unusually high when purchased. The highest rents are obtained when the property is attractive to tenants. If you must modernize, spend your money improving the bathroom, kitchen, landscaping and security system. These areas will give you the highest return on dollars spent.

- *Use leverage when purchasing.* Try to keep it under 10% Remember, when borrowing, never borrow more than the property will support, but never borrow less than the property will support. In other words, if the property will support a $500,000 loan, obtain such a loan, but if the property income dictates that it will only support a loan of $450,000, regardless of value, only borrow this amount. The exception to this rule is if you can see turning around the negative in thirty to sixty days, or if you borrow enough to put aside additional funds to cover the negative.

- *Try to get a return of 7 to 10% cash.* If your down payment is $100,000, your return each year should be $7,000 to $10,000 after all expenses, including debt service.

- *Buy smaller units in the beginning.* Smaller means anything up to twenty units. You will have fewer problems because you or a resident manager can do management. If you run into a "must sell" situation, it's much easier to sell a smaller complex than a bigger one because more people can afford such a purchase. The ideal investment is a four-family unit. They are easy to finance, easy to understand, and easy to sell if necessary. 100% financing is a possibility.

- *Look for condo possibilities*. Buy units that have this potential. It is possible to double your profits when this opportunity presents itself, even if you are not presently interested in taking this avenue.

- **Eliminate amenities.** If you are working with cheaper units, dishwashers and microwave ovens can be a nuisance. While swimming pools are nice, they are a headache when you are the owner, and you are subjecting yourself to a possible lawsuit. If you are working with singles as tenants exclusively, a swimming pool might be worthwhile, but otherwise try to avoid this problem.

- **Buy units where there is good existing financing** or where financing possibilities are available.

- **Buy only units with separate utilities.** The exception would be a complex where you can separate the utilities or charge the tenants for these costs.

- **Buy only for profit.** The tax benefits are many when purchasing income property of this nature, but buy for profit first. Always remember: You make your profit the day you buy. You realize that profit when you sell. Greater fools buy for tax shelter first—greater investors buy for profit first.

- **Understand values of apartment buildings.** You buy income property (over four units) for income. Therefore, it stands to reason that you value income property based on income. There are two types of income—the Scheduled Gross Income and the Net Operating Income.

The scheduled gross income is that income which the property produces if 100% occupied all the time. The net operating income is what the owner actually takes in after all expenses, except debt service. If a building is 100% occupied all the time, the rents are too low. In some complexes, the owner pays the utilities, and in some buildings the tenants pay. It stands to reason that if tenants pay their own utilities, the net should be more to the owner than if the owner paid the bills. Two buildings can have the same gross income, but the net is different. I prefer to net more, rather than gross more. The net you can spend—the gross you can't. Therefore, buy based on net income.

You may look at an apartment complex in many ways. The gross income is important to some realtors while others price the building based on square feet, number of apartments, or net income. The important thing to remember is to find out how investors are buying in your area and what they look for to establish value. Increase your value based on how others are buying. You increase income in one of two ways—either by raising the rents or lowering expenses, or a combination of both. If investors are looking to gross income to establish value, then simply increase the gross. If they are looking at net, increase the net. It's as simple as that.

Guide to Buying Single Family Homes

- *Try to locate properties that have been appreciating 7 to 10% per year.* Remember, with single family homes, you don't buy for income. The value is based upon supply and demand. If you buy in areas where people want to live, you will have an easier time renting it or reselling if necessary.

- *Buy the basic "bread and butter" home.* This price range could be between $20,000 and $80,000, depending on the area. Why? Because it's much easier to rent out a home in this price range and obtain a positive cash flow. It's predicted that the average $60,000 home will appreciate in value to $100,000 in the next ten years.

- *Buy and hold in good areas—Buy and resell in suspect areas.* Your criterion is five years. If you can see the value of a single-family home continuing to go up in value, keep it. If not, but the opportunity is just too good to pass up, buy but resell at a profit.

- *Buy properties below market.* Look for properties priced below what they normally should bring in price.

- *Buy "Subject To" existing financing.*

- *Look for seller "help."* These are situations where the seller will act as part or all lender.

- **Break even or positive cash flow.** You don't buy single-family homes for income, but you also don't buy them for a negative cash flow. Structure your offer so the house pays for itself.

- **Below-market rents.** Even though you don't buy single-family homes for income, a simple rent raise could make the difference whether a single-family home should be purchased or not.

- **Get paid for buying.** The one exception to buying a single-family home that can't be rented out for enough to meet the mortgage payment is when you get paid for buying.

Rule 3—Buy Only Bargains

If you buy only bargains, you can't help but be successful in the purchasing of real estate. As I've said, "Love is zero in tennis and in real estate, also." People buy their homes with emotion and their investment properties with logic.

If you are going to be logical in searching for properties, why not eliminate a lot of unnecessary time and effort by concentrating on those investments that will quickly return the greater profit. I call these opportunities or bargains. They are easy to find if you'll just take a few minutes each day to look for them. They exist in the newspaper, in the multiple-listing book, and along the streets where you drive to work.

There are many properties for sale where the seller is willing to sell only if he or she gets the desired price and terms. These are not the types of properties you want to buy. You want to concentrate efforts on properties that are for sale because the seller has to sell and because of this situation, the seller is willing to be flexible in either price or terms.

Example: If a seller is hung up on getting a specific price, then the person must be flexible in how he or she sells the property to a buyer. If a seller needs all cash, then the person should be willing to discount price.

Are there any clues to indicate whether a seller is flexible or not? Or, to put it more aptly, what makes a bargain?

Generally speaking, one of four things must take place to create a bargain. A seller wants to sell because of personal reasons, because of a management situation, the location isn't that good, or the person can't financially keep the property. Because of these reasons, the seller is willing to "help" the buyer with the purchase. Common sense suggests that as a buyer, you only want to look for sellers who fall under one of these four categories. Some experts refer to them as "opportunities." I like to call them "bargains." What are some of the things to look for?

- **Divorce.** When a couple is getting a divorce, you know a quick sell is almost always imminent. Often these couples list a selling price that is far below the market price for comparable properties.

- **Rundown property.** Look for a property that needs some fixing up. Through your own initiative and a certain amount of sweat, you can make thousands of dollars just by painting, repairing, and engineering other improvements which need not be costly. Drive a different route to work each day and keep your eyes open for the worst looking house in a neighborhood.

- **Transfer.** Whenever you run into a situation where the owner has to sell, you can bet that the person will be more flexible in price and terms.

- **Negative cash flow.** This situation occurs when the property doesn't produce enough income to make the expenses and mortgage payments. Perhaps you can see a way to turn this around.

- **Poor management.** Sometimes just by changing the management you can turn an "alligator" into a real money-maker.

- **Danger of foreclosure.** When an owner is running behind in mortgage payments, the person is generally more receptive to an offer at attractive terms. Look for "distress" ads in the newspaper or possibly develop a friendly relationship with one or more lenders who might guide you toward these people.

- **Foreclosures.** These are properties that have been foreclosed and put up for sale. Information regarding these possibilities is easy to come by. FHA and VA will put you on a mailing list, and a simple phone call to your conventional lender asking if REO's are for sale should provide you with adequate leads to work with.

- **Estate settlement.** Whenever a property must be sold to settle an estate, you can often find good opportunities.

- **Retirement.** Many times a retired person is looking to real estate to provide an extra income. Management may be a headache to this person, but a Sale on Contract basis could be all the aspirin the individual needs.

- **Out-of-state owners.** Often out-of-state owners don't know the true value of their real estate and will let it go at a price below the market. Besides, managing something from afar isn't all that easy.

- **Needs money to pay debts.** Persons under pressure from creditors will often make huge concessions to those offering to "take over" their debts and then make a settlement with the creditor on a small monthly payment or a discount for cash.

- **Seller doesn't know real value.** Many sellers are leery of real estate agents and don't want to spend money on an appraisal. More often than not, the price they put on their property is well below the market, which means you can pick up some real bargains if you keep your eyes open.

- **Get rid of partner.** Sometimes you'll run across a seller whose primary motive in selling is to pay off an unwanted partner. The average partnership is about sixteen months, and I've made some of my best buys under these circumstances.

- **Fear of economy.** This means fear of loss, and this is as strong a motivator as one can find.

- **Change of use.** All kinds of possibilities here—convert apartments to condos, offices, co-ops, etc.

- **Tax problems.** The IRS is threatening to attach a house unless the person sells—another super motivation.

- **Tax sales.** By law, tax-delinquent properties must be advertised for sale annually. Even though there is a redemption period, this method offers some strong possibilities. I personally know of one man who made over $600,000 in a seven-year period just buying tax sale properties.

- **Needs cash.** This is a person who needs cash more than price and, therefore, will discount the price heavily for all cash. Buy and then finance after ownership, recouping the cash.

- **Time problems.** This is a person who no longer has the time to mess with managing or taking care of a property.

- **Lost employment.** This person has lost a job and can't afford the high payments any more: "Must sell."

- **Balloon payments.** A big amount of money is due soon, and the seller doesn't have the money to make the payment nor does the person know how to solve the problem.

- **Double payments.** The person owns more than one house—must sell.

- **Property on market for a long time.** The seller is probably hurting because of having to pay mortgage payments.

- **Sickness—health.** Money means little when one is very ill, or it could mean a great deal. On the one hand, maybe the seller can no longer take care of the house or the seller may need money to pay doctor bills. Either way, the seller will probably be flexible.

- *Neighborhood troubles.* This could be a problem because of changing neighborhood from residential to commercial, too many kids or too few kids in the neighborhood, schools far away, and the list is long.

Sources of Opportunities

√   Newspapers—Watch for key headings indicating flexibility

√   MLS books

√   Estate sales

√   Foreclosure auctions

√   Attorneys

√   Lending institutions

√   Public records at the County Court House

√   Tax sales

√   Friends and acquaintances

√   Vacant properties

√   "For Sale by Owner" signs

√   Run your own ad

Rule 4—Always Ask Questions

Now that we've learned what to look for when buying, what's our next step? Since our purpose is to buy real estate with very little down payment and absolutely no personal risk, it's important that we not waste a lot of time with sellers who won't sell on our terms. They appear to have the right motivation for selling and apparently will listen to flexibility in an offer, so we're ready to take our next step.

There is a lot of real estate for sale and most of it is for sale only if the seller receives his or her price and terms. You can chase after that person hoping to get the individual to listen to an offer, or you can eliminate the individual from the chase right up front. Ask questions to see if a person qualifies.

- **Why are you selling?** The individual's answer to the first question will dictate whether you proceed to the next question at all. If the person is selling to solve a personal problem such as the ones we just discussed, then you will want to continue. If an individual is selling only to get a certain price and is not flexible, then thank the person very much and move to the next possibility.

- **How long have you been trying to sell?** The answer to this question is a great indicator as to how flexible a seller might be. When sellers first begin to try and sell, they sometimes get an inflated opinion of value and are less likely to be flexible, whereas if the property has been for sale for a long period of time, they are much more likely to listen to an offer.

- **Have you had any offers?** If not, why not? Perhaps you are asking too much. If yes, why didn't you accept the offer? Explain that you don't want to waste their time if you aren't even in the ball park pricewise or close to agreeable terms.

- **How long have you owned the property?** Very important. If a seller has owned the property only for a short time, something might be wrong with it, or perhaps the seller is trying to turn a quick profit at your expense. If a person has owned it for a number of years, though, chances are they have taken their tax benefits out and are more receptive to a "creative" offer.

- **How did you arrive at your price?** I love this one! Do you know how most sellers arrive at their price? By what they need—or I call it PFA (plucked from air). Most have no idea of value at all. Often this error works to your advantage since these sellers are pricing themselves under the market. I strongly suggest that you secure an appraisal. An appraisal will indicate the value after everything is in tiptop shape and tells you what is needed to get the property into that condition.

- *What major improvements are needed—What major improvements have you made?* You certainly should be aware of any problems that might occur when buying.

- *Do you have plans for the proceeds?* In other words, what are you going to do with the money? If you can get an honest indication from the seller, you can structure your offer accordingly. Example: If the person wants to use the funds to buy more real estate, find out the person's reason for buying. Maybe selling to you on a small down payment and taking monthly payments from you will satisfy the seller's needs. If the person needs the funds for other purposes, maybe you can furnish him or her with what they need to meet those needs.

- *Is there anything wrong with the property that would prevent you from investing in it?* Think about that for a moment. The seller can't really answer yes since that would discourage you from buying. If the person answers no, you can ask the seller to assist you with financing.

- *What is the existing financing on the property?* In other words, do you have loans against the property now, and what are they? You want to look for properties that have low interest loans that can be assumed at no escalation of interest, such as FHA and VA, or properties that have extremely high loans to value. It is important to check the due date on these loans. Avoid getting involved with loans that mature in less than five years unless you know how to handle them when they come due.

- *What rents and deposits does the property have?* Many times these escrows can be used to create a down payment.

- **_Is time for closing a factor?_** If you have to move soon, you might be more flexible. If the seller is not in a hurry to move, the person might agree to renting the property back or waiting for six months or so for a closing, giving you time to resell at a profit to somebody else.

- **_Have you had management problems?_** On income property, be sure to include this question. Along with this ask:

  a) How long has your longest tenant been here?
  b) How long has your shortest tenant been here?
  c) When was the last time you raised rents?
  d) How do the rents compare with other rents in the neighborhood?
  e) What is included with the sales price?
  f) Would you reduce the down payment or lower the price . . . depending on the situation?

    - If given a higher price?
    - To close in three days?
    - To get added security for you?
    - To be paid off more quickly?

You can handle these questions on the phone, in person, or by your realtor if one is involved. I suggest you write them down on a legal notepad and read from the pad. It is not necessary to memorize them, and in fact, doing so might hurt your chances in buying. Sellers like to feel comfortable with buyers, and if they think you know more than they do, you will have a problem negotiating with the seller. "The dumber you act, the better your chances for success."

Rule 5 – Check Location

When I sold real estate for a living, I always said that the three most important things in real estate were location—location—location.

Location can dictate whether you are successful in your investment program or not. It can also help you determine whether you keep a property for a number of years or whether it's in your best interest to use the property for what I call an "in-and-outer."

If the seller does not seem flexible or agreeable to questions, of course, thank the person and go on to bigger and better things. But, if he or she sounds interested in working with you, you're ready to take the next step—a visit to the property.

What should you be looking for? Basically, pride of ownership. If it is a "fix-up" property, you want the worst looking house in the area because you can make it more valuable by making it more attractive.

If it is a rental house, be sure that people will want to rent in that area and find out what rent other properties are bringing. Good locations command larger rents than suspect or bad locations. Good locations also attract better tenants, so concentrate your efforts on buying properties in good locations. What is a good location?

A good location is an area that is going up in value, not staying the same or going down in value. Try and find properties that are going up in value about 10% per year. The reason they are going up in value is that people want to live there and are willing to pay more because of this. A good location also provides amenities such as availability to schools, shopping, and transportation. A simple criterion is stability over the next five years. If you feel that a property will go up in value over the next five years, buy and hold onto the property. These will be growth areas most of the time where things are happening such as new shopping centers, new schools, and other growth producing developments.

If you've found a real bargain opportunity but aren't quite sure of the location, then consider the "in- and-outer" idea. Buy on soft terms and carry the financing. For the time being, just remember this approach—I'll cover how you do it later.

Who can you ask to find out whether this is a good location or not? There are several possibilities.

- **_Banker or Chamber of Commerce._** If it is a new town or city to you, consider asking a banker or Chamber of

Commerce representative which are the best areas in town.

- **_Look in directories._** Some cities have directories that list areas by streets and even show whether the people occupying the properties are owners or renters. They sometimes show the income average for the area.

- **_Realtors._** Look for sales signs in the area and call upon realtors having the properties listed for sale. They should have some feeling as to what is happening in the area.

- **_Professional management companies._** Since they manage properties all over the city, they can give you an idea as to how much rent you can expect to receive.

- **_Police department._** This is an excellent source to check for crime problems in the area.

- **_Utility companies._** I learned about a location from a telephone installer. He mentioned how much the area had improved in the past couple of years since telephone deposits were much less now than before.

- **_Mailman._** This is perhaps the best source of all. Here is a person who is in the area six days per week. The individual certainly knows who lives in the neighborhood, whether it be white collar or blue collar people, who is on welfare, who is having domestic problems, and other such valuable information. I personally know of one man who hired the mailman to be his manager. In case the tenant skips town without paying rent, who better to have on your side to track the person down than the mailman?

My Recommendation

Buy only in good neighborhoods initially. You will have fewer problems. Analyze what the area will do over the next five years. If it is going to continue to go up in value, keep the property. You should have no problem raising rents.

If you are concerned about the property continuing to go up in value, then consider buying and reselling, creating a nice income for yourself with no worries about the future. Look for "attractive" properties or properties that have a good appearance. Surveys from years back show that single people, married people, and family people all agree on this one issue. Their first impression of appearance determined whether they rented or not, regardless of location or other amenities.

Rule 6—Check Property

The property you acquire should be sound in two ways— structurally and financially. Don't buy a property that is falling down or needs lots of attention unless you are prepared or qualified to handle this problem. Have it inspected before purchase, even if you have to pay for the fee to have it done. These few dollars could save you thousands over the long haul.

I personally know of one couple that failed to do this and bought a property without any plumbing. Oh yes, it had tubs, sinks, and the likes, so it had the appearance of plumbing. The pipes were missing. An inspection will tell you the condition of the roof and furnace as well as if the structure has termites or other potential problems.

Secondly, you want to buy a property that is sound financially, meaning a property that can be financed conventionally. You may not wish to purchase using conventional financing, but it's awfully important not to get locked into a property that can't be financed conventionally at some future date.

Conventional financing includes government loans and those loans made at a local savings and loan or bank. Government financing is generally thought of as FHA or VA; however, there are also some HUD programs and FNME and GNME financing as well. Check with mortgage bankers or companies that specialize in this type financing.

If the property is free and clear of loans, you want to make sure that financing is possible on that property. That may sound funny to some of you, but surprisingly enough, not all properties can be financed, especially those properties located in a "negative location." This is yet another reason why you should concentrate only on properties in "good locations."

Rule 7—Check Financing Alternatives

If the property is something you would like to own, you then turn your attention to the financing possibilities. These are as follows:

- Seller financing
- Conventional financing
- Government financing

Conventional financing is a type of financing that most are familiar with. A person borrows the money from a bank or savings and loan and uses the proceeds to buy the property, most of the time putting up a down payment. Government financing is generally thought of as FHA or VA. Once again the buyer comes up with a cash down payment with the government programs furnishing the balance of the purchase price.

The cheapest form of financing to the buyer is when the seller gets involved either with part of the purchase price or all of it. In this case, the seller acts as the lender. The person can do this in several ways. Here are three:

- *Property fully paid for with no mortgage owed.* Instead of the buyer going to a savings and loan and borrowing money, the seller sells to the buyer for a small cash down payment and takes back a "note" secured by a Deed of Trust or a mortgage on the property. Instead of the buyer paying the savings and loan, the person now pays the seller.

- *Existing loans on the property.* The buyer agrees to take over these loans, but the seller also participates by taking a note secured by a mortgage for the balance of the purchase price. Now the buyer owes on two notes, the one taken over and the one owed by the seller.

- *Existing loans on the property.* Rather than allow the buyer to take over the existing loans, the seller can keep these loans in his or her own name and sell to the buyer on one note that includes these other loans. Instead of the buyer taking over existing financing and being responsible for it, the seller remains the responsible party. The seller can sell with existing loans on the property in one of two ways— either on Contract Sale or on a Wraparound.

If it is Contract Sale, the contract is notarized and recorded, but legal title does not pass to the buyer. The contract is evidence that the buyer is buying, so if done correctly, the buyer has little worry. The buyer is said to have an "equitable title" interest in the property. Once the buyer performs as agreed, the seller then deeds the property to the buyer.

Or, the seller can actually deed the property to the buyer at closing and take back a note for the balance. Since this note from buyer to seller includes the existing financing on the property, it in effect "wraps around" that financing, so it is called a Wraparound.

Anytime a seller helps with financing, whether it is a small amount or the entire purchase price, I highly recommend that you seek legal advice before proceeding.

Rule 8—Determine Value

A seller is asking a certain price for a piece of property. How do you know the price is right? You certainly don't want to pay too much for the property, so is there an easy way to determine its value?

First of all, it's important to understand that there are three approaches to value. They are the:

- Income Approach
- Comparison or Market Approach
- Cost or Replacement Approach

Let's examine each. We use the income approach on income property over four units in size. This means that we are going to buy a property of this nature based on the income that it produces. Every income property produces two incomes—one is called the "Scheduled Gross Income" and the other the "Net Income."

The scheduled gross income is that income the property should bring in if 100% rented at all times. It does not allow for vacancy or expenses. The net income takes into consideration all expenses, including vacancy. It is actually the amount of money left over to pay a mortgage payment.

It just makes common sense to buy a property based on what it nets, not what it is supposed to take in. One property may be for sale where the tenants pay the utilities and another property for sale where the owner pays the utilities. The scheduled gross income is the same, but the net will be entirely different because of expenses. You certainly want to buy the property that nets more.

It's important to know what investors are expecting in the way of a net return. They sometimes refer to this as the "Cap rate" or the "Capitalization rate." Simply put, this means what an investor would expect in the way of a return on money if the person paid all cash. If an investor expects a 10% return on money and the net income before debt service is $10,000, then the value to the investor would be $100,000. Be sure and buy based on what other investors in the area are paying and expect a return.

Get professional help to determine this amount. Your local MLS, realtor or appraiser can help. Remember: "You make your profit the day you buy real estate—you realize it when you sell." To pay too much up front can cost you—to buy right in the beginning can make you financially wealthy.

The Comparison or Market Approach is used to determine value on single-family homes to fourplexes. It's like comparing apples with apples. This is quite easy to do. Multiple-listing services have all the information you need. Realtors can also help, as well as title companies, and if worse comes to worse, you can always have the property appraised professionally. The Cost or Replacement Approach simply means that you should not pay more for a property than you would if you bought the land and built new.

To Review: Use the Income Approach when buying income property over four units, the Market Approach on one to four units, and the Cost Approach on something new. Hire an appraiser if need be.

How to Raise the Value of Your Property

Your objective in investing in real estate should be to make money. You can buy and hope, or you can guarantee that you make a profit by learning how real estate functions.

You should expect an immediate income because you will be buying properties that pay for themselves with the rental income from tenants. This is your starting point—a property that pays its own way.

Raising the Value on Income Property

You will recall that I said you should buy based on net income. It stands to reason then that the way to increase the value is by increasing the income. This can be done in two ways—either by raising the income rents or by lowering expenses, or both.

Example: an apartment complex of ten units nets, before debt service, $11,000 per year. If you wanted a 10% return on cash, the apartment would be worth $110,000, or ten times the net. By raising the rents a mere $10 per month, as an owner, you have increased value. You can now see why it's so important to buy right in the beginning.

Another highly workable technique for raising value is to buy "fix-up" properties. By improving the property, you make it more desirable, and it's quite easy to command a much higher rent. In fact, you can often increase your equity by many thousands of dollars in a relatively short time. Don't think this is an easy road to follow, however, because a great deal of work and planning has to be done in order to put the "fix-up" property in shape to command a premium price.

If you are a person who likes this type of thing or have a partner who can do the work, this road to success can come quite quickly.

My Recommendation

Try to avoid making your acquisition in a bad neighborhood where you may have trouble attracting the type of tenant willing to pay the higher rents you plan to ask after making necessary repairs and upgrades. A poor neighborhood can also cause problems when selling.

A safer move is to buy a property that is located in a good neighborhood but is being poorly managed and the rents are already low. This happens a great deal with out-of-state owners or owners who really don't care about raising rents because they don't need the income.

Single-family rentals come under different rules. Generally speaking, you buy single-family homes and condos for appreciation and income property for income. If you're fortunate, which is another way of saying that you've selected wisely, you may do very well on both counts. Raising rents on single-family homes will not increase the value—value increases in single-family homes by supply and demand. If buyers wish to live in certain areas over others, they tend to pay more to live in the area they like. This increases the demand for that area, making the value rise. Maximize your appreciation by buying in areas where buyers want to live.

The easiest way to increase your value is to buy below the market in the beginning, thereby guaranteeing an immediate profit. You do this by concentrating your efforts on those bargains that were earlier discussed.

Rule 9—Use Professionals

Most of us don't have the time or knowledge to participate in every facet of real estate investing, so to improve our chances of success, we surround ourselves with professionals to do the work for us. If we are careless in selecting them or just choose to ignore them entirely, in the long run we will lose. Let's examine who they are and what role they can play in the investment game.

- **Attorney**—This should not be just any attorney or a friend but should be an attorney who specializes in real estate.

Remember this if you remember nothing else about attorneys. They are not taught how to make real estate judgments, so do not ask them if you should buy or not. They will always answer no. Why? — Because if you take an attorney's advice on buying and lose money, you can sue the person. An attorney has to say no for personal protection. Just get an attorney for legal purposes. You do not need an attorney for every real estate transaction, but it is advisable most of the time.

- **Realtor**—Some of you will use a realtor, and some of you will not.

The unfortunate part about realtors in general is that they are not taught how to be creative. For the most part, they are taught how to pass a test to get a license, and that's it. They then go into a real estate office, are given an MLS book, a pat on the back, and are told by the broker to list and sell. Anything out of the ordinary pattern of normal buying and selling becomes negative in their mind.

The majority of properties for sale, however, are for sale through a real estate person, so your chances of dealing with an agent at some future time are almost inevitable. You might as well face this fact up front and pick the right realtor ahead of time. Who is that? He or she is someone who is willing to listen to your offers and work with you, the buyer.

I suggest you consider hiring your own realtor to work exclusively with you. We call this person the "Buyer's Broker." In this case, you the buyer, pay the realtor. The person's pay could come in the form of a note, sharing a commission with another realtor, cash from you, or even a partial ownership in the property. Your broker makes all your offers on your behalf. Look for an energetic person who is willing to "listen and learn." Make your agreement with the individual that you will buy everything through him or her as long as the person doesn't buy without first submitting the property to you. That will prevent your realtor from buying the "good deals" without first giving you the opportunity to buy.

- **Accountant**—A very important member of your investment team should be a qualified accountant.

Like picking an attorney, not all accountants are real estate-oriented. Pick one who knows real estate law and is willing to help you with your investment decisions. Don't ever sell without first checking with your accountant. It might be in your best interest to keep the property or exchange it.

Likewise, when you buy, it's very important to set up your depreciation schedule ahead of time. You can sometimes even set up a definite value for land and building at time of purchase.

- **Bank Loan Officer**—I've said it many times—A banker's oath is "We will not loan money to anybody who needs it!"

There will be a time when you need the help of a banker, so it's important to get his or her agreement when you don't need it. Try and create some borrowing power or line of credit for money before you actually need the money. Then, when it comes time for you to come up with cash, all you have to do is call the banker and the money will be ready. If you wait until you need the money to start your approach, much time will be lost, and you may not succeed.

My advice is to stay with the banker, not the bank. People make loans, not banks. If the banker moves to another bank, you move with the individual.

- **Insurance Person**—Look for an agent who looks to your needs, not sales. In other words, find an insurance person who will insure you for what you need and no more.

You may find that you need additional professional help as you progress. You may need assistance from a title company, an appraiser, a rental agency, or a management company. These are not as difficult to find as the four professionals listed, but you might want to keep them in mind for the future.

Rule 10—Establish Good Credit

Credit just doesn't happen. It has to be built! Unfortunately, in today's business world if you don't have good credit, or are associated with someone who does, you can run into all sorts of problems. You don't really need good credit to buy real estate, but if you have good credit, your path to success comes that much faster and easier. And having no credit at all is just as bad as having bad credit. In fact, you are penalized for paying all cash. And, in some cases, people and agencies won't even accept cash. Try renting a car without a credit card or checking into a hotel without this identification. So, if you must have credit, how do you start?

Build Your Credit

You start by building your credit. If you work for a firm, ask them if they will assist you in getting credit initially at a department store. Open checking and savings accounts and immediately apply for a Visa and MasterCard. Even use a co-signer if you have to. Stability is the most important factor. How long you have lived in an area, how long you have worked at a place of business, and how long you have been married are all factors that indicate to others your stability. Buy something on layaway from a department store. Pay for it over several months and then pick up the item after it has been paid in full. I don't care what kind of credit you may have, no retail store is going to refuse this request.

Pay Off Early

Cultivate bankers and pledge your savings account and borrow against it, paying off early. I know of one lady in Oklahoma City who created a $20,000 line of credit in one week starting with just $1,000. She opened a bank savings account for $1,000, waited a day and then applied for a loan. She offered to pledge her savings as collateral for the loan and asked how much the banker would loan her based upon this collateral. It's quite easy to borrow $1,000 using this method, but many times the banker will allow you to borrow more than the $1,000. In the case of my lady in Oklahoma City, the banker agreed to loan her $5,000. She then took $1,000 of the $5,000, put it into another bank and repeated the question. Within a seven-day period she repeated this at four banks and all of a sudden had $20,000 in credit built up. Gradually pay off the loans before due and repeat the process, but each time ask for more money. It's important to play what I call "the banker's game" when you do this. Don't go through the drive-in window but take the time to call on your banker once or twice a week. If nothing else, just be seen by the person regularly in the bank.

Correct Bad Credit

If you've experienced bad credit in the past and wish to correct it, buying real estate is a good way to start. Buy property that requires no qualifying, pay on time, and use this as a reference. If you have been charged with slow pay in the past, be sure that before you pay off the creditors, approach them and ask them to remove or refrain from giving you a slow credit rating. If you've already paid in full and they have socked you with bad credit, ask them nicely if they will remove the blot from your credit, or ask that your credit bureau write them a letter asking for an explanation of the situation. If the creditor doesn't respond in thirty days, by law, the rating automatically comes off your report. Sometimes the credit bureau will take it off on its own if you can prove that you paid in full.

If all else fails, consider associating yourself with a person who has good credit, either by paying the person for his or her signature and guarantee—or even making the person your partner. Try and get credit cards in both names or in your name alone with the partner co-signing for the bill. You sign the card alone and pay on time. After a period of time, you will have established yourself as a good risk. You might also consider establishing a business name and using that name to establish credit.

Your goal should be at least three major credit cards and a line of credit of a minimum of $5,000 each at three banks.

Rule 11—Understand Management

The very thought of having to manage real estate strikes fear in the hearts of many. You'd be amazed at the number of people who refuse to get involved with real estate just because they are afraid of management or don't want to get involved with it. Ask yourself these questions:

1.   Do I have to manage it myself?
2.   When should I consider hiring a management company?
3.   What should I look for in hiring a management company?
4.   How do I manage it myself?

Here's the Good News.

You don't have to manage property yourself. There are plenty of managers out there who are willing to do it for you. Personally, I hate management, so I have all properties managed with the possible exception of my single-family rentals. There really is little management involved with single-family homes, so I take care of these myself. However, there are those firms who specialize in this area, and if you own properties out of state, it's a must that you have professional management.

Management problems generally come right in the beginning when you fail to get the right tenant. Most of us make a decision on whether we will rent to a person based upon first impression. Don't do that. Before you let anybody move in:

- Do a credit check.

- Have the person fill out an application form and check answers thoroughly.

- Insist on references and check them out. Always remember, the person will only give you the good references, so do some digging on your own.

- Get a check, not cash initially. Why? Because it will indicate where the person presently lives, perhaps a telephone number, social security number, etc. It can also indicate stability. If a person wants to pay you in cash, look out.

- Always get a deposit with the application.

- Have the person fill out an employment verification and check with his or her employer. Also check with the previous landlord for history of payments. Caution: If the person has been *slow pay* for the previous landlord and has been asked to move, that landlord could give glowing reports just to get rid of the bum.

- Insist on rent on time. Be hard in the beginning and your problems will be easier later on.

- Use a lease with teeth in it, or better yet a month-to-month agreement. A lease ties you in for a specific period of time at the same rent. A month-to-month agreement allows you to raise the rent anytime with a thirty-day notice.

- Always inspect the property with the tenants before they move in, asking them to sign a form regarding condition of the house or apartment. Do the same thing when they move, using another form and compare the two. This will eliminate any problems you might have regarding damage or security deposits.

- An excellent book on management is Al Lowry's *How to Manage Real Estate Successfully—in Your Spare Time,* published by Simon and Schuster.

A few other ideas for you to consider:

- If it is a single-family rental, consider offering the tenant a "discount" on the rent for paying on time and not bothering with minor repairs.

- Be sure and include a penalty for not paying on time or a bonus for paying early.

- If you wish a tenant to stay one year, offer the first month free rent.

- I just recently rented three of my apartments during a difficult time by offering a "new free TV" if a person rented. You can buy a television for around $80. This is a small price to entice a tenant and much less expensive than a continually vacant apartment.

- In small complexes, stay with "resident managers" rather than professional firms. That person is there all the time and in many cases can be used for minor fix up.

- VERY IMPORTANT: Do not tell the tenants that you are the owner. If you are managing your own property, tell the tenants you are the "manager." In that way it will be much easier to raise the rents since you can always blame the owner. If it is a professionally managed building or you use a resident manager, ask the manager not to inform the tenants who the owner is. That way you will avoid midnight calls from tenants.

Should you manage yourself or hire someone? The best way for you to decide is to take the number of hours you are spending in managing and divide these hours into the cost of hiring someone. You will quickly decide whether you are being paid $10 per hour or $2 per hour for working.

How do you pick the right management firm? Getting recommendations from others is one way. I prefer to work with a company that specializes in management and that is its prime source of income.

Be aware that some companies manage property on the side, but their interests lie in real estate, insurance, and similar ventures. They are less likely to do you the job that a professional management company will. Fees are negotiable, but generally they charge according to the collections, so it is in their best interest to keep raising rents.

Ask to see other properties they manage and ask how often they raise rents. A quick view of other properties will be a good indicator of how well they take care of their properties, and periodic rent raises are a must. Ask them why you should let them manage your property as compared to another firm.

Rule 12—Negotiate from Strength

That all-important time has finally arrived. The seller has indicated a willingness to be flexible, the location checks out, the property seems to be sound, and the financing is available. All that's left is to get together and iron out any problems.

Ways to Negotiate

The negotiation can come in one of two ways. You can negotiate with the seller yourself, one-on-one, or you can have somebody else do it for you. Generally speaking, the worst person to negotiate for you is *you*. Why? Because you tend to become emotional when dealing for your personal desires or needs, but a third party looks at the transaction from an entirely different view, one of pure logic. It is important to remember that when negotiating for yourself to continually repeat this mental message: "I don't care whether I get this property or not, and if I can't buy it on my terms, I'm going to walk away."

Let's examine the rules we should apply and use.

- **Most important: Before you do anything else, build up trust and confidence with the seller.** If the seller likes you, the person is much more likely to adapt to your "creative" ideas. If the person distrusts you at all, your chances of success are very slim.

- **You do this by talking the "Fair Play" idea: "Mr. Seller, I'd like to buy your property, and I'm sure you want to sell."** All we have to do is work out the details so that both of us end up with what we want. Let's first talk about what is most important to you, cash or price? Cash— of course, I'll pay you all cash if that is what you want, but remember you will have to take less in price since all cash commands a better deal. Or—price. Fine, I'll give you your price as long as I can buy on my terms. I really don't care which direction you choose, Mr. Seller. As a matter of fact, let's consider several alternatives, one with all cash and the other with your price and terms, and you pick which offer you want.

- **Concentrate on relieving the seller of fears and show the person the benefits by selling to you under your terms.**

- **Be prepared before you begin to *not* fall in love with the property.** Always be prepared to walk away from it if you can't get it under your terms and conditions.

- **Point out flaws in a nice way.** Most owners don't view their personal property the same way they would properties they were viewing merely for investment purposes.

- **Keep your negotiations simple.** Don't use big words or come across as overly intelligent in real estate. Sellers immediately become fearful if they think the buyer knows more than they do. Play dumb, even to the point of asking the seller to help you.

- **Becoming a winner in negotiation happens because of persistence, attitude, and overcoming negative thoughts.** Don't tell yourself that the seller won't do this—tell yourself that the person will because you'll convince the individual that he or she should. You have the power to dictate what your future destiny will be. You can't win every time you negotiate, but if you don't try, or give up too soon, you'll never win. It's a proven fact that successful people actually fail more often than failures do. Why? Because they continually try and never give up. Within reason, you can get what you want if you believe you can.

Rule 13—Buy without Risk

If you are able to buy real estate without personal risk, you have few if any cares as to the condition of the economy or whether the tenants continue paying rent. If you have no personal liability, then you have nothing to worry about. Nobody can sue you or take away anything you presently own. How do you do this?

Eventually you will be asked to sign a contract to purchase real estate. It is extremely important to understand what you are signing and what the legal ramifications might be if you default for any reason in the purchase of that property.

Contracts call for the name of the buyers. I suggest you write in "John Doe and/or assigns" in this space. This will allow you to assign the contract at some future date to another person or take title in a name other than your own.

The contract will call for an "earnest money deposit," which can be any form of consideration from just a "promise to pay" to a check, cash, note or pledge of equity in another property. There is no set amount required nor is it required that you have to comply with this part of the contract. My suggestion is that you use as little as possible to tie up a property, and I prefer to use a promissory note due at closing to accomplish this. If you have to come up with cash, do not give money directly to the seller, but rather have it placed in escrow with a title company or the realtor involved.

The next area of concern is what happens if you sign a contract and then change your mind. Can the seller sue you? For the answer to this question, check under the "buyer's default" section of the contract. Make sure the liquidated damage clause appears as follows—and if it doesn't, put in this clause.

"The (cash) earnest money deposit will be retained by seller as total liquidated damages, in case of default by buyer."

With this clause, you can rest assured that if you change your mind, your only cost will be a forfeiture of the earnest money deposit. Without this clause, the seller can sue you for damages, plus perhaps force you to buy. Now let's see what happens if you own the property and everything falls apart and you end up losing the real estate via the foreclosure route. Will this affect your credit, and are you in danger of being sued by the seller or lender? It will not affect you in the least, providing you include the Exculpatory Clause with your offer:

"The liability shall be limited to the property itself and shall not extend beyond this."

This clause removes all personal liability from you personally in purchases and in the future. In short, a person can take the property, but not take *you*! Along with this, look for properties where you can take over existing loans with no personal liability.

How do you do this? You buy subject to the existing loans and do not agree to assume them. Under the section regarding financing, if the word "assume" and "agree to pay" are included, just slash them out and substitute "subject to." By doing this, the seller isn't really hurt, and the buyer's benefits increase. The buyer doesn't have to qualify for the existing loan since he or she is not assuming responsibility for it. Therefore, having a job or good credit doesn't come into play. In addition, there are no assumption fees for the buyer to pay.

When making an acceptable offer, especially the first property you buy, when that offer is accepted, you will panic. Is there any way you can protect yourself initially against making a mistake? Even though all you stand to lose is the earnest money, is there any way you can make an offer without the fear of losing anything? Yes, there is, and you do this by including certain clauses. These clauses fall into two categories: Weasel Clauses and Special Clauses.

9

Weasel Clauses and Special Clauses

A Weasel Clause is simply a vague conditional statement that allows you to back out of a contract anytime prior to closing. It's not your intention to back out, but it's awfully nice to know you have that option up until closing. Even if you have made a good faith earnest money deposit when you made your offer, that deposit should be returned to you if you change your mind. You can let your imagination do the walking, but simpler examples are as follows:

- *Subject to adequate financing or financing suitable to the buyer.* What's adequate or suitable? Whatever you want it to be—maybe 100% of the purchase price or even 150%.

- *Subject to my partner's approval.* Who is your partner? Your wife, husband, son, nobody.

- *Subject to my accountant's approval, attorney's approval, advisor's approval, inspection of records, books, and you get the picture.*

- *Subject to a soil test.* This is one of my favorites and also very important in many areas of the United States.

■ *Subject to an appraisal (paid for by either buyer or seller).* This is an easy clause to get in any contract, especially when the buyer agrees to pay for it. The buyer doesn't have to get an appraisal yet can use this as an excuse to back out of buying.

Your intent is to buy real estate, but you can always have second thoughts about whether you are making a mistake or not. With one or more of these clauses, you have right up until the day of closing to make up your mind.

Special Clauses

Exculpatory Clause

This clause allows you to buy without any personal liability. Note the wording: The liability is "limited to the property itself and shall not extend beyond this." In other words, if you default for whatever reason in your loan payments and the lender, or seller, is forced to foreclose and take the property, that is all they take. They do not take you. It also does not affect the credit of the buyer in any way. Whenever the seller carries part or all of the financing in the form of a note secured by real estate, I highly recommend that this clause be inserted right after the terms of the note.

Let's take an example: In the case, the price is $100,000, and there is an existing first mortgage balance of $60,000. The seller is willing to sell for a small down payment, or even nothing down, with the buyer taking over the first mortgage and the seller taking a note for the difference. The buyer buys " subject to" the existing first mortgage and includes the Exculpatory provision with the note to the seller. The buyer now has no legal responsibility if all goes sour.

Subordination Clause

Normally, if you have two or more mortgages against the same property and you refinance, the subordinate loans move up in security. Example: If you have a first mortgage of $50,000 and a second of $25,000 and want to refinance the first to $100,000, it will be necessary to pay off both the old first and second to accomplish the refinancing. This is because if you don't pay off the second, it automatically takes over that position.

Generally speaking, mortgage instruments do not spell out that they are first, second, or third, but they are called that because of time of recording. The first instrument recorded is the first, the second the second, and so forth. Anything other than a first could cause a problem because most lenders require a first position. If you'd like to keep the second in that position, for whatever reason, such as low interest rates or good terms, the use of a Subordination Clause accomplishes this. A property can now be refinanced without having to pay off the second. Used properly, this can be a very powerful tool in financing.

Performance Clause

This clause insures that you will always have a break even or positive cash flow since it calls for payments to be tied to the net income. Let's use an example of $1,000 per month mortgage payments and 80% of net operating income. As long as the net operating income is $1,250 per month, the mortgage payment remains at $1,000 per month since this is 80% of the net. However, if the net operating income falls to $1,000 per month, then the mortgage payment is reduced to $800 per month. If there are any worries about vacancies or reduced income for any reason, then this clause eliminates that problem. If a buyer had no income at all, there would be no mortgage payment.

Exchange Clause

This clause is used when a person desires to sell and postpone paying taxes. If you wish to accomplish this, I suggest you associate yourself with a competent exchanger.

Option Clause

There are two kinds of contracts that are used when purchasing real estate. One is called the Specific Performance Contract and the other a Receipt and Option form. Some states spell out which is which, while others use the clause regarding earnest money to distinguish the type of contract. An earnest money deposit is a good faith deposit indicating that the buyer has all intentions of purchasing the property. If, for some reason, the buyer changes his or her mind and decides not to go through with the purchase, then the earnest money and clause spelling out the conditions of that earnest money deposit come into play.

If the clause reads that the seller "may keep the earnest money deposit and take whatever legal action available to 'force' the buyer to perform or sue for liquidated damages," beware. This is a specific performance type of contract. If, however, you include the option clause that limits the seller to only the amount of your earnest money, the person can't sue you or force you to buy. Yes, the earnest money is lost, but that's better than the alternative. If your offer includes one or more "Weasel" clauses, you won't lose your earnest money.

Rollover Clause

This clause allows the buyer to rollover the loan for a like period of time, after the time is due in full. This is especially useful when a large balloon payment is coming due. If you can't get this clause in its entirety, I recommend that you at least have a clause that allows you to extend the note for an additional one-year period. You at least buy another year of time to solve your problem.

Wraparound Clause

Whenever a property is sold on a Wraparound, this is the legal clause used to describe the transaction.

Assignment Clause

This clause allows you to assign the contract to another purchaser or take title in a name other than the one used in making an offer. Example: John Doe and/or assigns.

Substitution Clause

This clause allows you to "move" the note secured by a mortgage from one property to another. I call your attention to a detailed example in the creative idea section under this heading.

A sample addendum is included for your use. Feel free to copy all or part of it and use it. All clauses may not apply to every property, but I take the liberty of crossing out those clauses that are not necessary in that particular purchase. If you don't know what to cross out, just copy as is. All of the clauses are important in individual ways. With these clauses, all your fears should be removed. You might even go one step further by including all the other clauses that are not contained in the addendum. In that way you've covered anything and everything that might occur.

I suggest the sum to be as small as possible—perhaps $500 and in the form of a note, not cash. Just write "$500 note" on this line. After "commonly known as," you write the address of the property. If you know the legal description, place it in the next section which reads more specifically described as follows: If you don't know the legal description, just put in "Legal to be Added Later."

Price Is Easy

Price is easy. The binder deposit is the amount of your note. The difference between the price and the deposit will be paid at closing. It can be paid by a new loan (d) by taking over the existing loan (e) or by seller help with financing (f).

Numbers 3 and 4 deal with who pays what. This part is negotiable. I recommend that you try and have the seller pay for everything if possible.

Note 5. The escrow is "assigned" to the buyer, meaning that you get all tax and insurance impounds that are on hand. Normally, these belong to the seller.

Note 9. This deals with default by the buyer. I strongly recommend that this paragraph remain as is and not be added to. This limits your liability to the amount of your binder deposit. The Weasel Clauses will eliminate even this, but I still recommend that you have it in your contract.

Under 23, "additional terms and conditions," write SEE ADDENDUM ATTACHED. Take from or use entirely the addendum I've included to cover any other problems that might occur. Sample ways to buy for no-money-down include:

- Buyer refinance; seller takes proceeds and carries a note for difference.

- Seller refinances with buyer taking over loan and seller taking back a note for difference.

- The buyer creates note secured by the buyer's property for down payment, with the balance coming from financing of purchased property. CAUTION: Make any note for at least five to seven years and make the terms of that note based upon the income from the property you are buying. Example: If the income is $200 more than the first mortgage payment, consider making a payment on the note to the seller. If the income is only sufficient to make the first mortgage payment and nothing else, then make the note with no payments, all due in five years.

- Note other ideas for other no-money-down techniques later in this book.

Suggestion: Find a form that you are comfortable with and fill in the blanks, asking for advice on how to do so. Use this form when writing offers. The only changes you should have to make are on the terms and financing.

Special Clauses to Use

To be added to any Standard Purchase Agreement.

Exculpatory Clause: "The liability shall be limited to the property itself, and shall not extend beyond this."

Subordination Clause: "The seller's mortgage (or deed of trust) shall be subordinate and inferior to the existing prior mortgage (or deed of trust) and to any extension renewal or replacement thereof."

Performance Clause: "The debt service, net of any impounds for taxes and insurance, shall be \$_____ per month, but not to exceed _____ percent (_____%) of the net operating income, subject to an independent audit."

Exchange Clause: (a) to be inserted after the stated cash at closing in lieu of other property. (b) (under special provisions) "This transaction is subject to a concurrent exchange for property or properties now held by other parties.

Option Clause: (To be inserted immediately after statement concerning right of seller to "retain said earnest money for liquidated damages.") As your sole remedy. NOTE: Strike out any provision such as: (or may enforce specific performance thereto) or (may take such action.)

Rollover Clause: "Purchaser (or lessee) shall have the right at the termination of this agreement to renew, for a like period, under terms contained herein."

Wraparound Clause: "Seller shall retain a Wraparound or all inclusive mortgage (or deed of trust) which shall include and be subject to an existing mortgage or (deed of trust) for which seller shall remain responsible."

Assignment Clause: After name, add "trustee" or if to a corporation, add "or nominee." Another possibility is "and/or assigns."

Substitution Clause: "The seller hereby agrees to accept a substitution of collateral for the amount of this note by moving the mortgage (or trust deed) to another piece of property which the buyer shall designate. The seller shall have the right to inspect such property to insure the security of the collateral and shall give approval to make the Substitution of Collateral, which approval shall not be unreasonably denied.

Addendum to Real Estate Purchase Contract and Receipt for Deposit

Dated_____

1. This sale is contingent to Buyer's approval of:

Income and expense statement.
All lease and/or rental agreements.
Physical inspection of the entire subject premises.

All of the above documents are to be furnished by Seller to Buyer within five (5) days of acceptance of offer, including information on all mortgages (trust deeds) presently on property, i.e., the name of lender, original amount of loan and all other terms. Buyer agrees to physically inspect the property within seven (7) working days of acceptance of offer. Failure to disapprove of same in writing within five (5) working days from date of inspection, shall constitute approval of same.

2. Seller agrees to place in escrow the following:

Tax bill and insurance policy.
Any existing leases and/or rental agreements.
Any inventory of all personal property presently being used on subject property, including carpets, window treatments, appliances, lighting fixtures, furniture and/or furnishing on subject property. Seller will deliver to Buyer in escrow a Bill of Sale of all such personal property.
Copies of any concessions and any other agreements which may have been made with any tenants.
Any existing contracts or agreements between Seller and management company and/or vendors.
Duplicate keys of each units; properly identified.
List of names, account numbers and addresses of utility companies that are presently providing service to premises.

All of the above documents are to be placed in escrow within five (5) days of opening of escrow. Buyer agrees to inspect the above documents within fourteen (14) working days from receipt of same in escrow. Failure to disapprove of same in writing within said time limit shall constitute approval of same.

3.   Seller warrants the accuracy of information supplied to escrow agent and/or buyer with respect to the subject property.

4.   Seller warrants there are no violations of any Zoning Ordinance or regulations of building and safety codes on said building, nor are there any encroachments onto the property nor does any part of property encroach onto adjoining properties.

5.   Seller shall warrant that all systems, i.e., plumbing, electrical, heating and air conditioning are in good working order at the close of escrow. Also roof to be in good condition.

6.   Seller warrants that all works carried out on subject property prior to close of escrow will have been paid in full by close of escrow, and herewith indemnifies buyer from any such claims that may arise on said property.

7.   Guarantees and/or warranties still in effect for repairs or replacements to subject property, shall be transferred to buyer at the close of escrow.

8.   Seller warrants that there are no known latent or patent defects in property or improvements including the plumbing, roof or electrical and other mechanical items on such property.

9.   Sewers are in, connected, and paid for.

10. Seller will furnish buyer through escrow a termite report/ clearance not over 120 days old from a state licensed pest control operator showing the accessible portions of subject property to be free of visible evidence of infestation caused by wood

destroying insects, fungi and/or dry rot. Seller will pay for such corrective works.

11. The liability shall be limited to the property itself, and shall not extend beyond this.

12. Oil, gas, water and mineral rights and leases thereto, for subject property owned by seller shall be transferred to buyer at close of escrow.

13. All names and trademarks relating to the property are to be made part of the sale.

14. Preliminary title report to be approved by Buyer prior to close of escrow.

15. This offer is subject to property qualifying for, and the buyer obtaining financing acceptable to the buyer.

16. Prior to close of escrow, buyer will notify escrow holder, the name in which title to the property is to be vested.

17. Buyer's broker to hold deposit check until all contingencies have been met.

18. Buyer has the right to inspect the property within 48 hours prior to closing escrow in order to verify inventory and that all systems are in good working order.

19. This agreement shall be binding on the heirs, successors, assigns and personal representatives of the parties hereto.

20. The seller hereby agrees to accept a Substitution of Collateral for the amount of his note, or notes, by moving the mortgage (or trust deed) to another piece of property which the buyer shall designate. The seller shall have the right to inspect such property to insure the security of the collateral and shall give his approval

to make the Substitution of Collateral, which approval shall not be unreasonably denied.

21. Purchaser (or lessee) shall have the right at the termination of this agreement to renew, for a like period, under terms contained herein.

22. The Seller's mortgage (or Deed of Trust) shall be subordinate and inferior to the existing prior mortgages (or Deeds of Trust) and to any extension, renewal or replacement thereof.
     This offer is subject to:

     ● My partner's approval

     ● My accountant's approval

     ● My attorney or advisor's approval

     ● A soil test

     ● An appraisal to be paid for by _____

     ● Inspection of all books and records

23. This escrow is to be opened at Escrow Company and will close _____.

24. Seller to pay all closing costs plus prepaid items.

25. The escrow instructions to be executed by the parties shall be in a form acceptable to Buyer's counsel.

PART III

FINANCING: THE KEY TO REAL ESTATE SUCCESS

10

Make Financing Work for You

Now that you know how to work a contract and you have found a seller who is willing to be flexible in terms, you are ready to ask questions regarding financing.

1. **How did you arrive at the price?** If you are not certain about the value, ask the seller to furnish you with an FHA appraisal. I suggest an FHA appraisal because it is made indicating a value after any "fix-up" is necessary. This appraisal will tell you if the roof is in need of repair or replacing, whether the wiring is adequate, if the furnace or boiler and plumbing are satisfactory as well as pointing out other similar potential problems. Once you have a feel for the marketplace, this step may not be necessary.

2. **What is the existing financing on the property?** Remember, you want to concentrate on FHA and VA existing loans because you can take over these loans without qualifying and with no personal liability.

3. **What is the loan payment and what does it include?** It could include just interest and principal or also include taxes

and insurance. If it includes all four items, it is referred to as including PITI (principal, interest, taxes and insurance). If the loan payment doesn't include all four items, you must take into account what the taxes and insurance will cost.

4. **What will the property rent for?** This is important because you want to buy properties that can be rented for enough to meet all expenses, plus pay the mortgage payment. In our particular example, the seller is willing to sell for $52,000. There is an existing FHA loan balance of $32,000 with PITI payments of $321 and the property can be rented for $350 per month. Assuming you have no other payments to make, the property provides you with a small positive cash flow. However, it will take a $20,000 down payment to keep the payments as such. You want to buy for nothing down and still maintain the cash flow.

You can do this by offering a "note" in lieu of cash as the down payment. A note is just a promise to pay at some future time. It can have payments or not, and it may or may not be secured. You might say something like this "I want to buy your property and am willing to take over your existing financing, but I want to give you my note for the down payment. I'm willing to pay your price and give you a quick closing if you are agreeable to these terms. Unfortunately, the income from the property isn't suffi-cient enough to make any monthly payments on

> *I personally know of two people who started with $19,000 equity in their own homes and used this equity (no cash) to become million-aires in one year.*

this note, so I'd like to compound the interest and pay it off in one payment five years from closing. At that time, I'll write you a check for the $20,000 plus whatever interest we agree upon."

You determine whether your note will have payments or not by the income the property produces. In this case, there is a $29 per month positive cash flow, so you could offer that, but you do need some reserves in case of a vacancy.

The seller will probably ask for security for the note. This can be accomplished by recording a mortgage or Deed of Trust against this property or another property the buyer may own. If using the seller's property and defaults, the seller can foreclose on the security and take back the property. However, because you have taken "subject to" and have gotten the person to agree that the total liability of the note is the property, you have no personal worries.

If you use another property that you own as security, then you have two properties at risk and could lose your own property in case of default. This possibility can be eliminated by using the Substitution Clause after your note, which allows you to substitute collateral for the note at some future date. Let's take it one step further.

Example: Your home has a fair market value of $50,000. This is the amount you could sell your home for if placed on the market, not what you necessarily paid for the home. You have a conventional 8% mortgage balance of $30,000. The difference between the fair market value and the mortgage in this case is $20,000 and that is what is referred to as equity in real estate. How can you get this equity out and use it inexpensively? Refinancing is expensive, and you would end up probably obtaining a new 80% loan, or $40,000 in this case, larger payments and (because of costs of appraisal, etc.) about $7,000 in cash. If you have a low interest loan, the best advice, most of the time, is do not refinance.

Do Not Refinance

You could also look into a second mortgage. This will not disturb your first mortgage, but the pay back plan will be shorter and the interest rate higher than refinancing. The lender will also lend 80% of value, giving you an additional $10,000, minus expenses of perhaps $2,000, or a total of $8,000.

The least expensive way to get your equity out of real estate, and the fastest, is to "create" paper against your equity. All that really means is that you offer a promissory note in lieu of cash and secure that promissory note by giving the seller of the property you are buying a subordinated mortgage on your property. You eliminate all costs, high interest rates, and are not bound by the 80% rule.

In fact, you don't need good credit to do this. And, you don't need money. You don't need a job, and you don't even have to live in the same city where a purchase is made. If you couple using the equity in your real estate with the Substitution Clause, it is possible to buy properties using your equity but never subjecting you or your property to any mortgages. Let's go back to our example:

Create a Note

Create a note for $20,000 for the down payment, offering the seller a subordinated mortgage on your home, after which you include the Substitution Clause. After closing, substitute the property you have just purchased for your own as collateral. This will allow you to buy for nothing down, have a small positive cash flow, and take absolutely no risk. Even if you don't own real estate, don't panic. Just offer an unsecured note or a note secured by the property you are buying. You'll be amazed by the number of people who will take such an offer. Not everyone will take these deals, of course, but you've eliminated that up front with questioning.

The income from the purchased property will dictate whether you make payments on the note or not. It is important to remember that every property should support itself. If there is a positive cash flow, then you might want to make payments on the note. If there is no cash flow, then offer your note with no payments.

I personally know of two people who started with $19,000 equity in their own homes and used this equity (no cash) to become millionaires in one year.

11

The Creation of Wealth Formula

You can actually create wealth or financial independence for yourself and do it with absolutely no cash. You do it totally with notes. I feel this technique is so important that I will take a few extra lines to go over the idea again.

- Let's say you own property A, which could be your home, rental property, or whatever. This property has a value of $50,000 and a $30,000 mortgage balance against it, giving you a $20,000 equity.

- You would like to buy property B. The owner of B is asking for a $20,000 cash down payment. In lieu of cash, you offer the owner of B a note for $20,000. The security for this note will be a Deed of Trust or mortgage against your real estate. Buyer B feels comfortable because he or she has two properties as collateral now, both your property A and property B.

- You now owe seller B $80,000 in two notes, one for $60,000 secured by B and one for $20,000 secured by A. Since property B is worth $80,000 and all you owe is $60,000, you have now transferred your equity position to property B. You now locate property C, offering a $20,000 note secured by a mortgage on property B. You have now transferred your B equity to C.

- You then use C to buy D, D to buy E, etc.

This is how you can become a millionaire with absolutely no cash. What is the worst that can happen if the market falls apart? You lose the properties and save your credit because you purchased all with no personal liability.

For those of you concerned about your property A — use the Substitution Clause after your note offer to buy property B. This clause simply states that you have the right to "substitute" collateral for your note secured by (A) at some future date and the seller of property (B) will agree to such a substitution.

After closing, substitute your property A $20,000 note for one on property B. You have now kept your $20,000 equity position in A – then use A to buy C, substitute later, use A to buy D, etc. Now, if the real estate market falls apart, you end up losing the other properties, but not property A.

More about Notes

What if you don't own anything? Can you still use notes to buy? The answer to this is yes. Only now you have to use something else as security or nothing at all. The logical choice is the seller's property. If the value is there, the seller should not hesitate to take back a note secured by his or her own real estate. You might also use anything else you own as security: car, horse, cow, whatever you have, or nothing at all. You could just make a promise to pay.

How to Pay Notes When Due

If a note calls for monthly payments, you, of course, pay off the note in that manner. But, what if the note has no payments and is due in one large sum? This is referred to as a balloon payment. Once again, it's very important to make the note for as long a time as possible, certainly no less than five years, unless you have specific plans to take care of it when it is due. But, what do you do in five years when faced with a large sum of money and don't know how to get it? Here are some ideas:

- Refinance the property. Real estate has been doubling in value every 7.3 years, so the equity should be there.

- Obtain a hard money second mortgage from a bank or other financial institution, using the proceeds to pay off your note.

- Get somebody else to pay it for you, such as a partner. Offer partial ownership in exchange for the person making the payment.

- Sell the property before the note is due. Sell for nothing down if you have to, taking a note for the down payment secured by something your buyer owns.

- Renegotiate with the holder of the note, asking for an extension, or offering some cash now and some later, or perhaps convert the note to monthly payments.

- If all else fails, you can always "give the property back" to the seller. What have you lost by doing this? Nothing really. Yet, you have benefited from the income and tax benefits over the term of the note.

Another Example

The asking price is $100,000 and there is an existing $60,000 FHA loan on the property. (Remember that you want to look for properties that have existing FHA, VA, or conventional loans that can be assumed without personal liability or qualifying.) The equity in this case is $40,000. The principles are the same in all properties, however, so keep that in mind when preparing your offer.

1. If the property is under-priced, meaning the property value is actually $120,000 to $150,000, you can finance the

property for 100% of the purchase price with conventional financing.

You do this by showing the lender the appraisal, not the purchase contract, asking for a loan based upon appraised value. If the lender says, "We will loan 80% of appraised value or purchase price, whichever is less," you take a more creative approach to achieve this end result. One way is to get the cooperation of the seller by having the contract show the appraised value as the selling price, with the seller taking back a note for the difference between what you actually wish to pay and the appraised value.

Have a separate agreement between buyer and seller, or buyer and broker and seller and broker, that this note will be discounted to $1.00 after closing and upon receipt of the cash purchase price. Another way would be to go to a bank and borrow the funds to pay all cash for the property. You now own the property free and clear, allowing you to refinance your own property. This should eliminate the problem of the lender loaning only 80% of the purchase price.

2. If the property value is $100,000 and the seller wishes all cash, you simply offer the person cash at a discount, such as $70,000 to $80,000, once again borrowing the money based upon appraisal to pay.

3. If the seller insists on a specific price, then change your tactic, offering to pay the $100,000, but with no-money-down.

4. If the seller insists on a set price and also requires a down payment, you take a different approach.

For illustrative purposes, let's say that the seller wants a $10,000 cash down payment but is willing to wait for the difference in purchase price. This means the person will take a note for the balance. The person can do this for the entire $90,000 yet owed, or just offer the difference between $60,000 (existing first) and $90,000, or $30,000.

Once again, if the existing loan is a low interest loan and can be assumed without problems, normally speaking, you should take it over. We talked about using a note secured by the property as a down payment or a note secured by something the buyer already owns. In this case, however, the seller wants $10,000 cash instead of a note.

One way to give the person cash and yet buy for nothing down is to ask the seller to take back a note secured by a Subordinated Mortgage. A Subordinated Mortgage simply means that it is subordinate, or inferior to, any existing mortgages on the property at time of closing.

Before closing, go to a lender and ask for a $10,000 or more loan on the property you are purchasing. As collateral, you can safely offer the lender a second on the property. At closing, take over the first of $60,000, borrow the down payment from the lender and the person records a second of $10,000 and the seller secures with a $30,000 note by recording a third mortgage on the property. In this case, you buy for nothing down, and the seller gets a down payment. If you need cash—tax-free, I might add—you could consider asking for more than $10,000, such as $20,000. You now owe $60,000, $20,000 and $30,000, or a total of $110,000, but you have been paid $10,000 for buying. In this instance, both buyer and seller get $10,000 at closing.

5. If the seller is unwilling to go along with this approach, consider raising the price to $105,000, with the seller agreeing to take a note, instead of cash, for $15,000.

Many times greed will take over, and the person will forget the $10,000 cash. If the person still insists on $10,000 cash and you wish to buy for no-money-down, make your offer contingent upon you (the seller or the realtor) selling the $15,000 note for $10,000 cash to an investor. Check your local newspapers for potential investors. There are tons of them around.

If you think about it, we have just come up with five different ways to buy a property, all with no-money-down on the part of the buyer.

1. A note secured by the purchased property for the down payment

2. A note secured by something the buyer owns or nothing at all for that matter

3. An inflated note which can be sold for cash

4. An all cash offer because of a discount in price

5. Seller agrees to subordinate a note, allowing the buyer to borrow the down payment. In this case, the buyer can be paid for buying.

The example used describes a property with substantial equity. Does this mean you should look only for those properties? No. Each property stands on its own, and each property, under the right set of circumstances, can be purchased for no-money-down. The possibilities are endless.

You are now at the crossroads of your plan to become a winner by investing in real estate. You have designed your game plan by understanding real estate in general and what to buy. You know the rules of the game and are now ready to develop that plan of action. If there is one way to guarantee your success and open doors, that key is financing!

12

Introduction to Financing

Unless a buyer pays all cash for real estate out of personal funds, a lender gets involved by loaning the buyer part of the purchase price. In return for this loan, the lender wants certain security insuring the borrower will pay back the loan. This allows the lender to foreclose on that security if the borrower does not perform. This is how it works.

The borrower borrows the funds, giving the lender a promissory note which is a promise to pay back the loan. As security for that promissory note, the lender wants collateral. In most cases, that security comes in the form of a mortgage or Trust Deed against a piece of real estate. Some states use mortgages as security while others use a Trust Deed. Either way, the lender has security.

In states where a mortgage is used as the real property security instrument, the borrower is called the mortgagor and the lender the mortgagee. You might best remember who is what by thinking "Simon Legree, the Mortgagee." It is a two-party instrument whereby the lender forecloses and takes over the property if the borrower does not pay. Other states use the trust deed as a security instrument. The borrower is called the trustor. The property is conveyed to a trustee, a third party (often a title company or bank) who holds title as security for repayment of the loan, for the benefit of the lender, called the beneficiary. This is a three-party instrument. If you do not pay, then the trustee forecloses on behalf of the lender.

Installment Land Contract, Contract of Sale, Contract for Deed, or Land Contract

The terms all mean the same. Basically this type of contract is an installment type contract between buyer and seller, whereby the buyer obtains the right to occupy but the seller retains legal title to the real property as security for payment of the purchase price. The seller agrees to convey title to the buyer upon fulfillment of certain conditions. During the term of the contract, the buyer is said to have an equitable ownership interest in the property. The buyer still owns and controls the property and can sell it, subject to the Land Contract, but does not have legal title in his or her name.

When using this type financing, I strongly recommend that a buyer obtain legal counsel before entering into such an agreement. I also call your attention to the chapter later which details in full how to use this instrument safely. The contract in this case is the security instrument and should be recorded. If there are any other loans against the property, it is the seller's responsibility to keep them current.

Wraparound Mortgage or All Inclusive Trust Deed (AITD)

This, too, is an installment type of contract between buyer and seller, or between lender and seller, but contrary to a Land Contract, in this case title is transferred to the buyer, and the seller acts as the lender. The seller is still responsible for other loans against the property. This also will be explained in greater detail in the book.

Acceleration: Due-on-Sale Clause

The term "Acceleration Clause" refers to a provision in a note and Deed of Trust or mortgage requiring immediate payment of the entire unpaid balance or principal and interest upon the occurrence of specified event or events.

One of the two common types of Acceleration Clauses, contained in most notes, makes the entire amount of unpaid principal and interest become immediately due and payable upon default, at the option of the lender. Although this right is usually stated without qualification, in most states there are laws that permit the borrower to reinstate his or her right upon payment within a specified period of time and upon reimbursing the lender for costs incurred.

The other type of Acceleration Clause, also referred to as Due-on-Sale Clause or Alienation Clause makes the entire amount of the unpaid mortgage on the property due and payable in full upon sale of the property, transfer and sometimes of further encumbrance of the property or any part thereof or interest therein, at the option of the lender. Acceleration is a lender's optional privilege, but without an Acceleration Clause the lender cannot accelerate the obligation upon default or transfer.

The Due-on-Sale Clause enables the lender to exercise or waive option to accelerate the payment date. The lender can, therefore, approve or disapprove of a buyer wishing to assume the loan. The lender can charge an assumption fee or demand an increase in interest rate.

Some states have ruled that the Due-on-Sale Clause is unconstitutional and cannot be enforced by the state-chartered institutions while other states have disagreed and seen fit to endorse it. In 1982, the United States Supreme Court reached the conclusion that federally chartered lending institutions have the right to enforce such a clause. This means that if you are buying or selling a property that has a low interest rate loan on it and the loan was made by a federally chartered institution, that institution has the right to call the loan due in full upon sale or make the new buyer qualify to take over the loan, pay a fee to do so, and pay a higher rate of interest. With that ruling in hand, it probably is only a matter of time until all institutions reach the same conclusion. There is disagreement as to what effect it will have on the real estate market in general, but everybody agrees that creative financing will play even a bigger role in the future because of this ruling. Later on I devote an entire chapter to showing you various ways to get around or deal with this ruling.

Assuming and Taking "Subject to" a Mortgage

A mortgage loan is assumed when a written assumption agreement is executed between the lender and the purchaser of the property. Thus the primary responsibility for repayment of the loan is placed upon the new owner. In this case, a buyer enters into a contract to purchase whereby the person agrees to assume any existing indebtedness already on the property. The buyer makes an appointment with the lender, and the lender then qualifies the buyer to see that the individual is acceptable to the lender.

This qualification of buyer includes a credit search, verification of income, expenses, and profession or job. If the lender doesn't feel that the buyer can qualify or feels that the buyer is not acceptable for any reason, the lender has the right to turn the buyer down as far as assuming the existing loan. If the lender is inclined to accept the buyer, then the lender has the right to increase the interest rate and ask for an assumption fee. Most of the time this results in a large fee for the buyer and a much bigger loan payment.

In the event no Due-on-Sale Clause is provided for in a mortgage or trust deed, or by state law, the lender cannot require a purchaser to sign an assumption agreement, nor can the lender raise the interest rate or make any other demands. In this case, the purchaser is said to buy the property "subject to" the mortgage loan, rather than "assume" it. Many good things happen if you buy "subject to" the loan rather than "assume" it. One, you don't have to qualify with the lender. The person has to accept you, regardless of your credit, whether you have a job or not, plus the person can't raise the interest rate or charge you an assumption fee. As a buyer, you have no legal responsibility for the loan, only the payments. If the buyer defaults, then the lender forecloses and takes the property.

What happens to the seller if a loan is bought "subject to" rather then assumed? How does it affect the seller? First of all, from a seller's point of view, when a mortgage is assumed, the assumption agreement between the lender and the new owner places the primary responsibility for repayment of the mortgage upon the new owner. Even if the mortgage is assumed by the buyer, many times the lender will also keep the original borrower on the loan in a secondary responsibility. If the terms are changed, the original borrower is supposed to be released of responsibility entirely, but be sure and check to see if this is the case when you sell and allow assumption.

If, on the other hand, the property is sold "subject to" the mortgage, the person primarily responsible for repayment of the mortgage debt is still the original maker of the note, and the buyer has no personal liability to pay back that debt. The buyer assumes the payments but not the mortgage balance. The fact that the new owner makes the payments after the sale is consummated does not place the obligation to pay off the mortgage debt upon the new owner, since he or she never agreed to do so in writing.

The Seller

Just how safe is the seller if a home is bought "subject to" the loan, rather than insisting on a buyer assuming it? For all practical purposes, the seller has little reason for concern unless the amount of the loan exceeds the value of the property. Only if the property does not bring sufficient proceeds to pay off the balance of the loan will the lender have legal recourse to recover deficiency. Some states, such as California, do not permit deficiency judgments against the original borrower where the loan was made for the purpose of acquisition of the borrower's home regardless of what the property is sold for at foreclosure. In addition, if you have purchased using the Exculpatory provision, the lender has no legal recourse. Get legal advice before you buy or sell.

My advice – look for existing financing that can be taken over "subject to" rather than having to be assumed. These include FHA, VA, some Life Insurance Company loans and some older government type loans made several years ago. If you're not sure, ask the lender.

Getting the Banker to Say Yes

Ever wonder why some people are always successful obtaining a loan while others never seem to succeed? Two different people can go to the same lender with the same loan request. One gets approved and the other doesn't – why? The main reason one is successful and the other isn't is that the successful person knows how to ask for a loan and has taken the time to learn how banks and bankers in particular operate.

All federally insured banks come under the same rules and regulations. What sets them apart is the banking officers.

Any bank officer can make a secured loan. What you want to find is a banker who is willing to make you an unsecured loan. An unsecured loan simply means that you can borrow money from that bank without collateral. The banker lends you money based upon your promise to pay back.

A former bank vice president offers these suggestions when asking for an unsecured loan:

- A banker likes unsecured loans of 20% of gross salary (example: if you make $50,000 per year, a $10,000 unsecured line of credit is not out of line). My banker tells me that the bank where he works prefers to keep this percentage at 10% of gross.

- A ten-to-one unsecured line of credit based on your average checking account balance is not out of line. Example: if you keep an average balance in your checking account of $5,000, you should be able to obtain an unsecured line of credit for $50,000.

- They look to your salary for a pay back plan. Other income is not that important. Example: if you have real estate income, bank officers tend to discount it some because of debt.

- Bankers like you to have a title. Give yourself as important a title as you can.

- Bankers want to know how you are going to pay them back. I recommend you say, "Just charge my account monthly." They like this.

- Don't mention the fact that you pay child support or alimony.

- If you are self-employed, a banker will want to see your last two years' income tax returns which could cause a problem, especially if you are in the zero tax bracket. Most lenders look at the "bottom line" of your income tax return. If you own real estate and have tax deductions that reduce your actual income down to almost nothing, you could have a serious problem obtaining a loan.

How Conventional Financing Works

Price : $100,000
Cash needed: $100,000

You, for whatever reason, wish to buy this property for $100,000, and you need all cash to make the purchase. Where do you get the money?

There are lenders who like to loan money on good real estate. If you are working through a real estate firm, ask them for assistance in this area. They should know who is making loans on this type of property. If you are not working with a real estate person, pick up the yellow pages and look under the headings "mortgages, savings & loans," and "mortgage companies or mortgage brokers." If it is a commercial loan rather than a residential loan, consider banks and insurance companies as well for your loan request.

Make an appointment to see the lender. Explain to the person that you want to buy this property and the asking price is $100,000. If you have a contract, take that with you. The lender will eventually ask to see your contract. Assuming that the property appraises for the $100,000 and qualifies for a loan, the lender will then look at you to see if you qualify. You will fill out an application, and the lender will analyze whether you can qualify for the loan. The person will take into consideration your credit, your ability to make the payments on the loan, and the fact that you have a down payment.

The lender will loan a percentage of the purchase price and will expect you to come up with the difference in cash, plus have on hand cash for the necessary appraisal costs, credit search, and closing costs. The loan could be anywhere from 65% to 100% of what you pay, depending upon the type of loan you are obtaining. If it is a new VA loan, it could be 100% of your purchase price. If it is a new FHA loan for your own home, your down payment could be as little as 3%, and if you obtain the funds through a savings and loan, your down payment could go as high as 20% of the overall purchase price.

When Lenders Feel Uncomfortable

If you have less than 20% of your money invested, lenders feel uncomfortable because they feel that you have nothing to lose in case of default. They feel that if you have money of your own invested, you are more likely to keep the payment current. However, it is possible for a buyer to obtain a higher percentage loan than 80% if the person has good credit and can prove to the lender that payments can be made. This still puts the lender at risk for the additional sums loaned over and above the normal 80% to value. To protect themselves, lenders require the borrowers to pay extra for mortgage insurance which guarantees the lender this extra 20% in case of default.

This is referred to as MIP or Mortgage Insurance Premium. The VA guarantees the lender that if the buyer defaults, the organization will pay off the lender while the FHA insures the lender against default.

Qualify on Work Income

The lender will qualify you based upon your work income. If you are on a salary, lenders will take anywhere from 28% to 36% from your gross salary to qualify you for a loan. If you are self-employed, they will want to see your last two years' tax returns and perhaps an up-to-date balance sheet. It is normally more difficult to qualify for a loan when you are self-employed than if an employee. If you have worked for a firm less than two years, you could have a problem qualifying because you haven't worked for that firm long enough to prove stability.

You could qualify for a $75,000 or a $90,000 loan. The amount you can borrow is dictated by the terms and conditions of the lender. The person may say you can only qualify for an $800 per month payment. This means that although the property qualifies for a

$90,000 loan, you might not be able to borrow more than $70,000 because you can't qualify for the higher figure. The difference between what you qualify for in the way of a loan and the purchase price is made up with your cash down payment. If, as an example, you qualify for a $90,000 loan, you must come up with a $10,000 cash at closing.

As security for loaning the $90,000, the lender will record a Deed of Trust or mortgage against the property you are buying. That is their security for making you the loan. If you default for any reason, they will foreclose and take the property.

All parties are present at the closing. The seller or sellers sign a warranty or grant deed deeding the property to the buyer. The lender pays off existing debt against the property, deducts other seller expenses, and gives the balance in cash to the seller. If the property is free and clear of all loans when sold, the seller will receive in cash $100,000 less expenses. If there is a loan of say $40,000 already on the property, this amount will be paid off out of the $100,000 proceeds with the balance going to the seller.

The seller sells for all cash – buyer pays all cash. The buyer's cash comes from personal funds and a lender who will loan based upon the value of the property being purchased. The buyer must have good credit, prove the down payment, and qualify for the loan.

When to Keep Present Financing

Instead of going the new conventional financing route, you could keep the existing conventional loan in place and just give the difference in cash to the seller. Most of the time you won't have a choice in what you do because the lender probably has a Due-on-Sale Clause in the mortgage documents. This means that the lender has the right to call the loan if any interest in the property is transferred. When ownership is transferred from seller to buyer, an interest transfer has taken place and the Due-on-Sale Clause can be enforced.

Lenders Usually Aren't Interested in Calling in a Loan

The lender normally isn't interested in calling in the loan but would be interested in changing it to fit into the current economy to make the interest rate conform to the going rate. That also gives them the right to qualify the new owner, check the person's credit, and charge a fee for such an assumption. If the present financing is a loan of $60,000 and you are paying $100,000 and you have to qualify anyway, you are generally better off to just get a new conventional loan and borrow as much as you can against the property. If the loan is $90,000 and you are paying $100,000, you could be better off keeping the present loan balance and just assume it. Your decision should be based on the difference in cost and interest rate and between keeping the old loan and obtaining a new one.

When Should You Refinance?

Even if you find a fully assumable loan that can be taken over without qualifying, sometimes it is better to refinance that loan and obtain a new one. Common sense will dictate your action. Let say that you presently have a 9% FHA loan and a new loan can be obtained for 7 to 7 1/2. As a buyer, you would prefer the 7% rate rather than the 9% rate. You wouldn't need to make as much to qualify, and payments would be considerably less.

So, if the present interest rate is 2 to 3% higher than what you can obtain on a new loan, go the new loan route. If the difference is minor, keep the old loan. The same rules apply when it comes to refinancing. Whenever the interest rate drops 2 to 3%, refinance at the lower rate. Again, anything less then the 2 to 3% won't pay. Also, if you are planning on selling soon, you probably would be better off keeping the present loan even if the rate is higher than what you can now obtain. Let the new buyer get the new loan. If you are planning on keeping your property for a long period of time, I suggest you consider refinancing at the lower rate.

Seller Financing

Instead of you going to a conventional lender and asking for a loan, many sellers will agree to act as your lender themselves. Let us use the $100,000 example (whereby you borrow $90,000 from a lender and combine that with your cash for the total purchase price).

In this case, the seller receives the $10,000 in cash but says he doesn't want the other $90,000 in cash now but prefers a monthly income. The person records a mortgage or Deed of Trust against the property for this $90,000, and you now pay the seller monthly instead of the conventional lender.

Obviously, if you can convince the seller to take this route, this is the cheapest and fastest way to buy real estate. In addition, there are no qualifying or closing costs. Why would a seller do this? One reason would be to spread tax liability. Another might be that the person can expect a higher yield by charging you interest rather than taking the money and putting it into a bank. And, of course, the person has a monthly income secured by the property. If you default, the seller gets the property back.

13

Creative Financing

It is possible to use both the seller and a conventional lender to buy real estate. In this case, the buyer obtains a loan from a lender for part of the purchase price, say $90,000, but is short on the $10,000 down payment requirement. The seller could agree to taking $90,000 in cash and a "note" for the other $10,000. This $10,000 promissory note can be unsecured or secured. If unsecured, the seller relies on the honesty and ability of the buyer to pay. If the person doesn't, the seller has little recourse other than to sue and "hope and pray" that he or she collects.

My Recommendation: Don't take an unsecured note.

Secured Note

A secured notes means that if you don't pay, the taker of that note can foreclose on the security and take the security away from you. Normal security for real estate is a mortgage. This mortgage can be on the property being purchased or any property that is agreeable to both parties. If it is not the seller's property, it will most likely be secured by the buyer's property. If the buyer doesn't own any property, the note could be secured by something else the buyer owns such as a car, boat, etc.

Seller Carries Financing That Includes Other Financing

Instead of the buyer obtaining a new loan and giving the proceeds to the seller with the seller taking back a note or cash for the difference, there are cases when the seller can actually keep the present financing in place and sell to a buyer including this financing. This is accomplished in one of two ways, either by selling on a Wraparound or Contract for Deed. In this case, the present loan, for example $30,000, is left as is and the seller sells to the buyer for $100,000, with $10,000 down, and the buyer gives the seller a note for $90,000.

The buyer could take over the existing mortgage of $30,000, give the seller a $10,000 cash down payment and a note for $60,000, but in this case, the seller is asking the buyer to give a note for $90,000. Since this $90,000 note includes the already existing $30,000, it is called a Wraparound mortgage. The title is transferred to the buyer at closing with the seller taking back a Wraparound mortgage. The seller is responsible for the making of the $30,000 existing loan but is receiving payments from the buyer on $90,000. The seller's benefit is that the person may be paying 7% on the existing $30,000 but collecting 10% on the $90,000 owed by the buyer.

Contract for Deed

It is also possible to sell under what is called a Contract for Deed, sometimes called a Land Contract. The difference here is that the seller retains the title and the buyer obtains what is called an "equitable title interest" in the property.

My Recommendation: Anytime seller financing is used, whether it is for the seller taking a note for just the down payment to the use of a Wraparound or Contract of Deed, *please* hire an attorney. There are many factors to be considered and much can go wrong. You could end up paying twice plus get stuck with the Due-on-Sale Clause.

One last piece of advice. With the exception of FHA and VA, most loans have a Due-on-Sale Clause connected with them. That means that the loan can be called in if an interest is conveyed. When you sell using seller financing, on a wrap or on a contract, an interest has been conveyed. You need the protection of a real estate attorney.

How to Qualify for a Loan

One method of acquiring real estate is for you, the buyer, to obtain a new loan and give the proceeds to the seller. In order to accomplish this, you will need to qualify for a loan. The reasons you can't qualify are many. 1) Maybe you have bad credit and no lender will loan you money, but you do have the necessary cash down payment. 2) You have good credit, but you don't have the down payment. 3) You have good credit and the down payment, but you can't qualify for a loan because you have no job or pay no income tax.

Solution to Number One

Let's assume that you do have the necessary down payment and the income to qualify for a loan, but your credit is such that a lender won't loan you the money. This is an unlikely event in as much as the real estate itself should be ample collateral for the loan and you secondary. Credit by itself shouldn't prevent you from buying real estate and obtaining a new loan, but in reality, this is often the case. If you need a new loan and the lender refuses to give you that loan because of your credit situation, use one of these methods to solve that problem:

- Get a co-signer who has good credit to sign with you. The ideal person is the seller who has nothing to lose. The person gets the property sold, gets all cash, and even gets property back in case of default.

- Ask the seller to refinance with an assumable loan that you can take over without qualifying.

- "Pay" somebody for the use of the person's credit. Find a person who has good credit and is willing to qualify and obtain a new "assumable" loan in that person's name. At closing, the person deeds the property to you and for this use of credit, you pay a fee. I normally pay $1,000 per unit of credit used or perhaps $2,000 if it is a fourplex.

- If it is an investment property, you could ask the seller to enter into a sell/leaseback arrangement whereby the person agrees to lease back the property from you on a net/net/net basis. This means that the seller is agreeing to pay all expenses including the mortgage payment. The buyer now uses seller's financial statement and lease to quality. I have done this many times.

- Do an equity participation whereby you grant a partial ownership to an investor in exchange for the use of the person's credit. I prefer to pay somebody for the use of credit, but this is an excellent alternative.

Solution to Number Two

Most lenders insist on you proving you have a down payment. Assuming you "need the cash" at closing but don't have it now—where might you come up with the required down payment or "proof" that you will have it?

- An easy way is to obtain a gift letter from a friend or relative. This will buy time until closing, but you will have to come up with the money at that time.

- Create some unsecured lines of credit with banks, or even secured if need be. Borrow the funds and place them in your checking or savings account to prove that you have the money on hand for the closing. Again, you will have to come up with the cash at closing from another source unless you can get your bank to go along for a period of time.

- Take out a second mortgage on something you already own for the necessary down payment.

- Obtain a number of credit cards that can be used for a cash advance for the down payment.

- Borrow from friends or relatives.

- Get a cash advance on your life insurance.

- If you belong to a credit union, contact them for a loan.

- Refinance or sell something you own.

- If you are buying below market value, consider creating a note secured by a second mortgage on the property, and sell that note at a discount at closing for the cash down payment. You will need to prove you have the cash on hand via another way, but this will get you the necessary cash for closing. Example: $10,000 cash down required. Create a note for $15,000 and sell it to an investor for $10,000. You now have two payments to make, one on the first and the other on the second.

- If the seller is receptive to taking a note for the down payment but the lender still wants proof of the down payment, you might approach the seller to loan you the money or place it into an account that can be verified by the lender. If the person refuses to do so, obtain an overnight loan from your bank for the down payment, and get the seller to "rebate" back to you the cash in exchange for the note. For other ways, check my other materials.

Solution to Number Three

First of all, I am going to assume that you can make the payments, not just qualify as far as the lender is concerned.

- If you have a job, but your job verification is not adequate for lender approval – the reason being you have not had that job long enough or you don't make enough money, it will be necessary for you to show "additional" income to help you qualify. A second income should satisfy this requirement. Have somebody verify that you also work for his or her company. This person could be a friend or relative. As an example, once when my daughter needed to buy a car, she didn't qualify for a car loan, so I put her on my payroll for $100 per month, which allowed her to qualify.

- Form a company and become an employee of that company. As an owner of a company, it is difficult to qualify, but as an employee it is easy. Why? Because lenders call and verify your "gross" income, not net income. They subtract their percentage requirement and qualify you based on what is left. If you are self-employed, you have to produce your last two year's income tax returns and that could be a problem if you pay little or no income tax.

How Do You Form a Company?

Go to your courthouse and ask who is in charge of fictitious names. Pick a company name, and you are in business. Pick a title, but certainly not president. If you have to be the president, be prepared to be asked if you are also an owner. Lenders won't ask that question if you are a vice president or regional sales manager. I suggest you use an out- of-state address for the home office, but you can get a local post office box number and a second phone in your home. Out-of-state works best, however. Use a relative or friend in another state for verification. Your relative or friend can forward the mail back to you, and you can easily verify your income.

I qualified for a loan and didn't have to come up with my tax returns by asking my accountant to send a letter to the lender verifying my "gross income" for the year, not net.

It is important to note here that I am not suggesting you lie about your income. To do so could put you in prison. I am only offering suggestions on how you prove an income to qualify for a loan. You could, however, get fired from your company or second income source. In this case, it's not your fault.

Seller Wants $100,000, All Cash

Price: $100,000
Cash needed: $100,000

If the seller wants "all cash" for a property, the only time you should be buying this property is when it is priced at 15 to 25% (or more) below value. That means that this property should be worth $125,000 but the seller is willing to sacrifice for all cash.

If the property is worth $125,000, you should be able to obtain an 80% loan to value, or $100,000, if that is the sales price or the value when refinancing. How do you buy at $100,000 and pay the seller all cash?

Be Careful How You Approach the Seller

Ask the seller to refinance to 80% of value and sell to you with you assuming the new loan. You have to be very careful in how you approach the seller to make this request. The person could decide to refinance and keep the property and the borrowed money tax-free and then rent it for a break-even cash flow. Or, the person might decide to refinance and sell with a small cash down payment or a note for the down payment, thereby increasing his or her overall return. This is an alternative, but not the best in my opinion.

Get a lender who will commit to loan 80% of appraised value if owned by you. Ask the seller to deed it to you and take a note or other security for a few days until you refinance what has now become "your" property. If you have ample security to give to the seller in exchange for deeding the property to you, this might work. A better suggestion might be to take your commitment for an 80 % loan to value, or $100,000, to a short-term lender, a bank, and ask that the loan officer advance you the $100,000 for a few days. Your security for such a loan – your loan commitment. The bank gives you the loan for $100,000. You pay all cash and later refinance, paying back the short-term lender. I have done this numerous times and find that it works beautifully.

Use my buddy system whereby you enter into a contract to buy for the $100,000 and turn right around and enter into a second contract to sell to "your buddy" for $125,000 subject to the person obtaining a $100,000 loan. The person takes this contract to the lender, and you close both properties at the same time.

Your buddy will have to qualify and prove a down payment and closing costs. If the person can't buy, but you can, substitute that person in your place, and you take the larger contract to the lender and borrow the $100,000.

If your buddy takes title, the person deeds it back to you at closing. For this, you might pay a small fee. The fee is negotiable.

Seller Wants "His" Price — $100,000

Price: $100,000
Terms: Flexible

In this case, the seller is hung up on price, not cash. That generally means that the property is not worth $100,000. You only purchase this property with a no-money-down deal and on terms and conditions that are suitable to you. Why would you pay more for a property than it is worth unless it makes sense?

Offer This Suggestion

You could offer no-money-down, no personal liability, and the financing to be carried back by the seller. Your interest rate and payment should be what you can afford if it is your own home and not more than what you can rent the property, if it is a rental property. In other words, if you can afford $500 per month, make your payments $500 per month and that includes PITI (principal, interest, taxes and insurance). The same applies to a rental property.

I do suggest you try and make your payments slightly less than the mortgage payment in case of vacancy or repairs. Use the Exculpatory provision to protect against default and a lawsuit.

If the seller wants some cash, ask the person to refinance and take back a note for the difference with the terms of that note being dictated by the property's income. In other words, if the first mortgage payment is $500 per month and that is all you can afford, make your note to the individual with no payments.

Or, you the buyer could obtain a new first mortgage, and the seller could take back a note for the difference. The bank will loan on value in this case. At least, that is what I suggest you have the bank do.

If the property is only worth $90,000, but the seller wants $100,000, borrow 75% of the $90,000, not the $100,000. In this way, if you ever default and the first forecloses, you will have enough equity to avoid being hurt with a deficiency judgment. I recommend an FHA loan if possible.

To Review

Only pay more than what the property is worth if you can do it without personal liability and on terms that fit that property. This includes using none of your own money and having your payment not exceed the rental income.

Seller Wants Some Cash but Not All Cash

Price: $100,000
Terms: Flexible

First of all, find out how much cash the seller really wants or needs. These funds should come from the equity in the property being purchased, not yours.

Example: existing first of $40,000, leaving an equity position of $60,000. Property is worth $100,000, but seller doesn't need all cash.

A lender will agree to loaning $80,000 (80%) based upon the value of $100,000. This means there is $40,000 cash available through new or additional financing. That money can be used for a cash down payment to the seller. Your alternatives in acquiring this cash are:

- Keep the present $40,000 first and either the buyer or seller obtains a second for an additional $40,000. You would want to keep the first if it is a low interest rate loan and assumable without qualifying such as an FHA or VA loan.

- Refinance this first into a new first position of $80,000. Either the buyer or the seller can do this. As a buyer, your offer might read–$100,000 price, $80,000 cash and the seller to take back a note for the difference, or $20,000. $40,000 of the $80,000 is used to pay off the existing loan with the remaining $40,000 going to the seller. Something the buyer owns or the seller's property can secure the $20,000 note.

An Offer to Avoid

There are those who preach overfinancing which allows the buyer to put cash in pocket but at the same time puts the seller at risk.

In this case, instead of offering the seller $40,000 in cash over and above the existing first and a note for $20,000, you offer $30,000 in cash and a note for $30,000. This allows you to refinance for $80,000, use $40,000 to pay off the old first, $30,000 to give to the seller, and you as a buyer would walk away with $10,000 in cash and debts totaling $110,000 ($80,000 first and $30,000 second).

The problem with this is that the property is not worth $110,000, and it would be quite easy for the buyer to default on the first and disappear with the $10,000 in cash. The seller would have to step back in and take over the new loan, losing $10,000. *Do not make this offer as a buyer and do not accept this offer if you are selling.*

However, you can walk away with money if you give the seller a note secured by something other than the seller's property, say, something the buyer owns. In this case, the buyer offers the seller $30,000 in cash and a note for $30,000 secured by $50,000 (example) equity in buyer's property. The buyer still owes $110,000, $80,000 on seller's property and $30,000 on his or her property but walks away with $10,000 in cash, and the seller has no concerns or worries since the buyer's property is worth more than the loan against it.

Rules When Buying for No-Money-Down

- Make sure your payments (PITI) do not exceed what you can afford if you live in the house or exceed the rental value.

- Ask a seller – what is more important to you, price or terms? If it's price, I'll buy on my terms, no-money-down. If it's cash you want, fine. I'll pay you all cash, but I'll pick the price–75% of appraised value.

Finance the property based upon the appraised value to pay the seller all cash. You do this by asking the seller to refinance, deed the property to you, and allow you to refinance, get a short-term loan and pay the seller cash and then refinance or use my buddy system.

- Use the Exculpatory Clause with all seller financing. This limits the liability to the property itself.

How to Get Paid for Buying Real Estate

You can take money out of closing several different ways. One is something that I'm presently doing. In order to get rid of a problem, I'm offering to "pay" someone to buy my property. Why would I do that? This deal allows me to get rid of a large negative cash flow and at the same time allows the buyer to buy below market value and get paid.

A good friend of mine had lots which he wished to sell. His asking price was $5,000 per lot. A creative buyer said he would take the lots if the "seller" paid him $5,000 per lot to do so and in return he would give back a note to the seller for $10,000 on each lot.

The seller was motivated to get rid of the lots, but this was a bit strong, so the two of them negotiated a $1,000 cash rebate to the buyer and a $4,000 Zero Coupon Bond due in ten years in exchange for a note of $10,000 on each lot. If you have something you don't want, offer to pay the seller cash and/or bonds in exchange for the person buying the property from you.

The normal way to take cash out at closing is through financing. One way was discussed in "Buying for No-Money-Down." In this case, the seller took some cash and a note secured by something the buyer owned. The seller ended up with his selling price of $100,000, which was received in cash and a note, but the note was on the buyer's property, not the seller's property.

This is a version of the "Creation of Wealth Formula" whereby you create notes secured by your equity and use them in lieu of cash as a down payment. As long as the seller is flexible, there is no end to what you can do with this formula.

Example of Substitution of Collateral

You own land free and clear worth $100,000. Seller owns house free and clear worth $100,000, and the person will sell for no-money-down or some cash down and take back a note for the difference. Instead of offering the person a note secured by the person's property, offer a $100,000 note secured by your land.

The person still gets a monthly income, but now the person's security is your land, not his or her house. Finance the person's house for $80,000 and walk away with $80,000 in cash and $20,000 in equity.

That's not a bad deal.

Bad News

Problem: You now owe the person $100,000 and the lender $80,000.

Solution: Put your land up for sale under the following terms: No-Money-down, Take Over Loan.

Think about it. You've just sold your land for "all cash" and yet your land buyer is buying for no-money-down. What a great way to get rid of an alligator. If the person wants some cash, make your note on the land less and still sell for no-money-down taking a paper loss on something that's not worth $100,000 anyway. Besides, this is a cash sale if you think about it, and if anyone pays cash, the person is entitled to a discount.

The Rebate Method

Another way you can take cash out of a closing is through rebate. In this case, the seller is willing to pay you to buy, but this will reduce the purchase price. This means that the lender will only want to loan based upon what you are paying, not the actual value.

If you show a rebate in your contract, this will reduce what you pay, and you can't borrow the same amount of money. Have a separate agreement between the buyer and seller whereby the seller agrees to rebate back to the buyer at closing a sum of money. Be sure and call this rebate an allowance for something such as appliances, landscaping, decorating, etc. By doing this, the seller can deduct this amount from the selling price, and the buyer gets the funds tax-fee.

Let's Review

You get cash back at closing because of financing or the seller paying you cash. You finance the property for more than what is needed to pay the seller, keeping the difference, or you ask the seller to pay you to buy the property. Setting the proper closing date and possible discounting of existing loans are a few other ideas.

How to Overcome Lender Stating . . .

One of my most often asked questions is as follows: "How do I overcome the lender stating that he will loan only 80% of the purchase price or value, whichever is less?" Your objective should be to buy only bargains and certainly a property that you can buy well below market value is a bargain. To take advantage of these bargains, you generally must pay all cash. For example, if you have an opportunity to buy a $100,00 property for $75,000 cash and if you show the lender the $75,000 contract, the person will only loan you 80% of this, or $60,000. Because the property is worth $100,000, if you can show that you are paying $100,000, you can then borrow the $80,000. The difference is quite substantial in addition to the fact that you can put $5,000 cash in your pocket at closing if you use the higher figure.

How to Solve the Problem

If the seller is agreeable, you could ask the person to refinance for the $80,000 and pay you the difference in cash and allow you to assume the loan. This might work, but my experience has been that for the most part if you tell the seller this, the person refinances and then sells it to somebody else for the no-money-down and "keeps" the $5,000. I like the next suggestion better.

The "Buddy" System

Use my "buddy" system to overcome this problem. I have used the buddy system more than 200 times successfully myself so it should work for you. In this case, you need a buddy or friend to help you. This could even be a corporation that you own, but it is better if it is a person.

You ask your "buddy" to enter into a contract to buy property "A" for the $75,000 figure and immediately upon signing of that contract, your buddy enters into a contract to sell to you for the $100,000 cash value.

You show this contract to the lender and borrow accordingly. This is not a case of overfinancing but rather a case of borrowing at a percentage of the actual value. The closings are done simultaneously. The seller gets cash, and your buddy gets the cash difference plus your down payment of $20,000. The person later rebates back to you the $25,000. For this favor, you might take the person to dinner or pay for the use of credit. If it is done correctly, your buddy pays no taxes on profit. If and when your buddy finds something to buy, you reverse the position and help the person acquire property.

Look for Seller Financing First

Eighty percent of real estate failures are not due necessarily to lack of financing but are due rather to lack of knowledge about financing. We tend to overlook that the largest source of financing is actually seller financing. In fact, over 50% of all real estate sales include some sort of seller help with financing. Yet, most of the time, seller financing is only thought of as a last resort and much of the time not thought of at all.

Why? Lack of knowledge is probably the most important reason. A seller may want all cash and may think that he or she can't get cash if asked to take a note for part of the purchase price. A seller may not know what to do with a note nor know that the note may be turned into cash or used as cash. Yet, a buyer can actually buy at "his price" and "his terms" even if the price and terms are different for each. In addition, realtors can make many thousands more in commissions each year using seller financing.

It all comes down to these questions. Why does the seller want to sell, and what is the person going to do with the money? To put it another way—what is more important to the seller, selling the property or getting cash. Naturally, if the person is mostly interested in selling the property, the person is a prime suspect to help make that sale by helping with the financing. However, even if the seller insists on all cash, don't rule out the possibility of seller help because it still is possible for the person to receive all cash and assist with seller financing at the same time. How?

When a seller sells property and takes back a note and mortgage or Deed of Trust for part or all of the selling price, the person becomes a lender in that transaction. Just like any other lender, the person has a piece of paper stating that he or she owes a specific sum of money. That paper is secured by the recording of Deed of Trust or mortgage against the property. That paper has a value and can be used as cash or turned into cash. Let's examine five ways in which you can use this real estate paper to create cash.

- **Trade the paper as cash:** Let's say the seller sells the property for $100,000, takes a $10,000 down payment and a note for the balance of $90,000 secured by the property. If there is no other financing on the property, this $90,000 note can be traded to somebody else as cash. If there is an existing loan on the property and the seller just takes a note for the difference, this difference can also be traded for cash. Example—new loan secured from conventional source for $75,000, buyer puts down $10,000 and seller carries back the difference of $15,000 secured by a second mortgage on the property.

- **Sell the note for cash:** In this case, instead of trading it to somebody else as cash, you sell the entire $90,000 note, or $15,000 note, for cash. In order to make it enticing to a buyer, it will be necessary for you to discount the overall note. The amount of discount is dictated by the interest yield which the buyer of the note wants. Example: If the note calls for 10% interest only and the buyer wants a 15% return, the person will discount it accordingly to yield the 15%.

- **Sell the payments:** Instead of selling the note itself, you could sell a portion or all of the income stream (payments). Actual example: payments of $430 per month for next seventeen years. In order to make the sale work, it is necessary to come up with over $20,000, so the $430 income stream is sold over the next 10 years for $26,652. This means that instead of collecting $430 per month for the next 10 years or $51,600 total, the investor or buyer of the payments received this much and paid $26,652 to obtain it.

- **Borrow against the note:** If cash is needed but the seller is unwilling to sell a note at a discount, it is possible, through a mortgage brokerage firm, to borrow up to 100% of equity of that note. The collateral for this borrowing would include the payments.

■ **Use a combination of each:** In fact, let's take an example or two and show you how this might be accomplished. Look for a super bargain. For example, a property you wish to purchase is valued at $300,000. The owner has run into difficult times; the lender is threatening foreclosure, meaning that the owner stands to lose all equity in the property. The person only owes $125,000. Nobody is looking or buying, so the seller reduces the asking price to $200,000. This is, indeed, a super bargain.

The problem is that the seller must have at least $50,000 in cash. You don't have $50,000, but do have equity in real estate and paper due you from a sale you made earlier. Perhaps this equity and paper could be used to acquire the property whereby the seller gets the $50,000, and you take advantage of an opportunity. A student of mine had just this opportunity, and this is how he solved the problem.

First of all, he had a $25,000 equity in a small rental property which he owned. The seller agreed to take this property and equity for $25,000 of the $75,000 needed to make the sale. The $75,000 is arrived at by subtracting the $125,000 owed to the lender from the purchase price, in this case $200,000.

My student used to own an apartment complex which he sold on contract. The balance owed him was $90,000, and he was receiving $1,200 per month in payments. Even though he had $90,000 still coming from this sale, he himself owed a lender $40,000 which the lender had secured with a first mortgage on the property. The payment to the lender was $500 per month on this loan. In other words, my student sold his property and took a note for $90,000 which included or wrapped around the existing note of $40,000, making his equity $50,000 on this note.

If he were to sell this equity, he would need to discount the present $50,000 value, leaving him short on making the deal. Instead, he contacted a mortgage broker and arranged for a $50,000 "loan" against the equity, pledging the $700 per month cash flow to make the payments. This was the end result:

The seller received $50,000 cash and $25,000 in equity for his $75,000 equity. He used the cash to bring the payments and taxes current, leaving him with $35,000 in cash and $25,000 in equity on an appreciating real estate property. The buyer got in without using any of his own money by using his "paper" equity in other real estate. This is an example of using both a trade and borrowing against equity.

Another Example Using Paper

You say: "You set the price, and I'll set the terms, or you set the terms, and I'll set the price." Or, "Seller, what is more important to you, price or terms?" In other words, are you more interested in all cash or getting your price? If the seller wants a specific price and cash, you aren't dealing with a motivated seller, and my advice is to walk away.

However, if the seller is flexible, it is quite possible to put together a deal, even if you don't qualify for a new loan or have any money. In this example, the seller was willing to sell his property for $50,000 cash when the actual value was $60,000. A buyer was found that was willing to pay the $60,000 value and had a down payment of $15,000, but he couldn't afford the terms and conditions of the $45,000 difference.

At the time, interest rates were quite high, and even if the loan had been $35,000, the buyer still couldn't afford the payments. Again, a mortgage broker was called and the mortgage broker arranged for a buyer of this newly created $45,000 note which the buyer of the property was preparing to sign. Only, in this case, instead of the buyer being dictated to by the lender and being told the terms, the buyer was actually able to make his own terms which he could afford.

The note was sold for $35,000. This, plus the $15,000 down payment, gave the seller the $50,000 which he required. The buyer, on the other hand, paid $60,000, but under "his terms and conditions" which he could afford. This is an example of "selling the paper" to make a transaction work.

Incidentally, the mortgage broker could also have found a "lender" to loan $35,000 against the $45,000 note.

So, we might close by saying, don't overlook a mortgage broker or a creative realtor as an additional source of financing. However, please remember that realtors are not taught creativity, so it will take a specially trained realtor to work one of these transactions. A mortgage broker should be knowledgeable, however.

14

Creative Ideas for Notes and Loans

Now that we know how to make offers without personal risk or loss, what do we look for when buying? I suggest you stay with what I call "good deals" only. These include:

1. Sellers who are agreeable to being flexible as far as financing is concerned. If they insist on a high price, that's okay as long as they will be flexible on terms, such as a low-down or no-money-down deals. If they insist on all cash, they must be prepared to discount their price considerably.

2. Properties priced below market value. When a property is listed at 15% or more below market value, it can be bought for nothing down.

3. Under 10% down payment required.

4. A seller will carry back part of the purchase price in the form of a note. I suggest at least 25%.

5. You can take over existing low-interest rate loans with no qualifying or escalation of interest. Look for older existing

FHA or VA loans to accomplish this. You may have to qualify with newer loans.

6.   Where a seller will take a Substitution of Collateral for a note as part or all of the down payment secured by your property.

7.   Where you can use the Subordination Clause.

8.   Where a seller will agree to a rebate to you for buying.

9.   Turn around situations. Example: Buy for $9,000, with $2,000 down and $100 per month. Fix up or just resell at $15,000 with same down payment but higher monthly payments, giving you a nice positive cash flow without owning real estate.

10.   "Fixer upper" properties are those where the seller will deed the property to you and take a note for the entire purchase price with no payments for 6 to 12 months. Fix up the property. Finance at increased value and pay off seller or sell at higher figure and pocket profit.

11.   Properties with several low-interest loans that can be assumed at the existing rate. Consider discounting loans. Note chapter on mortgages on how to do it.

12.   Properties for sale with seconds. Note MLS idea in my creative ideas section for the method of use.

13.   Properties that can be bought "subject to" existing loans but can be resold on a wrap for the same down payment and price but a higher interest figure.

14.   Properties that can be optioned rather than being purchased.

15.   High equity situations. This allows you to be creative in purchase. Note my ideas later.

Now that we have an idea of what to look for, how do we go about buying those properties?

Buying in Spite of Bad Credit

Surprisingly enough, buying real estate when you have bad credit is quite easy. If you can afford the payments but can't qualify for new financing for one reason or the other, try this:

1. Look for existing loans that can be purchased "subject to" or assumed without qualifying. These include FHA, VA and other types of government financing.

2. If the existing loans have no Due-on-Sale Clause or Escalation Clause, anyone can take them over.

3. Look for sellers who will carry all of the financing. No qualifying is necessary.

4. Offshoot of above. Ask the seller to refinance and then sell to you on a contract. The seller gets a cash down payment.

5. Ask the seller to co-sign with the buyer on a new loan. The seller really can't lose since the property is sold for cash. While still on a mortgage, the person is in an excellent position to take back the property if the buyer defaults.

6. Take in a partner other than the owner. In exchange for the person co-signing or obtaining a loan on the property, the person gets partial ownership, a fee or security other than the property.

7. Use a compensating balance to guarantee payment. Deposit money with the lending institution in the form of cash which is to be held by the lender as additional collateral in case you don't make the payments. Even though the buyer's credit is suspect, the lender is protected because of the cash on hand.

8. Use a "buy/lease" back plan whereby the seller agrees to lease back the property from the buyer on a net/net/net basis. This means that the seller agrees to pay everything, including taxes, insurance, mortgage payments, etc. The buyer uses the seller's financial statement and lease to obtain the loan. The buyer's credit is not important in this case because the lease guarantees the mortgage payments.

9. Add collateral. In other words, give the lender more collateral than the person needs. This collateral could be in the form of other real estate, stocks, or similar items.

10. Have the seller insure the top percentage of the loan. Note a more detailed explanation in the creative ideas section, but basically the seller insures the lender that the buyer will perform, and if the buyer doesn't perform, the seller stands to lose. In actuality, the seller really can't lose if it is handled properly.

11. Borrow more than you need. Ask the lender for more money than you need, agreeing to leave the extra funds on hand with the lender to be used in case of default.

Using Notes to Buy Real Estate

In today's world of creative financing, sellers are often asked to take a note for part of their entire selling price. Many sellers would willingly take these notes if they understood them or knew what to do with them. Most have been accustomed to thinking "cash" and anytime a new term such as a "note" is introduced, people become totally confused and usually negative because they don't understand what a note is or what to do with it..

Let's first examine what constitutes a note. Actually, it's a promise to pay or an IOU. People in general think nothing of signing a note when purchasing furniture, a car, or real estate. This note comes from a furniture store, a car agency or bank, or savings and loan. It is common practice to borrow money and pay cash for whatever is being purchased. The lender asks for a note to be signed which states that the money loaned will be repaid.

This note generally calls for monthly payments over a period of time, until paid in full. As security for the note, the lender records a security agreement against whatever it is the person is buying. In real estate, this agreement is called a mortgage. This agreement is collateral for the note, and if the loan isn't paid as agreed on the note, the lender forecloses on the security. In this example, the seller gets all the cash, with the help of the lender, and the buyer pays back the lender.

It is possible to eliminate the third party or lender and work directly with the seller. Ask the seller to take the place of the conventional lender. Instead of the seller getting all cash, the person takes the buyer's promise to pay the cash in monthly payments rather than all at one time.

Why would a seller consider such a proposition? Most have been programmed to think cash only, so why would a person want to take a buyer's promise to pay instead of cash? There are a number of reasons, but basically it means that the seller gets a sale at his or her price. The person can move quickly and doesn't have to worry or wait to see if the buyer can qualify for a loan. But then the question becomes remains the same. "What do I do with the note?"

1. ***Sell the payments for cash.*** Example: a note for $20,000 calls for $250 per month for four years, and then the note becomes due in full. A buyer of notes might be interested in buying this cash flow.

The person might say, "Look I'm not interested in the note itself, but I will buy your payments." You have $12,000 coming in the next four years at $250 per month. I will give you $6,000 cash for that $12,000 payment schedule, and you assign the payments to me. As far as the note is concerned, you can keep it, meaning that whatever is left of the note balance in four years belongs to the seller.

2. ***Sell the note.*** Here you sell the entire note, including the payments. You probably will get more money but still less than the note. This automatically means that you should expect a discount.

3. ***Sell part interest in the note.*** Offer a part interest only for sale, such as 25%. Put an ad in the paper or contact investors offering a 25% interest in the $20,000 note for $5,000 cash. There are more people with $5,000 than $20,000. Because you are keeping 75%, investors are much more likely to feel comfortable investing with you. Suppose you get four people who want to buy a 25% interest? Whoops! Sorry about that, but you have just cashed out on your note, 100%.

4. ***Pledge the note for a loan.*** Use the note, secured by a mortgage, as collateral to borrow money from your bank. In this way, you need not discount the note, and while you are paying interest to the bank, the interest is tax deductible and payments are being made by the originator of the note.

5. ***Trade the note as cash.*** Offer the note instead of cash when you buy something. Example: If a $20,000 down payment is required, offer the seller the note for $20,000 instead of cash.

Seller Hesitates to Take Note

If the seller is still having a tough time making up his or her mind, you might offer further inducements such as:

1. Sign to personally guarantee the note

2. Throw in a car, furniture, or other real estate as additional collateral in case of default

3. Offer a life insurance policy on your life for the amount of the note

4. Use a co-signer as additional guarantee to seller

I suggest, however, that you use none of the above unless absolutely necessary

How about Collateral for Notes?

There are two kinds of notes, one that is unsecured and one that is secured by something. An unsecured note is a promise to pay-- period. There is no security or collateral connected with the note. If the giver of the note defaults, the person taking the note can sue the giver and tie up everything that the person owns until the note is paid in full. If the person owns nothing or happens to declare bankruptcy, the taker of the note could lose his or her money entirely.

The second type of note is one with security. That security can be in the form of anything: car, furniture, horse, personal property, real estate, or whatever. If buying real estate, I recommend that the security be some form of real estate, either the property being purchased or another property which the giver of the note may own.

You might say something like this: "Mr. Seller, I want to buy your property, but instead of me giving you cash, I would like to give you my promissory note as the down payment or for the entire purchase price. I will pay you _____ interest and _____ per month with it all due in _____ years. As security for this note, I will give you a mortgage secured by _____. If I default, the security pledged goes to you."

Whether you offer a note as a down payment or accept one from somebody else, be sure that the note is secured by something and be sure that the security offered is worth more than the face value of the note.

In case you are wondering what kind of form to use to accomplish this, I call your attention to the "sample" form that follows in chapter 15.

Use Notes to Get Paid for Buying

This is just one method, of several, that we will be discussing that allows the buyer to get paid for buying. Create a note for the down payment, or even the entire purchase price, secured by something other than the property being purchased. This security could include any item you own.

The important thing to remember is to make the security for the note something other than the property being purchased. That way you secure your investment.

If you are creating a note for just the down payment, make your offer cash plus a note secured by other collateral. Be sure and make the cash part less than what can be borrowed against the property.

For illustrative purposes, we will use a $100,000 property. An $80,000 new first mortgage is possible. To begin with, you might offer $70,000 cash and a note for $30,000 secured by the other collateral. This offer totals $100,000. You could then finance the purchase for $80,000, giving $70,000 to the seller and keeping $10,000 for yourself. There are many advantages here and taxes is one of them. Remember that since this is borrowed money, it is also tax-free. The buyer now owes $80,000 on a first mortgage on the something else or a total of $110,000 overall. It is important to be sure that the property being purchased provides enough income to make both mortgage payments, or be prepared to do so yourself.

This method is just one way to use notes to buy. For other examples, check the chapter on buying for nothing down and having no mortgage payment. There are endless opportunities if you keep your eyes open for them.

15

Becoming Wealthy Using Notes

In my travels across the United States, I've been privileged to make many friends and help countless numbers become financially independent. One such friend is Paul of Cleveland. Paul is one of those "seminar junkies" who takes every seminar that comes his way. I'm proud to say that I started Paul on his way many years ago, and he has, in fact, written his own book.

I recently received a letter from Paul in which he states: "Now you can appreciate how your teachings through me as a former student of yours have trickled down to affect many lives in a town that you've probably never seen."

Paul took one idea using notes and applied it to helping a realtor in a small town in Ohio do more business in one month than he did in all of the previous year. And, every month since then they have sold 10% more than they did the month before. Paul reports that this office is now responsible for approximately 80% of everything sold in that town.

You don't have to be a realtor to do it. The idea works for the average investor. Not every lender will agree to such a program, however, so it will be necessary to seek a lender or lenders who will cooperate. It's a win/win technique since the buyer buys for nothing down and the seller gets the majority of the selling price in cash. Here's how it works.

For example, the offer is made for the full purchase price of $35,000, "subject to" the buyer obtaining a new mortgage up to 70% of the sales price. You may be able to obtain an 80% loan which makes it even better.

The seller will take a note from the buyer for the balance of the purchase price, at simple interest accumulative with no payments for five years. The total amount due should be spelled out in the contract. The seller also agrees to pay all of the buyer's closing costs up to a specified amount. The note can be secured by a mortgage on the purchased property or by nothing at all. I recommend it have security, however. You might want to make your offer in this manner:

- Price: $35,000

- Earnest money deposit $1,000 (in the form of a note)

- $19,000 more in cash at closing

- Balance of $15,000 to be carried on a note by seller at 9% simple interest payable in 60 months after closing. Total due in 60 months to be $21,750. Seller agrees to pay all of buyer's closing costs not to exceed $1,000. Contract and offer are subject to the property and buyer qualifying for a new $20,000 mortgage plus inspection and approval of property by buyer

With this last clause, you can make offers all day long without even seeing the property until your offer has been accepted. That's all there is to it. It's a simple, straightforward offer to purchase. I suggest you make the cash consideration dependent on what the property will produce in the way of an income. For example, if the property will rent for $300 per month and only supports a $20,000 mortgage, then that is the amount you should borrow. If the rent will support a $25,000 mortgage, then you increase your cash offer accordingly.

If the seller is agreeable to the above idea but the lender isn't willing to cooperate for one reason or the other, you could have problems. Just what do lenders object to with this technique? They might object to a second being placed on the property. They also want proof that you have the down payment. It makes no difference that you don't need it. They will want to know that you have it. How do we handle these problems? Here are some creative ideas for you to consider.

Problem: Lenders Won't Allow Second Mortgage

In our example of the seller getting some cash, but not all cash, and you buying for nothing down (via new financing on the property) many lenders object to making a new first mortgage and allowing the seller to take a second, even though the seller is willing to do so. FHA and VA are prime examples of this. They don't mind the seller taking a note secured by something else for the down payment, but they object initially to the seller securing that note with the seller's property. How do we get around that problem?

1. Create a note for the down payment but secure it by something the buyer owns temporarily and later move it to the purchased property. This can be accomplished by the use of the Substitution Clause after the terms and conditions of the note.

2. If the buyer owns nothing that can be used as security, the seller might consider taking the buyer's note unsecured until after the closing takes place and then record the mortgage.

3. Ask the seller to refinance and sell subject to this new loan, taking a second for the difference.

4. Buy under a Contract for Deed or Wraparound and later refinance as the owner. Since you are already the owner, the lender's objection to a second becomes obsolete.

5. Use somebody else's property (your partner or relative's) temporarily as security for the note. Later move it to the sellers' property.

AGREEMENT BETWEEN PURCHASER AND SELLER OF _____

Seller of said property hereby agrees to provide purchaser a _____ year loan for $_____ at an interest rate of _____ percent with monthly payments of $_____ including principal and interest to begin _____days after closing. The loan will be secured with a (mortgage or trust deed) on the referenced property and the unpaid balance due and payable in its entirety on _____, 20 _____. If property is sold and deed transferred prior to this due date, the loan balance will be payable at that time. There is no prepayment penalty. In the event any monthly installment is more than _____ days late, a charge of _____ of the monthly payment will be charged.

_____

Purchaser   Seller
_____

Purchaser   Seller

Dated this _____ day of _____, 20 ____.

Overcoming Seller's Need for a Down Payment

These are ideas you can use when the seller is willing to act as the lender for the buyer but requests a cash down payment from the buyer. If conventional financing is used, a down payment is easy to manage; however, since our purpose is to buy with no-money-down, if possible, and use the seller 100% for financing, it is important to try and satisfy the seller and yet buy with little or no-money-down. In order to accomplish this, you need to know why the seller needs or wants a cash down payment. Maybe you can satisfy the seller with other means. Let's look at some ideas.

1.   Point out the tax disadvantages to the seller of taking a cash down payment. Uncle Sam takes part of the down payment immediately in taxes. If the seller insists on cash, suggest that the seller borrow the down payment, with the buyer paying

back the loan in monthly payments. Since the money is borrowed, it is tax-free to the seller. The seller pays taxes only on the monthly payments.. Both win in this case – the seller gets a cash down payment and the buyer buys with nothing down.

2. Many times sellers want a down payment because they need the money to buy something else or perhaps pay off existing debts. Consider buying them what they want: car, boat, furniture or whatever and charging the purchase to your credit card.. If they want money to pay off debts, consider taking over these debts and then settling with the creditors on small monthly payments or at a discount.

3. If the seller wants cash to buy other real estate, show the person how to use your note to accomplish the same thing. Also, find out the person's reasons for wanting to buy real estate. Perhaps you can satisfy that requirement with the person's own property. If, for example, the person doesn't want to handle management or have the headaches of ownership yet wants a monthly income, consider offering all this on the person's property. You take over these responsibilities and pay the person a monthly payment.

4. If the seller wants money to put into the bank strictly for interest, show the person the advantages of taking your note instead. Offer more interest and perhaps increase the individual's incentive to take your note by increasing price. Example: $10,000 down payment wanted. Offer a $12,000 note.

5. Letter of Credit. Many times a seller doesn't need or want a down payment and doesn't want to get property back if you default. If the person knows you are good for the money and can rest assured that if you do default, he or she can sue and get something in addition to the property back, the person could feel much more comfortable selling to you with no-money-down. Get your bank to issue a Letter of Credit on your behalf indicating that you are good for the

amount, with the stipulation that if you default on your payments, the seller can call the Letter of Credit, but as long as you are current in your payments, the letter is not to be called. If you do this, I suggest you try and put a time limit on the Letter of Credit such as one, two, or three years until your equity is such that the seller should no longer be concerned.

6.   Offer additional collateral which you will forfeit if you default in your obligations. This offer could be in the form of a note secured by other real estate, land, or car. In this case, there is no payment on that additional collateral and it will remain the property of the buyer unless the buyer defaults. Example: $100,000 purchase price, no-money-down. Offer an additional note for $10,000 secured by something else you own.

This note calls for no payments and will only be honored if the buyer defaults in the purchase. If you do this, I suggest that you set a time period for this additional collateral, such as two years or perhaps until the property goes up the value of the additional collateral. In this case, that would be $110,000.

Let's Review

Sellers want down payment for some reason. Try and find out what that reason is and satisfy it by a means other than giving cash. If the person just wants to know that you are good for it, then offer additional security or a Letter of Credit to relieve the person's fears.

PART IV

MORE ABOUT LOANS, NOTES, AND OTHER CREATIVE IDEAS

16

Managing Payments

Balloon Payments

A balloon payment is used when a large sum of money is due all at once. It is something you should know about and be aware of because it apparently will be a way of life from now on when it comes to financing real estate. Instead of amortizing a loan over a long period of years until it has been paid in full, lenders have gone to the 25 or 30 year amortization schedule to lower the payments but make the loan due in full in a shorter time, anywhere from 1 to 10 years, but generally 3, 5, or 7 years.

It is something that can be very costly if you don't understand it fully and plan ahead as to how to handle that payment when it comes due. I strongly suggest that you stay away from a balloon payment due in less than three years unless you have a plan to handle it before you actually buy. Just about any balloon payment can be handled if you don't panic and if you buy under the right terms. Here are some ideas to help you make that big payment when it comes due.

1. If you make the note for 5 years or more, chances are that the value will have gone up enough to refinance and pay off the balloon.

2. Instead of refinancing entirely, if the balloon is secured by a second on the property, consider getting a new second from a conventional lender.

3. Try re-negotiating with the holder of the note, asking for an extension on the note. I suggest you try for a one-year extension option when you first enter into the note. Your intentions are to pay it off when due, but if worst comes to worst, you have bought yourself an extra year.

4. Take in a partner. In exchange for the person making your balloon payment, offer a partial ownership in the property.

5. Secure the funds by selling something else you own or refinancing another property. If the property purchased doesn't go up in value enough to refinance, then this could work.

6. Trade the property for something else before the payment comes due. In this way you won't have to make it.

7. Sell. This is perhaps the easiest way out. Even if you can't come up with a cash buyer, consider taking your buyer's note for the down payment, making it a nothing down purchase. Be sure and take the note secured by something other than what you are selling in case your buyer can't perform either.

8. Offer something else in lieu of cash, such as car, boat, lot, or similar item.

9. If you have bought the property without personal liability and with nothing down, you can always give the property back. You lose the property but have had the use of it plus the tax advantages over that period of time.

No-Money-Down and No Mortgage Payments

Now, we're really going to get creative. To avoid paying a mortgage payment, many of us have been taught that you must pay all cash for the property. It may surprise you to know that if the circumstances are right, it is quite possible to buy with nothing down and never have a mortgage payment. Here are ten ideas for you to consider:

1. ***Delayed close***. A delayed close is just exactly that, a delay in actual closing.

Here is how it works. Find a property that is priced well below the market for the area. It works best with "fixer upper" properties. For example purposes, let's say this property is available for $40,000 cash in a neighborhood where similar properties are bringing $80,000 or more. This property will probably be underpriced because of the work it would take to bring it to market value.

Many potential buyers will waste considerable time seeking a lender who is willing to make a $32,000 loan, and then, in addition, go scrambling for a loan to improve the property. Even if you could find both lenders, you'd end up with monthly payments during the "fix up" period and most likely have no income to make these payments since you'd probably vacate the property in order to work on it.

A better method is to approach a lender and obtain a one-year commitment for a loan based upon the value after "fix up." Using our example of $80,000, it should be possible to obtain a commitment of, say, 80% or $64,000. What this lender is saying is that upon completion of all work and based upon the fact that the improvements that are being made increase the value to $80,000, he or she will commit to a long-term loan at that time of 80% of $80,000, or $64,000.

You may have to pay a small fee for this commitment and perhaps the lender won't commit to an interest rate one year down the road, but try and get a committment to something, even if it is market interest at that time. This commitment will come from a long-term lender, such as a savings and loan or insurance company. We call this a "take out" loan. Once you have this firm written commitment, you can take it to a short-term lender, generally a bank, and borrow up to 100% of the long-term commitment. They are eager to do this because they have a locked in "take out" in one year. In other words, they know that they are going to be paid back in one year by an S & L.

You might draw $40,000 to buy the property and maybe an additional $10,000 or so for the fix up. There won't be any payments on this draw so you won't have to worry about making mortgage payments. The total sum will be due in one year. If there are quarterly interest payments, consider borrowing enough to make these payments when due. When the loan comes due one year later, the long-term lender pays it off.

If you can live with a mess, move into the house and live "rent free" for one year. At the end of the one-year period, finance the property for $64,000, pocket the difference in cash, tax-free I might add since it is borrowed funds, and start paying on your new mortgage, rent it out for enough to make the payments, or sell it. If you don't like messes, then stay where you are and remodel. Here you have purchased with no-money-down, have no mortgage payments, yet the seller gets all cash.

2. ***Credit cards.*** We don't generally think of credit cards as a possible financing tool when we buy real estate, when, in fact, credit cards could provide us with a down payment or maybe even the full purchase price. Here is how to do it.

Get as many Visa and Mastercards as you can. You are not limited to one or two as you might think. These cards can provide you with instant funds any place in the world. All you have to do is walk into a bank and hand the cards to a teller. The person will call to find out how much credit you have on each card and then give you that amount in cash. The more cards you have, the more money you can obtain. Take this cash and buy the property, either using it for the down payment or the entire purchase price. When the bill comes due on the cards, take other cards into the bank and borrow against them, paying off the first card's bill in full. Reverse the procedure the next month.

You may wonder how Visa and Mastercard like this. They like it just fine. Most of the time they charge interest from the day you take the money, so they don't lose. You establish yourself as a good risk and because you always pay on time, they probably will increase your line of credit. You have no mortgage payment as such if you pay all cash with the cards. If it is a rental property and you wish to keep it, use the income from the property to pay back the borrowed funds.

3. ***Letter of Credit.*** A bank Letter of Credit is an excellent way to buy and have no mortgage payment. In this case, the Letter of Credit guarantees the seller that he or she will receive cash at some later date. In the meantime, the buyer controls the property without having to make a mortgage payment.

4. ***Use a partner.*** This is a fantastic way to buy real estate for no-money-down and have no mortgage payments.

Find a property that can be purchased for nothing down. In this case, there will be payments that somebody will have to make, but it won't be you. Advertise for a partner, offering a 50% ownership in the property in exchange for the partner making the mortgage payment. The partner could even be the existing tenant, future tenant, or just an investor. Sure—you give up 50% ownership for doing it, but remember you bought for nothing down and 50% of something is better than 100% when the cost becomes a hardship.

5. ***Buy/leaseback.*** This method allows you to use the seller to 100% finance the property and at the same time guarantee that you won't have to make mortgage payments.

You need a strong seller to accomplish this and one who is selling to crank cash yet still wants to control owned property as far as occupancy is concerned. You agree to buy only if the person will leaseback his or her property from you on a net/net/net basis. This means that the seller will pay everything from maintenance to taxes, insurance, and mortgage payment. Take this lease to any bank, and if the seller is strong enough, the bank will loan you the money based on the lease and strength, not yours. If you can't finance enough to pay the entire price, then get the seller to take a note for the down payment. Since the seller is agreeing to a net/net/net lease, the seller is actually paying back your note for you.

6.   *Use the property itself.* Often it is possible to use part of what you are buying to create either a down payment or the entire purchase price.

Some ideas include mineral rights, water rights, trees, equipment, furniture, etc. Example: Sell the mineral rights or the water rights off the property for enough to pay all cash. Many times these rights are worth more than the property itself.

7.   *Options—don't buy.* If your intention is to buy and resell at a profit, consider not buying but rather optioning the property.

An option takes far less cash and eliminates much of your risk. In fact, the option deposit is a write-off if you don't exercise your option. So even if you don't end up with the property, you can take a taxable loss on that option deposit. Incidentally, an option deposit doesn't have to be cash. It could be equity in something that you don't want such as land, boat, car, etc. You'll see more detailed information on options later.

8.   *Moratorium on payments.* One of the easiest things to do, yet is hardly ever considered, is to ask for no payments, or a moratorium on payments. You might even ask the seller to make the payments for you for a period of time. Ask, and you may be surprised by the answer.

9.   *Unsecured note due when property is sold.* I have seen this technique work best on "fix up" properties where the seller just wants out.

Offer a note for the entire purchase price, no interest, no security and no payments, all due when the property has been fixed up and financed or sold. You might place a time limit such as one year on the note for doing the work.

10.   *Use a Substitution of Collateral.* This is explained in great detail in the section on creative ideas, and I suggest you read the explanation thoroughly.

Basically, what you are doing is using another piece of real estate to secure the note due on the purchased property. If you make the note due in twelve months or less, for all practical purposes it's about the same as paying cash. This works especially well if your property value is substantially higher than the purchased property. If it is a "fix up" property, you get the title without any mortgage, so you have collateral to pledge to borrow for the "fix up" money. Once upgraded, its value increases, allowing you to finance at a higher value and better selling price. Either way, your note is paid off with the proceeds.

Overcoming Negative Cash Flow

A negative cash flow is created when a property does not produce enough income to support all expenses, including a mortgage payment.Except in unusual circumstances, I recommend that you stay away from such a property, unless you can see turning it around in 30 to 90 days. How do you turn around a negative cash flow, how do you deal with them, and can anything be done to correct one that popped up when you least expected it? A negative cash flows can also be a blessing in disguise since it will allow you to buy at bargain prices. Here are 15 possible solutions.

1. ***Put a moratorium on principal and interest payments.*** There is no law that says you have to make payments. Keep the income from the property and later use it to cover any negative that might occur over and above the mortgage payment. Lenders are in the lending business and not the owning business. They don't like to foreclose and take back properties. Explain your problem to them. You'll be surprised how much they will cooperate.

2. ***Refinance.*** I just recently went from a negative cash flow to a nice positive cash flow by refinancing at a lower rate of interest. Consider this possibility.

3. ***Seller financing.*** Get the seller to wait or carry the financing at a low interest rate. The lower interest rate will bring the payments down, thereby eliminating a negative cash flow.

4.   ***Sale/leaseback.*** We talked about this before. Use the seller to make the payments.

5.   ***Performance Clause.*** It ties the mortgage payment to the income stream.

6.   ***Get more money.*** Borrow more money than you need, leaving the overage in an escrow account to cover negative cash flow.

7.   ***Delayed close.*** This is discussed in great detail in another section of the book.

8.   ***Get a partner.*** Offer partial ownership in exchange for a partner making the payments.

9.   ***Equity participation by lender.*** Give the lender a partial interest in the future growth and appreciation in return for lowering the payments.

10. ***Make the tenant a partner.*** Give the tenant a partial ownership in exchange for the person making the payments.

11. ***Give rent back to the tenant.*** You can rent anything at just about whatever you want if you agree to give part or all of the rent back to the tenant at some future point in time. In fast appreciation, consider giving it all back while at slow times just a portion is refunded. This eliminates a negative cash flow for the time being, but if you use this method, be sure and plan for the eventual time when a tenant moves or asks for money.

12. ***Option.*** Insist that the tenant take an option to buy with the lease. This works extremely well on houses.

13. ***Rebates.*** The seller actually pays the buyer to buy. The seller is agreeable to doing this because the person gets a sale at his or her price. The buyer may or may not want to pay the higher interest rates so is reluctant to buy. In addition, the income may not be enough to support the high mortgage payments. However, if the buyer is paid $10,000 for buying,

a negative cash flow takes on less significance since the $10,000 can be set aside to cover the negative for a long period of time.

Precautions When Using a Land Contract

When we think of sellers helping with financing, we usually think of them helping in one of three ways. They can take a note secured by a first, second, or third mortgage. If there is already a loan against the property, the buyer can buy "subject to" that existing loan and ask the seller to take a note for the balance of the purchase price secured by the sold property or by another property which the buyer may own. Or, the seller can sell and act as the total lender as far as the buyer is concerned. If the property is free and clear of any encumbrance and the sold property is collateral for the note and mortgage, the mortgage is called a first mortgage. If the property has other mortgages against it, however, the seller now carries back a note and is still liable to pay on the existing loans. The seller can either carry back the note in the form of a contract or as a Wraparound. Let's examine what is meant by a Contract Sale, how it works, and whether it's safe.

A Land Contract, Contract of Sale, or Contract for Deed is an installment type of contract between buyer and seller, providing for periodic installment pay-off of the purchase price while the seller retains the title to the property as security for the payment of the purchase price. The seller agrees to convey legal title to the buyer at some future date, upon fulfillment of certain conditions. During the term of the contract, the buyer has an "equitable ownership" in the property.

Even though the buyer does not have what is called "legal title" to the property, the person is still the owner, has all the tax advantages of owning, can sell and even create notes against equity. It is recommended that if you use this type of installment sale, you record the contract. This recording protects the buyer against the seller selling the property to somebody else or placing additional liens against the property.

The major concern that the buyer has is to be sure that the seller is keeping the other mortgage payments current. If the buyer pays the seller but the seller doesn't pay on existing loans and the first lender eventually forecloses, the buyer could end up paying twice.

In order to prevent this from happening, it is my suggestion that both parties hire an escrow agent or company to act as the collector of payments and payer of mortgages. This could be a title company, bank, attorney, realtor or anybody who is not connected with the transaction. The cost is very small and certainly whatever it is, this type of protection should be used to protect both buyer and seller. I recommend that you escrow four items:

1. ***The mortgage payment from buyer to seller.*** The escrow agent has instructions to divide this sum up in whatever way the mortgages call for and pay them monthly. The balance is then sent to the seller. In this way, the buyer knows that the mortgages are kept current.

2. ***Taxes and insurance.*** The seller wants to know that the taxes and insurance will be paid on time, so I suggest that every month one twelfth of both taxes and insurance be escrowed. When the tax and insurance bills come due, the escrow agent makes the payment.

3. ***Warranty Deed*** (called a "Grant Deed" in California) — deeds the property from seller to buyer. This deed should be signed by the seller and notarized, but not recorded. It is held by the escrow agent. The agent has instructions to record only when the buyer has performed as agreed.

This method is suggested for a couple of reasons. 1) The seller may be on a trip when the buyer performs in full and, therefore, is not available immediately to execute a deed. 2) What happens if the seller dies and the buyer still owes money on the contract to the seller? Without the benefit of a deed being placed in escrow, it could cause a delay in title being transferred. However, if a deed is placed in escrow, this constitutes evidence of delivery on the part of the seller, and even if the seller has been dead for ten years, the deed can still be recorded and be considered perfectly legal. The seller cannot simply place a signed, notarized deed in the person's lock box at the bank and achieve the same results.

> **4.   *A Quit Claim Deed from buyer back to seller.*** Sometimes
> a Quit Claim Deed is treated like a Warranty or Grant Deed,
> so be sure and examine the law in your state. Generally
> speaking, though, a Quit Claim Deed simply means that the
> person signing and giving the deed does not warrant
> anything. The person is simply stating that all personal
> interest in the property is being deeded to the other party.

This deed is signed by the buyer, notarized and given to the
escrow agent with instructions that if the buyer defaults, the escrow
agent is to record the deed. This removes the contract as a cloud on the
title and gives the title back to the seller. I suggest you get an attorney
involved if this happens because it is more of a scare tactic than
anything else, and the buyer does have some recourse in most states.

To Review

Selling on a contract simply means that the buyer obtains an
equitable interest in the property and has the right to occupy the
property but does not hold legal title. Recording the contract is
evidence to all that the buyer is buying the property and, therefore,
can sell it, write notes against the equity, and take all the tax deductions
offered. A Contract Sale is not advised or acceptable in some states,
so be sure that before you enter into this type of agreement you check
with legal counsel. A Contract of Sale is safe and is an effective tool
of financing in most areas if handled properly. A Contract Sale differs
from a Wraparound only in terms of who is in title. In a Wraparound,
the buyer immediately goes into title, so escrowing the deed is not
necessary. Everything else is the same. With that in mind, let's now
direct our attention to Wraparounds!

So . . . .What's a Wraparound?

The Wraparound mortgage, or All Inclusive Deed of Trust
(AIDT) has been in existence for more than 60 years but has not
come into its own until fairly recently. The concept itself is very basic.
A simple definition is a purchase money agreement that is subordinate

to, but includes all encumbrances (or underlying loans) to which it is subordinated.

What this means is that a seller, who is currently paying on a mortgage with lower than the market rate of interest, sells property and takes back a mortgage which contains not only a portion of the equity, but also debt, and continues to pay the underlying debt out of payments received. While the same thing is true when you sell using a Contract of Sale method regarding responsibility for existing loans, in this case, the title is transferred immediately to the buyer via a recorded Warranty or Grant Deed.

You must be careful to determine whether or not the existing loans — first, second, or third — have an Alienation or Acceleration Clause written into the contract. If they do, you may not be able to use the wrap or AITD unless you are successful in removing these through negotiation with the lender.

Another area of caution when writing the deposit receipt is in using the term "assumption." Unless you are willing for your buyer to go through a new credit check and negotiate a new loan at higher interest rates, do not use the term "assumption" and do not write "buyer will assume existing loans." If a buyer assumes the existing loan, the person assumes responsibility for that loan, or loans, and can be sued on a deficiency judgment in case of foreclosure when the property does not sell for enough to satisfy all debts. Rather, have the buyer buy "subject to" existing financing. In this case, the buyer is not the principal guarantor of the note, and the most he can lose in case of default is his equity in the property.

When using a Wraparound, remember that the seller retains responsibility for the existing loans but transfers the title in the property to the buyer. This is a much stronger position for both parties. If it is necessary to foreclose on the property, the seller can repossess through foreclosure without having to obtain a court judgment.

There are a number of good reasons why a seller should sell and a buyer should buy under a wrap, particularly during fluctuating economic conditions. For example, there's the matter of flexibility alone. The number of variations that you can structure into this type of sale is almost limitless. The seller and buyer can work out virtually any terms they want. No bank loan officer or anyone else can dictate what they must do in this type of transaction. Because of this situation, the seller can frequently obtain a higher price for the property. As a general rule, the easier the terms, the higher the price is likely to go.

Terms of the sale under a wrap are not subject to rigid rules nor bound by the inflexible customs of some lenders. The seller is able to amortize the loan over as long a period as is necessary to structure the conditions for the convenience of both parties. Does the buyer need lower monthly payments? Then amortize for 50 years instead of 30. How about setting up lower monthly payments with a balloon payment at the end of the contract? Does the seller require additional funds or a monthly income to aid in purchasing another house? Then go ahead and structure the deal so that the person may enjoy a positive cash flow that can be counted on as additional income that will help the individual qualify for a future purchase. Or, perhaps the seller has too much equity in the house. In that case, a Wraparound installment sale and the resulting tax benefit may be just what the person is looking to obtain.

Another important advantage of a Wraparound to both buyer and seller is the speed with which one can be closed. The time saved by not having to shop for new loans is substantial. Add the time it usually takes to make and process new loan applications, and clearly the time saving really adds up.

If the seller is reluctant to enter into this type sale, there are several strong arguments that may sway the person. Explain the effective interest rate that can be earned by utilizing the earning power of the Wraparound. By retaining the lower interest loans and selling in this manner, the seller can actually earn money on money the person owes. Where else can you do that?

Note this example in which property is offered for sale for $100,000, and the seller is willing to wrap a $90,000 note, meaning that the buyer comes up with a $10,000 down payment. There are two existing loans on the property, a first for $40,000 at 7% interest and a second of $30,000 at 8% interest. Even if the seller were to charge just 9% on the $90,000 wrap, the person's overall return would be 14½% and that is because of the low existing interest rate loans.

Let's take interest alone for a moment. The seller collects 9% on $90,000 the first year, rounded to $8,100, yet only pays 7% on $40,000 or $2,800 on the first mortgage, and 8% on $30,000 or $2,400 on the second. This totals $5,200. Subtracting $5,200 from $8,100, we come up with a difference of $2,900. To determine the yield, we divide the equity, in this case $20,000, into the difference in the amount of interest the seller nets. If we divide $20,000 into $2,900, we will see that the seller actually nets 14½% effective interest return the first year.

You can Retire on Wraparounds

You don't have to like real estate to make money; you only have to understand it. You don't need money either. Quite literally, you can acquire a monthly cash flow for yourself of $500 to $10,000 just by utilizing the Wraparound technique.

Consider this idea. Buy the property shown in the example by offering a $10,000 down payment, assuming the first and second mortgages, and getting the seller to carry a third mortgage of $20,000 at 9%. Then turn right around, prior to closing if you wish, and find another buyer. Offer the property to that person for the same price of $100,000 and the same down payment of $10,000. You even offer to carry the financing on a wrap at 9% interest. In addition to the $2,800 and $2,400 you are assuming by taking over the first and second mortgages, you will also owe the seller 9% of $20,000 or $1,800 the first year. However, you will be collecting $8,100, thereby netting $1,100 the first year. You don't need money to do this, and you run no risk since you own no real estate.

Take another example of a building priced at $100,000. There is an existing $60,000 first at 8%. Consider offering $10,000 as a down payment with the owner carrying back a second of $30,000 at 9%. You agree to assume the first of $60,000. You then resell the property, on contract, for $100,000, obtaining a $10,000 down payment and agreeing to carry the entire financing of $90,000 at 11% interest, or $9,900 per year.

This means that you will be paying out 8% on $60,000 or $4,800 per year, on the first mortgage, and 9% on the second mortgage of $30,000 which the previous owner will be carrying. This amounts to

$2,700, or a total of $7,500 in interest, that you will be paying each year. You are, however, collecting $9,900 or a difference of $2,400 in interest income. On this one transaction, you have made yourself $200 per month and yet you own no real estate and have no headaches.

Follow this formula several times, and you will end up with a very nice monthly income and no risk. There are a number of people I know who have used this technique to retire. One lady I know used it until she acquired a $2,500 per month income, and then quit her job. Another lady nets over $100,000 per year!

How Do We Start?

There are two questions that will lay the groundwork for successful Wraparound or AITD sale, and their importance cannot be overstated. Always ask the seller: "What do you intend doing with the money?" and "Is there anything wrong with the house that would prevent you from investing some of your money in it?"

The answers to these questions will give you an insight into whether or not the seller is a likely candidate for a Wraparound. Without this information, you're flying blind when making an offer.

Let's review some of the pros and cons of working with wraps from the viewpoint of both seller and buyer. First, here are some of the circumstances when you'll find it most desirable to use them:

1. When there is a locked-in loan in the subject property

2. When the seller is anxious to sell but has a poor-risk buyer with a small down payment who is wanting to purchase

3. Where there is an overpriced property and the seller is firm regarding price but flexible as to terms of sale

4. Where the seller does not want to lose the benefit of a present low-interest loan but is still anxious to sell, thereby retaining the use of funds already provided by existing financing

5. Where there is little time available to shop for loans and/or little likelihood that the buyer will qualify for a loan

6. Where there is insufficient cash down payment offered and the seller must carry back a large purchase money agreement

Advantages to the Seller

- The seller retains the good terms of present financing in the event it becomes necessary to repossess the property at some future date.

- It is probably the only practical way the seller has of disposing of a property which has a lock-in loan against it without being forced to renegotiate with the lender.

- The seller can obtain a much higher effective interest on the true value of the wraparound.

- Because the seller can afford to give better terms on the balance, the person can usually ask a higher price for the property.

- The seller can cash out of the Wraparound at a lower discount rate than a similar purchase money agreement because of the higher effective rate of interest generated.

- The wrap is better for the seller than a Contract of Sale because the property may be repossessed by foreclosure while the former may require a court judgment in order to be canceled. Remember — check your state laws to see which is better for you.

Advantages to the Buyer

- Can acquire a much larger property for the same down payment

- Can purchase a property for which the person might not be able to qualify were it necessary to apply for new financing

- Can generate greater tax benefits through adjustment of the price and terms

- Saves the buyer the cost of new loan appraisal fees, new loan points, and loan escrow fees

- Saves the time and effort required to shop for new loans and process the necessary paperwork

- Can tailor the cash spendable return to suit personal needs

- Receives title to the subject property with an owner's policy of title insurance; with the Contract of Sale, the person would not receive title

- Can afford to overpay for the property by adjusting the terms of the wrap to compensate for the overall payment

- Buyer is responsible for only one loan payment rather than two or more

Important: If you should decide to deal with a Wraparound, either as a buyer or seller, you should be sure to consult your attorney or real estate advisor. This route possesses numerous advantages, but it can also be rather tricky. With the advent of the Due-on-Sale Clause being considered legal and enforceable, it is all that more important to be sure you are protected. However, the advantages of using a wrap are certainly desirable and worth the effort regardless. Take time to study the procedures involved in setting up a wrap and learn all you can about the precautions that protect both the buyer and seller.

17

Managing Your Transactions

Getting Rid of Alligators

We think of alligators being green in real estate because they eat money. In other words, alligator type properties are those properties not producing income or enough income to make the mortgage payments. We find ourselves paying out money each month to keep the property instead of taking money in the form of income from that property. Non-income producing properties are generally land, but they also could be a vacant building or a building that doesn't produce enough income to meet all expenses and pay the mortgage payment. Here are some ideas to help you dispose of your alligators.

- Contact surrounding owners to see if they are interested in buying. Since they live or own in the area, they are good possibilities. This idea is especially good with land. If it is an income property of some kind that doesn't produce enough income, try contacting owners who own similar properties.

- Ask the former owner to buy it back. Maybe times have changed and the person now has a use for the old property.

- Inflate the price and offer terms, selling the note for cash. Example: You want $4,000 cash for a lot and nobody will pay you $4,000 in cash. Increase your price to $6,000 or $7,000 and offer it for sale for nothing down or a very small down payment. You volunteer to act as the lender in this case, taking a note secured by a mortgage or trust deed on the land as security. Then sell the note to an investor for $4,000 cash. The buyer gets in with attractive terms, the seller gets all cash, and the investor gets a $6,000 or $7,000 mortgage for $4,000 cash. Now, the buyer pays the investor monthly payments. Everybody wins.

- Exchange the equity into something more salable or useful. This could be anything—car, house, motor home, whatever works.

- Sweeten the equity with cash. If you can't find somebody who will exchange with you, try adding cash with your equity. Example: A $20,000 lot, plus $20,000 cash. You don't need cash to make this deal, but you do need to exchange for something that will provide you with the cash, such as a house. Take a free and clear $40,000 house and finance the house for the $20,000 cash. In this way, you literally cash out on your alligator and at the same time get something that is income-producing.

- Use as a commission. Buy something and offer the realtor the lot in lieu of cash as a commission. If that is the only way the person can get a sale, the individual will be willing to cooperate.

- Use an option deposit. Option a piece of property that you wish to own, and instead of coming up with a cash option deposit, offer your alligator as the deposit. If you don't exercise your option, the person gets to keep your property.

- Donate it. Have a tax problem? Consider donating your alligator to a charitable organization. You don't get cash, but you do get that amount as a tax benefit that can apply to other income.

Problems and Solutions

You must manage your transactions, and the only way to be a successful manager is to know your options, know the seller or buyer's options, and know what strategies you can successfully use.

When a seller wants a down payment in cash for a reason, take time to find out that reason. How? As we've said, by asking questions.

Problem: Seller wants cash to buy something else or pay off debts.
Solution: Purchase what the person wants or assume the person's debts, using your credit in doing so. Instead of the seller taking your note, you now owe the creditors, car dealer or whatever.

Problem: Seller wants cash to buy other real estate.
Solution: Offer your note as cash with the stipulation that the person the seller is buying from will take your note. This note can be secured by the individual's property or your property.

Problem: Seller wants cash to put into a bank in a savings account.
Solution: Offer your note with a higher interest rate than a bank will pay.

Problem: Seller wants to be sure you perform on the purchase. The individual feels much safer if you have something invested in the property.
Solution: Secure your note with something you own, not the purchase property. Seller now feels comfortable knowing that you have something to lose.

Problem: Seller says, "I don't want my property back, and I don't want to worry about collecting and perhaps having to spend money foreclosing."
Solution: Offer something else as collateral for the note, such as Single A, Double A or Triple A Bonds. These can all be purchased at a discount and offer immediate cash, can eliminate the problem of foreclosure, and can even be purchased at a positive cash flow many times. Note my explanation of this in the creative ideas section.

Problem: Seller just wants or needs cash and doesn't understand notes.

Solution: Increase the size of the note, such as raise it from $10,000 to $14,000, and sell it to an investor for $10,000 cash. The seller gets the down payment, the buyer buys for nothing down, and the investor gets a great investment.

Problem: Seller says, "What do I do with a note?"

Solution: Show the 5 ways to turn it into cash or use it as cash.

Problem: Seller says, "Why don't you turn it into cash and just give me the cash?"

Solution: Explain to the person that it really shouldn't make any difference as long as he or she gets the cash, but it makes a big difference to you. Besides, if the seller takes a note instead of cash, the person doesn't pay income tax on that note until the money is collected.

Possible Sources of Down Payment

- Create paper against home equity

- Obtain an equity loan

- Get a credit union loan

- Borrow against permanent life insurance

- Have seller refinance for down payment

- Obtain a Title I Improvement loan

- Advance on wages, bonuses, profit sharing

- Use personal property

- Borrow from relatives

- Use your credit cards

- Hobbies

- Stocks

- Realtor's commission

- Proper closing date

- Sweat equity

- Professional services in lieu of cash

- Use Letter of Credit

- Life estate

- Use additional collateral

- Seller take note secured by owned property or nothing

- Seller carrying and selling note

- Let seller stay rent free for one or more years

- Sell part interest to partner

- Trade stock in your corporation

- Line of credit

How to Handle a Realtor's Refusal to Submit Offers

Another part of management is knowing how to manage a real estate agent. As we have said, a real estate person may not be of much help. Some, as we have said, will refuse to submit an offer normally under the following set of circumstances:

- Wonders how to get paid a cash commission when offered nothing down or a note

- Doesn't understand the offer because it isn't the normal way of making an offer

- Realizes that you are buying for nothing down, so the realtor sets himself or herself up as protector of the seller by advising clients not to take an offer

- Says the owner turned down more than that last month.

- Says, "Yes, I will submit it, but I'll advise the owner not to take it."

Possible Solutions

- Show the agent how to get a cash commission even though the offer is no-money-down.

- Remind the agent that all offers must be submitted. Mention the Civil Rights Act 1968, Title VIII, which states that it is "illegal" for a real estate person to discriminate in "terms or conditions of financing." Ask if you can accompany the agent when submitting the offer.

- Just because a seller turned down less than that a month ago doesn't mean the person won't accept it now.

- Hire your own agent to work for you. In this case, your representative is working on your behalf.

- The easiest way to get around an agent's objection to submitting an offer is to make multiple offers at one time, giving the seller a choice. This should overcome any agent's objections.

Actual case study: $100,000 market value or appraisal.

Offers

- 90K on a three-year lease-option

- 80K with seller deeding the property to the buyer immediately, taking back a note due in 3 months. Buyer to refinance as owner giving seller cash

- 10K cash and 100K in 10 year U. S. Treasury Bonds

- 65K all cash immediately

As a seller, which offer would you take? In spite of the fact that every offer except the last one gave the seller more than 65K, the seller opted to take 65K cash.

The possibilities and opportunities using this technique are endless. First of all, find a seller who is flexible in either price or terms. It really doesn't make much difference which is more important to the person, price or cash, but it works best if the seller wants all cash. Naturally, if the person wants all cash, the seller should be willing to discount the selling price. The bigger the discount, the more profit you'll make. The more expensive the property, the more profit you'll make.

An Example

For this example, let's say you find a seller who is willing to sell a $100,000 market value home for $80,000 cash. For whatever reason, the seller needs cash now and is willing to discount to get that cash quickly. In today's market, this transaction should be easy.

In fact, if you take the time to look, you will probably find all kinds of sellers willing to discount anywhere from 15% to 30% just to get that required cash. Find a lender who will allow you to borrow 80% of market value, in this case $100,000, not 80% of the purchase price. If a lender says, "We will loan 80% of market value or purchase price, whichever is less," use my buddy technique.

Have two sales, one with your buddy purchasing at $80,000 and you buying for $100,000. Use your $100,000 contract to secure an 80% loan, or $80,000. Schedule a simultaneous closing. In this case, you qualify for the loan and pay your buddy $100,000. The person now has a $20,000 profit which is quickly refunded back to you after closing as a credit for improvements of some kind.

The "Buddy" System

If you can't qualify yourself, have your buddy qualify. You enter into a contract to buy for $80,000 and sell to a partner for $100,000 who obtains the loan and then deeds it to you. For this favor, you would pay a fee, such as $1,000 or $2,000. I suggest you get the assistance of a qualified attorney in this case, so the partner doesn't end up paying taxes on a profit that doesn't exist.

Another alternative would be for the seller to refinance to $80,000 obtaining an assumable loan and sell to you with you taking over the loan. This may or may not work, although I did have one student do this 35 times in one year.

Interest rates are negotiable and the less exposure the lender has, generally speaking, the lower the interest rate. As an example, if you put up 50% in cash as a down payment, your interest rate should be lower than if you put up 15%. Likewise, if your loan runs for only 15 years instead of 30, you should be entitled to a lower rate of interest since the exposure on a "fixed" loan is not quite as long with a lender. I normally suggest you get as long a loan as possible, but in this technique I'm going to suggest you only ask for a 15-year loan.

Here's How It Works

Let's say the going interest rate for a 30-year mortgage is 10%. In all likelihood, you probably can negotiate this rate down to 9% by getting a 15-year loan. You now have a fixed rate loan of $80,000 at 9%.

Turn right around and offer to sell it for no-money-down at the market value of $100,000 and 10% interest over 30 years. You act as the lender and "carry" the financing. That means your buyer won't have to qualify. If you are interested in a "lot of cash" in 15 years, I suggest you put a 15-year balloon on this financing. If you want a monthly income of close to $900 per month for the rest of your life, or for another 15 years, just keep the time fixed at 30 years. If you aren't sure, why not put in a 15-year call with the option of a rollover at the discretion of the lender.

Let's see how it works. If you obtain a 15-year, 9% fully amortized loan of $80,000, your payments will be $811.47 per month. On the other hand, you are selling for $100,000, no-money-down, 30-year amortization and 10% interest. The payments you receive on this loan amount to $877.58 per month, meaning that you have just produced for yourself a nice positive cash flow of $66.17 per month and have none of the problems connected with owning real estate. Over a 15-year period that amounts to a total cash return of $11,910.60.

In addition, your 15-year loan will be completely paid off, but your buyer will still owe you a balance on the $100,000 which the person originally agreed to pay. If a balloon is due at that time to you, guess how much you have coming — $81,700. Add this to the $11,910.60 you've already collected, and you now have an overall return of $93,610.60 on a property you purchase for no-money-down, and the seller got all cash.

Why is this the case? In the beginning, most of your payments are interest, and you really don't see the loan balance coming down until the last 50% of the loan period. Since the buyer loan to you is for 30 years, not 15 as yours is, that loan won't move much until after the 16th year. And, remember, the person's loan to you is $100,000 while yours is only $80,000.

If you want to use this, and several similiar transactions as a retirement income, leave the 30-year loan in place, and you now have a positive cash flow of $877.58 per month coming in for the next 15 years. This increases your yield on this one house to just under $170,000. Do this 6 times this year, and what's your overall return over the next 30 years? *One Million Dollars*. Yet, you purchased every property for no-money-down.

Get $2,500 Tomorrow Morning, Unsecured

One of the least known money-making secrets, yet one of the best, is a loan called an FHA Title Loan. I'm utterly amazed at the number of realtors who are not aware that such a loan opportunity exists. It is possible, in most areas, for you to borrow up to $2,500 unsecured on every property you own.Some lenders insist that you can only do it on your own home, but nevertheless the loan is available if you look.

Banks, credit unions, and some savings and loans make them. In my area of Kansas City, banks actually advertise they are making them and invite you to apply. You do need good credit, and the loan will have to be repaid, but if you need $2,500 immediately and want to pay it back over the next 10 to 15 years, look into a Title I Loan.

The FHA Title I Loan was intended to be an improvement loan. Lenders make them and FHA insures them. You don't need an existing FHA mortgage to get one either. You can borrow more than $2,500, perhaps as much as $27,500, but then a lien is placed on your property.

It is also possible to get one on commercial property as well. I suggest you call around to see what banks in your area are making them or call FHA for their recommendations. The Money Store in many areas makes such loans. They can be reached by calling 1-800-LOAN-YES.

Interest rates and length of loan may vary depending on the lender. Your best rates should come from your local banks. You might even be able to get a commitment for one before you own something. Where I live, all one needs is proof of ownership. In my case, this means a copy of a recorded Warranty Deed or Grant Deed.

Since $2,500 is unsecured, you can either sell your property with the buyer assuming these payments, or you can sell and keep the loan personally. If you borrow more than $2,500 and the lender places a lien on your property, this loan may have to be paid off when the property sells, so check out this possibility as well.

Borrow 115% of Your Equity

Some lenders will not allow you to 100% finance your property; however, with a Title I loan, it's not only possible, but in some cases you can actually finance more than 100%. Where I live, if you owe $75,000 on a $100,000 property, it is possible to obtain a $25,000 FHA Title I loan, bringing your financing to 100%. Even if you are 100% financed, you can still get an additional $5,000 with a Title I loan.

Some lenders allow you to do even better. The rule in California is $15,000. If you are 100% financed at $100,000, you can actually borrow an additional $15,000, secured by a second or even a third on that property.

Anything over $15,000 that you may want changes the bank's requirements to 100% maximum. So, if you borrow $25,000, as an example, the most you can finance that property is 100%.

I recommend that you try and get the lender to allow you to sell with the buyer assuming your Title I loan. In that way, you could sell for no-money-down and yet pick up $15,000 cash. Finance for $115,000, $100,000 with conventional financing and the rest with a Title I. Sell for no-money-down for $115,000. If you can't accomplish this, think in terms of selling on a Wraparound or contract.

Make $250K a Year with Your Fax Machine

A blind man called me a few years ago and said he needed to make $5,000 within two weeks. He wanted to know if I had any ideas to help him. I told him to place two ads in the newspaper, one reading: **We pay cash for properties in 10 days or less. Call!** The second one was to read: **Wanted.Investors who want to buy bargain real estate at wholesale prices. Call!**

When people responded to the first ad, I told him to ask specific questions such as location, number of bedrooms, baths, reason for selling, existing financing and what would be the least they would take to move. Many times people answering this ad are behind in payments and most anxious just to get out and save their credit. You want to be sure that their price is much less than the market value. Write down this information on a 3 x 5 card, or in this man's case, have somebody do it for you.

> *Many times people answering this ad will be behind in payments and most anxious just to get out and save their credit.*

When a person replies to the second ad, find out what the person wants to buy, where, and what the person's criteria is for selling. You will have a 3 x 5 card filled out with each person's requirements.

It's not necessary that you look at the house until you think you may have a match between what is available and what somebody else might want. You then enter into an agreement with certain contingencies, of course, to buy for less than what your investor has told you he or she will pay.

For example, the investor wants to buy at 70% of market value and will pay all cash. You enter into an agreement to buy at 65% of market value and then assign your contract to the investor, pocketing the difference at that time, which should be at least $5,000.

All you are doing is matching up buyers with sellers for a referral or finder's fee. However, you enter into a contract as a buyer and assign this contract, so you don't need a license to operate. This is your profit when selling.

My experience has been that you will receive many calls from people who want to sell but not many from people who want to buy since they are not reading these ads or actively looking to buy.

I had one student do both ads on a Sunday after listening to me speak, and she got eight calls from people who wanted to sell but none from investors wanting to buy. If such is the case, where do you find these investors, and how do you contact them?

The Fax Connection

I spoke in Orlando recently and one of my students came up to me with this suggestion. He told me that he is making $250K per year using his fax machine and the only cost is the paper.. He too isn't having any problem finding sellers, but finding investors is more difficult, so this is what he did.

He called every attorney's office, accountant office, dentist, doctor and professional person and asked for a fax number. He then proceeded to write a letter asking them if anybody in their office would be interested in buying real estate at wholesale prices and, if so, what were the conditions.

If you merely mailed such a letter, the chances of everybody looking at it are slim, but if you send a fax, everybody looks at it. Plus, you don't need to pay postage when you send your letter nor do you have to send to everybody in the office. The fax does your work for you.

This student goes one step further by telling the accountants that if they know of somebody who really needs this additional tax shelter that he will see to it that the person gets a referral fee if that individual buys a property.

I personally see nothing wrong with this since many people often ask their accountant for advice on what to do to shelter their income. Real estate is just one way to do it; plus it's a great way to make some extra money. This is certainly a bargain opportunity for those are willing to be creative and put these ideas to work.

In addition, the investor/buyer doesn't have to spend time looking for such a bargain. All the leg work is being done for the person. So, if you desire to make money, be creative.

The next time you want to make another $5,000 or $10,000 per week or month, try this unique approach. It works!

18

More Ways to Grow Rich

There are so many golden opportunities for gaining wealth, but it is up to you to give them a try. Today's market is ever changing, and bankers are some of those who have come around to a new way of thinking. If you capitalize on this potential source, you can grow rich in a relatively short period of time.

In addition, some foreclosure banks are also seeing the light. They end up getting back properties that they can't sell for what they have in them. Bankers are short-sighted when they tend to think of cash instead of considering practical ways to recoup loses.

When selling for cash, bankers have to discount their asking price. Instead of getting back the $150,000 they have invested in the property, they sell for all cash for $100,000, taking a $50,000 loss. Here are three alternatives to solving this problem, two of which are presently being done and the third should be another alternative. Who knows, maybe it will be used sometime in the future after some bankers read what I have to say.

The first way to handle a foreclosure is with a lease-option. A purchaser moves in, with no-money-down, and the bank credits them with all of their payments for 1 or 2 years and finances them 100% beyond.

The bank gets their price, and the bank complies with the banking regulations stating that the buyer should have something invested in the property. The second method is relatively new as of this writing but may be commonplace by the time this book is in print. A student of mine, who makes over $500,000 a year buying real estate but not keeping it, has been using this method for himself and finally convinced two of the larger banks in his area to do the same thing.

What He Does

Using a foreclosure example of $250,000 value, this man buys directly from the bank for $180,000 to $200,000 cash. The bank takes a loss for cash. My student finds a buyer who can qualify for a new loan based on a selling price of $250,000, the value of the property. He qualifies and receives a $200,000 to $225,000 loan, gives my student this amount in cash, and gives my student a note and mortgage or Deed of Trust secured by this property for the difference between what he borrows and the $250,000 selling price.

My student gets either $20,000 or $25,000 in cash at closing plus a note for the balance, buying from the bank for all cash and making $50,000 to $70,000 on each purchase. The buyer buys for no-money-down and makes payments on the first and the second to my student. Both win. Banks have once again changed their attitude toward seconds and as of this writing are allowing sellers to take back a note secured by a second for the down payment. A banker from one of the largest banks in the United States met with my student and asked him how was he reselling properties for $250,000 when they couldn't.

My student replied that he was selling them all for no-money-down and explained in detail how he was doing it. He said, "Why don't you do the same thing instead of discounting for cash?" Two lenders that I know are presently doing just that.

The third method I'm suggesting can be applied to all loans a lender might make, not just foreclosures. Let's examine this technique.

Negotiate for the Best Deal

Or, put another way—negotiate—negotiate—negotiate.

Most of us are prone to pay back what we might owe or pay what is being asked instead of attempting to negotiate a different price. This applies to just about anything we have to sell or buy. I recently negotiated a reduction of a hotel charge by $35 per night. I know of another person who looked to buy a new fur coat. The store was asking $9,000, and this man ended up buying that same coat for under $3,000.

> *I literally danced around my desk when hanging up. I just made $10,000 making one phone call.*

A lot of us simply don't want to go through the hassle of negotiating, even though the results might be outstanding, and others do it on anything and everything, treating it much as a game. I don't view negotiating as a game but rather as good business strategy that can either make or kill a deal. You can negotiate either as a buyer or a seller when it comes to real estate. Let's examine how you might use it when selling.

I once purchased a moving and storage company in Colorado Springs, Colorado. I later sold the company but kept a warehouse. I purchased the warehouse from the developer of the industrial park where it was located, and he financed it over a number of years. I didn't have the warehouse for sale, but I did receive a cash offer to sell that was acceptable. This meant that I would be paying off my loan to the developer.

Did I tell him I would be paying him off? No. I called and said "Times are tough, conditions are rough, and the economic situation is terrible. However, I do have an opportunity to come into some money, and I might consider paying you off if you will discount and take less than the balance owed." Note that I didn't lie. I was coming into some money since I sold the warehouse. I just didn't tell him the warehouse was sold.

He immediately asked, "How much less?" Here's where I had to negotiate. Chances are the person you are negotiating with isn't going to take the first offer, so make it higher than you expect to receive. I said, "How about $20,000?" He immediately replied that was way too high but he would discount $10,000 if I paid him off by a certain date. Now comes the game part. If you jump too quickly at this offer, the person will feel the discount he or she just offered was too deep.

I said, "I'm not sure that's enough of a discount. I'll call you back." Is that enough of a discount? Anything is enough, isn't it? He gets the whole thing if he doesn't discount, but he doesn't know this.

I literally danced around my desk when hanging up. I just made $10,000 making one phone call. I called him back a short time later and said, "It will be tough (yeah, real tough), but I'll do it." He said he'd write a letter of agreement and put it in the mail. I said, "Write the letter, and I'll be over in ten minutes to pick it up." I did not want to give him time to find out that I had sold the property. He would quickly have changed his mind on the discount.

Most of you reading this would not even have attempted to discount this loan. You'd just pay what you owe. But let me ask you a question. What if the developer had said "No, I won't discount." What would I have lost? Nothing! But if you don't ask, it's like a no anyway, so it doesn't hurt to ask.

People Are Willing to Discount

In today's economy, many people are willing to discount for cash. Maybe you have a loan with a private party and an opportunity to refinance that loan at a lesser interest rate. In that case, you would approach the present lender and ask if he or she would be interested in discounting for a quicker payoff since you have an opportunity to refinance the property. It wouldn't pay you to refinance unless they consider discounting what they have coming.

The U.S. government has admitted that somewhere between 50% and 90% of all Adjustable Rate Mortgages (ARM's) have been done incorrectly. It' very possible that if you have such a loan, you are entitled to a refund of some kind. The average return is $1,500 per loan. They could very well consider discounting if asked.

Other conventional type loans may be for more than the property value. I helped one man in Omaha save over $8,000 on his mortgage because he couldn't sell his house for what he owed, and that included selling for no-money-down. That's an unusual case, but it does happen. His buyer would only pay a certain price and that happened to be $8,000 less than the mortgage balance.

The seller thought his only option was to not sell or come up with the difference to satisfy his loan. A realtor friend of mine asked if I could help. It took about three phone calls, but the mortgage company did agree, after some prodding on my part, to take less for a payoff. For the first half of any loan, almost all of your payment is interest so any discount they might give you really doesn't hurt their loan. They basically are forgiving or discounting interest, not principal. If you are a seller, ask your lender or lenders for a discount.

Use It to Buy

I recall one lady who listened to me speak in Tampa saying, "You've just told me how to buy my first home. I'll get the existing lenders to discount what they have coming, and I'll refinance it at the appraised value, pay them off, and put cash in my pocket at the same time."

I asked her who the lenders were, and she replied they were private. I said, "This is good." I then asked her what the interest rates were, and she stated, "16% and 18%." I said, "This is bad." They probably wouldn't discount. She replied that she thought she could talk them into it and would let me know how she came out. She called a week later to report that both lenders discounted what was owed, and she ended up buying that property and even "got paid" to buy it.

I had a student who purchased a million dollar property with no money. Don't get hung up on millions. You might just make thousands. I've always said the only difference between a million and ten dollars is a bunch of zeroes.

This particular property had a first mortgage of $400,000, a second mortgage of $300,000 and a third mortgage of $200,000, or a total of $900,000. The seller said, "Give me $100,000 in cash and take over my loans." I suggested that my student look into discounting the existing loans and refinancing to come up with the $100,000 needed for the down payment. That is exactly what he did.

The 2nd and 3rd lenders both agreed to a 50% discount if paid in full by a certain date. That meant that the 3rd could be settled for $100,000 and the 2nd for $150,000. Each lender issued a statement to that effect which was used as their "payoff" amounts. The 1st lender, in this case, wouldn't discount. Sometimes that's the case, but if there are enough other lenders who will discount, discounting still works.

The end result was as follows:

Needed to pay off loans and down payment: $750,000. $400,000 to pay off the 1st, $150,000 to pay off the 2nd, and $100,000 to pay off the 3rd. Add the $100,000 needed for the down payment, and it totals $750,000, not the 1 million asked, even though the property was worth 1 million. The student got an 80% loan to value, or $800,000, and walked out of closing with $200,000 in equity and $50,000 cash. It was all accomplished through discounting the mortgages. The lenders were happy, the seller got what he wanted, $100,000, and the buyer purchased a million dollar property for $750,000. Everybody won in this case. Why didn't the seller do it himself? Because he didn't know how, nor had he heard me speak, or the person hadn't read this book.

And, just don't limit discounting to real estate. I also applied the concept once when renting a car. Several years when I leased a car, I was quoted a ridiculous payoff figure, much higher than I anticipated. After a series of telephone calls, the company reduced their payoff amount over $5,000. Not bad for just a few phone calls. Once again, remember to NEGOTIATE — NEGOTIATE — NEGOTIATE!

19

Other Techniques

This technique has been around for several years, but I can't remember a better time for you to consider this than right now. It has been referred to by three different names: Equity Participation, Shared Appreciation Mortgages, and Co-Ownership.

It's a win/win technique whereby "everybody" wins, except maybe the banks. Let's approach it first from a buyer's standpoint. To borrow money from a bank to buy real estate, certain requirements must be met.

- You will need a cash down payment, generally 10% to 20%.

- You will need a good credit history.

- Banks like job stability of at least two or three years.

- You will have to qualify for a loan based on your income.

- You will have to pay loan fees for borrowing the money.

Equity Participation, shared Appreciation Mortgages (SAMS) or Co-Ownership eliminates all of this. This unique strategy enables the buyer to buy a home no matter what the market conditions are like and do it with a small deposit only. There are no loan fees, credit checks, income verifications, need to show job stability, or big cash down payment.

With this technique, there are absolutely no bank rules to have to worry about because banks simply are never involved. Basically, this is how it works:

- Instead of the buyer becoming the new 100% owner, the person becomes a 50/50 partner with the seller.

- Generally speaking, the buyer gives the seller a completely refundable deposit of between $1,000 and $5,000. This is to show good faith in the partnership.

- The buyer moves into the property and begins to make payments to the seller. Try and make the payments the same as if the buyer had put up a 20% down payment and had borrowed the balance from the bank. Depending on what you might pay for that particular property, those payments could be anywhere from $500 to $2,000 per month. In this manner, in effect, the seller is financing the property for the buyer.

- The buyer is responsible for taking care of the property, both interior and exterior.

- At the end of the fifth year, the home is appraised. Assuming it went up in value, which is why these deals are generally structured for five years, each party is entitled to 50% of the profit.

- At this point, the buyer has two choices. The person can either buy the property outright or can choose not to buy at all. If the person chooses to buy, the extra appreciation is paid to the seller in cash. As an example, let's say the property went from $100,000 in value to $120,000, not much even with a small appreciation factor. This means that the seller would be entitled to $110,000, minus the refundable deposit. The buyer, on the other hand, receives the tax benefits over this period of time, including deductions for taxes and insurance paid on the home. If part of the person's payment applies to principal, the seller will receive $100,000 less this amount also.

Question?

What happens if the home doesn't go up in value or actually goes down in value? The buyer wins again. The buyer didn't put up the 20% down payment normally required by banks, so the person, in effect, has controlled this home for 5 years, has taken the tax deductions, yet stands not to lose a penny in money.

If the property goes down in value, the buyer can again negotiate with the seller and offer the new value instead of the originally agreed upon price. For example, if the property goes from a value of $100,000 to $80,000 over that 5-year period, instead of losing $20,000 in equity, the buyer can negotiate a new purchase price of this amount or the seller loses when the property is sold at the end of 5 years. The buyer does not share in any loss, just gain.

Let's take it one step further. Let's say that you, the buyer, lose your job or get injured and can't work anymore during this 5-year time frame. In other words, you can't make the payment. You can either rent the house to a third party or give the property back to the seller, losing only your initial deposit.

This shouldn't affect your credit since you are not dealing with a lender, just a homeowner, and the person probably won't report it to the credit bureau. For the buyer, this technique is more profitable, less risky, and smart.

Now let's examine it from the seller's viewpoint. Naturally, if a buyer comes along and pays the seller the asking price and offers the seller's terms, the seller won't consider this technique.

However, in many markets there aren't that many cash buyers and this technique allows the seller to sell at the asking price with the prospect of getting even more if the property goes up in value.

In addition, the seller saves a real estate commission because a realtor is not involved. This alone could mean many thousands of dollars in the seller's pocket. Let's briefly examine the seller's advantages, and there are many.

- The seller makes it very easy for a buyer to purchase because of terms and just a small refundable deposit if the buyer performs as agreed.

- The seller receives more in payments than would happen if renting.

- The seller doesn't have to be concerned about a partner since he or she knows the buyer will maintain the property perfectly in every aspect because the buyer, too, knows that if the property goes up in value, a gain is possible.

- Depending on the monthly income, the seller can pledge this security to obtain a new maximum loan to value on the property, putting cash in pocket at the same time. The buyer makes the loan payments. If the seller's loan payments are less than what he or she is receiving, the seller also has a very nice positive cash flow.

- The seller stands to make additional monies if the property goes up in value because the person is a 50/50 partner in the appreciation.

If the property goes up in value, perhaps to $120,000, the seller receives an additional $10,000 over and above what was originally asked and receives cash on refinancing and any positive cash flow over and above what the person owes on the loan as opposed to what the buyer is paying.

When a Buyer Defaults

Both the buyer and seller are in this for one thing and one thing only, to split any future profit of the home 50/50. However, if the buyer defaults at any time during the 5-year period, the seller automatically gets the property back and the buyer loses everything. Let's examine just what the buyer loses:

- The buyer loses the security deposit.

- The buyer loses all money that was invested on a monthly

basis plus any improvements that might have been made to the property. This could be a tremendous loss since the buyer probably could have rented a similar home for less money.

- The buyer loses the 50% of appreciation.

- The buyer loses all rights to the property immediately and, according to partnership laws, must vacate within 45 days. During this 45-day period, the seller has an opportunity to find another buyer under the same terms.

When the Five Years Is Up

If the home goes up in value, the buyer can choose to buy the home or put it on the market to be resold at the increased value. Or, the seller can offer to keep the home, pay the buyer the equity in cash, and do it all over again. If the property has gone up enough, it shouldn't be difficult for the seller to refinance at the new value to come up with enough money to pay the buyer the profit.

If done correctly, both the buyer and seller stand to win. Nobody really loses. If the property goes down in value, the buyer can offer to buy at the lesser price or walk away, writing off the expense of owning the property for the five-year period. Instead of collecting rent receipts, the buyer can actually write off almost the entire monthly payments during that time frame.

As a buyer, I recommend that you get the right to "sublet" the property if need be. In this case if you, the buyer, can't make the monthly payment, you can always rent it to someone who can or do what one of my students is doing. This student is finding sellers who will sell for what is owed on their mortgage if the buyer will take over the payments. This is a nothing-down transaction. Often, however, the loan is not assumable meaning that he must qualify to take over the existing seller loan. Unfortunately, he can't qualify nor does he want to assume liability for the loan, so he is going about it in a different way.

When this is the case, he offers to take over the loan payments and makes the seller a 25% equity owner in any appreciation over the next five years as well. The seller ends up making more because he is getting rid of something that he wants to give away and stands to make another 25% in appreciation over the next five years.

If the value goes up, he makes money, and if it goes down, he's no worse off than he is now. My buyer takes it one step further, however. He may or may not want to move into the home, but he is interested in making a quick $5,000. He sells 50% of his 75% appreciation to another investor for $5,000. This investor gambles $5,000 on the hope that the property will appreciate over the next five years. If it does, he gets 50% of the profit over and above the existing mortgage. The seller gets 25%, and my student gets the other 25%. My student gives up 50% in exchange for $5,000, guaranteeing himself a nifty profit up front.

Why not just assume the seller's loan and get 100% of the appreciation? Because he must qualify and assume. In this manner, the existing owner still is the owner of record and no assumption is necessary. He is, in effect, using the seller's credit and financial statement to make the transaction work. Pretty creative in my opinion.

I'm taking the liberty of including a sample contract. I'm told this contract is IRS approved in every state, so it should work for you. However, I'm not an attorney and am not giving legal advice, so please contact your attorney for verification that this will work in your area. Also please remember that this contract is for illustrative purposes only.

Good luck.

AGREEMENT:

This agreement, dated this _____ day of July, 20___, by and between Sam Seller, of his town (here-in-after referred to as Seller), and Betty Buyer, of her town (hereinafter referred to as Buyer).

WITNESSETH:

That Seller owns a certain parcel of land with improvements thereon, located at 10 Main Street, His town, more particularly described on Schedule A, attached hereto and incorporated by reference hereby, (hereinafter referred to as Premises), and That Seller owns the premises in fee simple subject only to those encumbrances listed on schedule A and to a mortgage to Bank or other financing (hereinafter referred to as Bank). Seller has constructed on the Premises a single-family residence on the premises for which a Certificate of Occupancy has been issued by his town and for which all necessary permits and approvals were obtained by Seller.

That Buyer desires to occupy the premises and seller agrees to allow Buyer to occupy the premises pursuant to the terms and conditions contained herein.

NOW THEREFORE, in consideration of the mutual promises contained herein, both Seller and Buyer agree as follows:

INVESTORS CONTRIBUTION:

Seller will be paid X-amount per month interest for tenants in common partnership. Both parties agree that the value of the Premises is presently (market value). Seller has a current, existing outstanding mortgage balance of (loan balance) which leaves a balance of (Seller's equity). There will be an allowance of _____ for the finishing of the following items: linoleum, carpets, appliances, and light fixtures.

CO-INVESTORS CONTRIBUTION:

_____ is to be given to Seller plus _____ per month for 50% equity sharing partnership. The partnership agreement states that 50% of the future equity above agreed value is Buyer's and the remaining 50% is Seller's. The _____ will be held by Seller as a security. At signing of contracts, Buyer will pay Seller _____ down payment. The _____ is refundable if Buyer does not default, explained within this document.

(1) TERM:

Unless sooner terminated pursuant to this Agreement, the term of this Agreement shall be for a period of five (5) years.

(2) OCCUPANCY:

Buyer agrees to take occupancy of the Premises on June 15, 20___, and to retain occupancy of the premises until June 15, 20___ unless

Buyer's rights to the Premises are terminated pursuant to this Agreement, or extended by subsequent written Agreement executed by both parties hereto.

(3) PAYMENT:

Buyer shall pay to Seller the sum of _____ DOLLARS on a monthly basis throughout the term of this Agreement in consideration of Seller allowing Buyer to take possession and occupy the premises.

Seller will pay the Homeowners Fire and Casualty Insurance Policy which insures the Premises against fire or other loss.

Seller shall supply a receipt of payments to Buyer. Seller shall supply proof of such taxes and insurance payments on the Premises. Buyer shall make his payments on a monthly basis to seller on the first of each month, in advance. It shall be considered an act of default by Buyer in the event Seller does not receive payments due pursuant to this Agreement on or before the tenth day of any month during the term of this Agreement.

FOR ILLUSTRATIVE PURPOSES ONLY

(4) VALUE:

Both parties agree that the value of the Premises on the date first above mentioned is _____ DOLLARS.

(5) MAINTENANCE:

Buyer agrees that he has examined the property and is fully satisfied with the physical condition thereof and has entered into this Agreement with full knowledge as to the value quality and character of the land, the buildings and improvements thereon, as well as the condition of the fixtures and systems therein. Seller represents that all fixtures and systems, including the heating, plumbing, and electrical systems are presently in working order. A one-year new home guarantee by (his state) law is in effect.

Buyer shall, during the term of this Agreement, maintain the Premises in at least the same condition as the Premises were in on the date this Agreement was entered into, reasonable wear and tear excepted. Said maintenance shall include, but not be limited to, all exterior maintenance including grass cutting, leaf raking and snow removal where appropriate.

Seller's obligation to repair or replace as above mentioned shall not obligate Seller to repair or replace any of the following at the premises:

(a)   Natural or normal wear and tear;

(b)   Conditions which are the result of characteristics common to materials used or to be expected of them;

(c)   Conditions resulting from condensation or normal expansion or normal contraction of materials;

(d)   Damage due in whole or in part to any act or neglect of the occupants of the premises or any other person even though caused in part by any defect;

(e)   Loss or injury caused in any way by extraordinary weather conditions or acts of God;

(f)   Hairline cracks, nail pops, slight ridging of sheet rock, slight separation of walls or floors resulting from normal expansion, shrinkage or settling;

(g)   Normal driveway and lawn settlement.

(6) INSURANCE:

Buyer agrees to insure the interior of the Premises during the term of this Agreement, as well as any possessions Seller may have inside the Premises and to provide proof of same when requested by Seller. In the event of a fire or other casualty loss at the premises during the term of this Agreement, both parties agree to share equally the cost of repair or replace such loss which is not covered by the aforesaid insurance policies, unless such loss is occasioned by the act or failure to act of one of the parties hereto, in which event that party is solely responsible for the uninsured cost of the loss.

(7) EQUITY SHARING:

The parties hereto acknowledge that the purpose of this Agreement is to allow Buyer to occupy the premises and share in the equity increase along with the benefits of tenants in common partnership, in the Premises pursuant to this Agreement, if any, and to allow seller to own the Premises during the term of this Agreement.

(A) Buyer shall have the option to purchase the Premises from Seller upon the termination of this Agreement or by mutual Agreement of the parties to terminate the Agreement earlier than June 15, year.

In order to exercise such option, buyer must notify Seller ninety (90) days in advance of such date in writing of his desire to purchase the premises from Seller. In the event Seller receives such notice in a timely fashion, Seller shall convey the premises to Buyer in fee simple, subject only to the exceptions listed on Schedule A. Seller shall convey the Premises to Buyer by way of Warranty Deed with warranty covenants.

(B) In the event Seller terminates this Agreement before June 15, year, the price shall be determined as follows in paragraphs (i), (ii) and (iii).

(C) In the event Buyer does not desire to exercise his option to purchase the Premises from Seller pursuant to the Agreement, Seller agrees that the property should be sold to a third party, (who may be Seller).

The price shall be determined as follows:

(i) In the event both parties can agree on the then value of the Premises, they may do so in writing and the agreed upon value shall be the then value, subject to (iii) below.

(ii) In the event the parties cannot agree on the then value, each party shall select a local recognized real estate appraiser who shall perform immediately a long form appraisal with comparable sales. In the event the value of the Premises that each appraiser finds is within five (5%) percent of each other, the two values shall be added together and divided by two. This sum shall be the then value of the Premises, subject to (iii) below.

In the event the value of the premises that each appraiser finds is not within five (5%) percent of each other, the appraisers shall select an independent appraiser who shall immediately perform a long form appraisal with comparable sales. The values found by the three appraisers shall be added together and divided by three. This sum shall be the then value of the Premises, subject to (iii) below. Both Seller and Buyer shall share equally in the cost of all required appraisals.

(iii) Once the value of the Premises has been determined pursuant to the above paragraph 7(i) or 7 (ii) , the following sums shall be subtracted from that value:

(a) State and Local conveyance taxes.
(b) Usual closing adjustments pursuant to the customs in the Town.
(c) Real estate commission (if any).

This shall be the value of the premises.

Buyer shall then be entitled to a "credit" equal to fifty (50%) percent of the difference between the value of the premises determined as above and (the agreed value of the Premises on the commencement of this Agreement).

Buyer shall then pay to Seller within 45 days of the date Seller received the notice of Buyer's intent to exercise his option to purchase the value of the Premises as determined pursuant to paragraph 7 (i) or 7 (ii) above, less the above mentioned "credit" to Buyer. Said payment shall be made by bank check or certified funds. Upon such payment, Seller shall convey the Premises to Buyer.

(D) In order that the Premises be sold, the Premises shall be listed with an agreed recognized real estate agency. The listing price shall be the value of the Premises as determined pursuant to paragraphs 7 (i) and 7 (ii) above. The property shall be listed for sale on the earlier of the date the parties agree to terminate this Agreement and sell the property on June 30, year and stay on the market until sold. The parties agree to accept any bona fide purchase offer within five (5%) percent of the listing price. The parties further agree to review and, if appropriate, to change the listing price every three (3) months that the property remains unsold in the event no such offers are received.

In the event that an offer to purchase from bona fide purchaser within five (5%) percent of the then listing price is received, Seller shall enter into a standard real estate Contract for Sale with the bona fide purchaser. Buyer agrees to vacate the Premises and leave the same in as good an order of state and repair as when Buyer took possession of the premises, reasonable wear and tear excepted, and to leave same in broom clean condition, no later than June 15, year. Seller agrees to cooperate in order to facilitate said sale to the bona fide purchaser.

On the date of the closing between Seller and the bona fide purchaser, or in no event later than the close of business on the following business day, Seller shall tender to Buyer by bank check or certified funds fifty (50%) percent of the difference between the sales price to the bona fide purchase less the following costs of closing:

(a) State and Local conveyance taxes.
(b) Reasonable Attorney's fees for Seller.
(c) Usual closing adjustments.
(d) Real Estate commission paid 50/50 by both parties and (the value of the Premises on the commencement of this Agreement).

(e) In the event, through no fault of either party, the premises decreases in value, said value determined pursuant to paragraph 7 (i) and 7 (ii) above, Buyer shall pay seller Fifty (50%) percent of the difference between _____ and said value by bank check or certified funds on the earlier of the date Buyer purchases the property from Seller by exercising his option to purchase pursuant to this Agreement or the date Seller sells to a third party bona fide purchaser to this Agreement.

(8) DEFAULT:

The following shall be considered acts of default by Buyer:

(i)   Failure to tender any payment to Seller pursuant to paragraph (3) above within ten (10) days of the date it is due.

(ii) Failure to remain in possession of the Premises for twenty (20) consecutive days, unless written notice is received by Seller of such absence in advance.

(iii) Failure to maintain the Premises pursuant to this Agreement.

(iv) Failure to perform any obligation of this Agreement.

(v)   The voluntary or involuntary bankruptcy or insolvency of buyer.

In the event of an act of default by Buyer, this Agreement shall be considered terminated at the option of Seller, said termination to be effective upon Seller delivering to the premises written notice thereof.

In the event of such termination, Buyer shall vacate the Premises within thirty (30) days of the date of such written notice of termination of this Agreement. Buyer shall be solely responsible for any damage or destruction to the premises, reasonable wear and tear excepted.

Further, in the event Buyer defaults pursuant to this Agreement and Seller exercises his option to terminate this Agreement, buyer shall NOT be entitled to any credit or equity sharing pursuant to this Agreement. In the event buyer remains in possession more than 45 days after the date of the termination notice, Seller shall have the right to summary process eviction of Buyer and any other occupant from the premises. Buyer agrees to pay reasonable attorney's fees and all costs of such eviction action, as well as any damage or destruction to the premises, reasonable wear and tear excepted. The following shall be considered acts of default by Seller:

1A. The voluntary or involuntary bankruptcy or insolvency of Seller.

2A. Failure to supply Buyer with proof of mortgage payments, proof of taxes and insurance payments on the premises.

3A. Encumbering the property beyond 80% appraised value.

(9) UTILITIES:

Buyer agrees to pay promptly as they become due all utilities at the premises, including, but not limited to, gas, oil, water, electricity.

(10) ASSIGNMENT:

The rights, duties and obligations hereunder are assignable by either party without the expressed written consent of the other party. Such consent shall not be unreasonably withheld. A consent to one assignment shall not be deemed a consent to any subsequent assignment.

(11) DEPOSIT:

Buyer has deposited with Seller the sum of _____ DOLLARS for full and faithful performance of all of Buyer's obligations and duties hereunder. Said deposit shall not bear interest. In the event Buyer fully and faithfully performs all of his duties and obligations hereunder, Seller shall return said deposit within thirty (30) days of termination of this Agreement pursuant to its terms. Said deposit shall not be used towards payment by Seller of his monthly payment obligation hereunder.

(12) INSPECTION:

Upon written notice dated three (3) days in advance, Seller shall be allowed to physically inspect the interior and exterior of the premises.

(13) NOT APPLICABLE:

(14) EFFECT:

This Agreement constitutes the entire agreement between the parties. No representation or warranties of any nature, other than those made herein, have been made by Seller, and Buyer has not entered into this Agreement in reliance upon any representation or warranty. This agreement may not be amended or modified unless such amendment or modification is reduced to a writing and signed by all the parties hereto. In the event a word, clause or paragraph is deemed unreasonable, illegal or unconscionable by a Court of competent jurisdiction, only that word, clause or paragraph shall be stricken from this Agreement. All the words, terms and covenants herein contained shall be for and inure to the benefit of and shall bind to respective parties hereto and their heirs, executors, administrator, personal or legal representatives, successors and assigns.

In all references herein to any parties, persons, entities or corporations, the use of any particular gender or the plural or singular number is intended to include the appropriate gender or number as the test of the written Agreement may require.

(15) USE:
Buyer agrees that he shall lease the Premises during the term of this Agreement as a single-family residence and that he shall not permit the Premises or any part thereof to be used for the conduct of any offensive, noisy or dangerous activity that would increase the fire and liability insurance premiums on the Premises; the creation or maintenance of a public or private nuisance or anything that is contrary to any law, rule, or regulation of any applicable public authority which affects or may affect the Premises.

(16) ALTERATIONS:
Buyer shall have the right to make alterations to the interior of the premises, provided same are non-structural, and provided such alteration:

(i) shall not impair the structural soundness or diminish the value of the premises, and

(ii) shall not involve any expenditure in excess of FIVE HUNDRED ($500.00) DOLLARS without Seller's written consent, and

(iii) shall not be undertaken until Buyer has procured and paid for all required permits and authorizations, if any, for such work. In the event any alteration requires demolition or construction of any part of the premises, Seller shall have sole right to choose the contractors to perform such work.

(17) NON-LIABILITY:

Buyer, his invitees and other occupants of the Premises pursuant to this Agreement agree not to hold or attempt to hold Seller liable for any injury or damage to persons or property whether proximate or remote, which injury or damage is occasioned by the occupancy by Buyer in the premises or the carelessness, negligence or wanton or willful act of Buyer. Further, Seller shall not be liable for the loss of or damage to any property of Buyer or others by theft or otherwise; neither shall Seller be liable for any latent defect in the Premises. In so far as Buyer makes all the payment obliga-tions under this Agreement, Buyer shall be entitled to fifty (50%) percent of the mortgage interest and tax benefits. Failure by Buyer to make any payments or adhere to his obligations shall result in an automatic forfeiture of his right to claim tax benefits and forfeiture of his equity benefits.

In so far as Seller failure to adhere to page 9 1A, 2A, and 3A, his obligations of this contract Agreement shall result in an automatic forfeiture of Seller's rights to claim equity sharing benefits to Buyer all over _____. Seller is entitled to 100% of the depreciation plus 50% of all the future equity all over _____ DOLLARS as explained within this contract. In so far as Buyer makes all the payment obligations under this Agreement, Buyer shall be entitled to 50% of the equity all over _____ as explained within this contract.

Witness:

_____

_____

_____   _____
                                                            Sam Seller

_____

_____   _____
                                                            Betty Buyer

STATE OF _____

                                                            _____
                                                            A.D.,

COUNTY OF _____

Personally appeared, Sam Seller, signer and sealer of the foregoing instrument, and acknowledges the same to be his free act and deed before me,

STATE OF _____

A.D., _____

COUNTY OF _____

Personally appeared, Betty Buyer, signer and sealer of the foregoing instrument, and acknowledges the same to be their free act and deed before me,

_____

20

Lease-Options

In the current buyer's market, a lease-option can be the ideal solution to many real estate difficulties, and it can create special profit opportunities for buyers and sellers. The problem is not buyer demand for lease-options but how to satisfy that demand. There are never enough lease-options available. That's why smart buyers and sellers create lease-options.

What Is a Lease-Option?

A lease-option is a combination real estate rental, sales, and finance device. Its major benefit for buyers is there is usually little up front cash required to move in and start building equity toward the down payment. The major benefit for sellers is, when properly structured, a lease-option practically assures the sale of the property. But even when the tenant-buyer doesn't exercise his or her purchase option, the owner-seller is still usually happy because (1) the tenant paid above-market rent, (2) the seller gets to keep the forfeited option money, and (3) the seller retained all the ownership benefits during the lease-option.

The lease-option is a simple lease, typically for one or two years, but for as many as 30 or more years, combined with an option for the tenant to buy the property, usually at an agreed price. The purchase price is usually locked in at the time of signing the agreement (although I have seen lease-options where the purchase price is to be determined by appraisal in the future –but I don't think this is fair to the tenant-buyer).

From the tenant's viewpoint, the longer the lease-option period the better. But from the property owner's viewpoint, the shorter the lease-option the better. Lease-option property sellers often get hung-up on the issue of setting the option price. My opinion is the option price should be set at today's market value. The tenant-buyer should benefit from any appreciation in market value just as the tenant-buyer risks that the property value might decline.

But some greedy sellers feel they should profit if the property goes up in value during the option period. I disagree. Since the tenant-buyer is paying the property owner rent for the property, and the owner retains all the ownership benefits, including income tax deductions, I think the tenant-buyer should benefit from any reward which might be received for the risk undertaken by the buyer. To minimize the seller's risk that property values might skyrocket, I recommend sellers agree to only one or two-year lease-options. Of course, this conflicts with my earlier recommendation that lease-option tenant-buyer, try to obtain the longest possible lease-option term.

When to Use Them

A lease-option is appropriate whenever the seller does not absolutely need a cash sale now. For example, if you haven't been able to sell your home due to the current slow buyer's market, a lease-option is a better alternative than just renting your house to a tenant who has no possible future ownership interest in the house.

Lease-options tenants usually take excellent care of the property, treating it like owners, because someday they expect the property will be theirs. Yes, some lease-options tenants don't exercise their purchase options, but my experience has been that most do.

Which Are the Best Candidates?

Which are the best candidate properties for lease-options? Except perhaps where the property owner must have a cash sale, such as to provide a down payment for another home purchase, virtually any property is a lease-option candidate. Although we are discussing houses, lease-options are also widely used for commercial properties. For these deals, I find houses which are either vacant, have been listed for a long time, or have been advertised in the newspaper classified ads under "houses for rent." These are the best lease-option candidates.

The owner usually has given no thought to a lease-option (until you present your lease-option offer) because most property owners don't know about lease-option or how to work with them.

The Biggest Obstacles

As illustrated by the situation where I bought my home on a lease-option, most real estate agents are not enthusiastic about these deals. Why? Because 99% of real estate agents do not understand the lease-option benefits for agents, buyers, and sellers.

The primary reason is because real estate agents generally do not receive 100% of their sales commission up front with a lease-option. However, the smart agents realize lease-options are like money in the bank. But, the agents can't be sure when the full sales commission will be received. I feel the agent should receive part of a commission, from the non-refundable option money paid by the tenant-buyer, up front and the balance when the option is exercised.

Benefits for Buyers

- **A person can move into the house for little cash.**

Most people who want to buy a home for the first time earn good income but haven't saved money for a down payment. The lease-option solves that problem because the monthly rent credit forces the buyers to build up a down payment.Surprisingly, most of these first time home buyers have a very good income but no will power.

- **The amount of up front cash for a lease-option is negotiable**.

I generally run a newspaper ad under both "houses for sale"and "houses for rent" and put this headline in big bold letters:"$5,000

MOVES YOU IN!" Lease with option to buy. Cute 3-BR, 2-BA house, $1,500 per month, $500 monthly rent credit toward down payment. 1234 Easy Street. Open Sunday 1-3 PM."

You may have noticed my phone number is missing. The reason is the phone won't stop ringing with an ad like that. But, I post an information sheet in the house's front window with my phone number on it, so I know anyone who phones has already driven by the house and is a serious prospect.

Of course, you can change the amount of up front cash required to move in, depending on the price of the house. One realtor reports he received $100,000 nonrefundable option money for a $2 million vacation home for which the tenant-buyer paid $10,000 per month rent with no rent credit! From the $100,000 option money, he got a $50,000 commission and received the $90,000 balance of his 7% sales commission when the tenant exercised her purchase option. This agent knew the benefit of a lease-options.

- **This plan allows the prospective owner to try out a house and neighborhood before committing to long-term payments.**

For trying on a house for size, lease-options are especially advantageous for out-of-town transferees. Since the landlord pays for maintenance during the lease-option, if the house turns out to be a lemon, the buyer doesn't have to buy until the problems are corrected.

- **It is easy to build up a rent credit toward the down payment.**

The major lease-option advantage for tenant-buyers is building up a rent credit toward a down payment. The general rule is "The larger the rent credit percentage, the better the chances the tenant will buy the house." If you really want to get the house sold, give a 50% to 75% rent credit. But if you don't care, give a more modest 33% rent credit, as I do. However, I feel it is unfair to the tenant-buyer to give a very low rent credit such as just 10% or a mere $100 per month. If you are highly motivated to sell, give a 100% rent credit, and you'll almost have a guaranteed sale!

- **You can exercise the purchase option when you have arranged the best mortgage terms.**

Most lease-option buyers are short of cash, so they have to shop carefully for the best mortgage terms. I've discovered that some mortgage lenders won't count all the rent credit toward the down payment (because of the stupid rules of secondary mortgage market buyers Fannie Mae and Freddie Mac). The result is lease-option buyers must usually borrow from a portfolio lender who keeps the home loan and does not have to sell loans to tough Fannie or Freddie. If the buyer wants an adjustable rate mortgage, however, lenders are generally happy to loan to a lease-option buyer because the originating lender retains most ARMs.

- **You can control the property.**

It is usually far less expensive to rent a house than to own it. Yet, the result is virtually the same—controlling the property. With the 15-year lease-option I mentioned earlier, it was much cheaper to rent that house, for if I had owned it and had to make mortgage payments, it would have been more costly. But the major lease-option disadvantage for the buyer is the lack of income tax deductions. However, as an investor, I don't find this to be a serious disadvantage, but if I were a tenant-occupant, I might find the lack of tax deductions to be disadvantageous.

- **This plan provides for minimum monthly payments.**

As mentioned earlier, renting is cheaper than owning (on an out-of-pocket basis). But the rent credit compensates the tenant-buyer for the lack of income tax deductions. However, this lack of tax deductions will create a major incentive for lease-option tenants to exercise purchase options.

Benefits for Sellers

Most home sellers, and their realty agents, think there are no lease-option advantages for sellers. I disagree. But the seller advantages are far different:

- ## You will have lots of prospective buyers.

If you and/or your agent have been unsuccessful selling your home in the current buyer's market, try offering a lease-option. Then, presuming you do everything right, get out of the way of the stampede.

- ## There will be no argument about the top-dollar option price.

I've found that a major lease-option advantage offers leaves little if any room for negotiation over the option price if it is reasonable. The owner can set the option price at the top end of the range of market values and usually won't encounter any objections from the tenant-buyer. Why? Because the tenant-buyers are so happy to be getting into the house for very little up front cash that they forget about negotiating price. My suggestion to owners is to get a professional appraisal of the house before advertising your lease-option. Then, you won't set the option price too high or too low.

- ## Get top quality tenants with this deal.

As mentioned earlier, lease-option tenants are usually outstanding. They treat the home especially well because they know someday they will probably own it. The biggest problem I have is they add improvements without permission.

- ## Another owner advantage is obtaining higher than market value.

For example, most of my houses would rent for about $1,200 per month. But I get $1,500 per month rent on a lease-option. However, since I give $500 per month rent credit, the tenants view the situation as paying a bargain $1,000 rent with $500 going toward their down payment.

- ## Option money is not immediately taxable.

The option money can either be reported as taxable rent received or included as part of the down payment when the option is exercised. Of course, if the option is not exercised, then the option money is ordinary income in the year the option expires.

- **Another significant lease-option advantage for sellers is retaining the income tax deductions for mortgage interest and property taxes during the lease-option period.**

Depreciation is also available, but many tax advisors recommend against taking depreciation if the seller contemplates using the Internal Revenue Code 1034 "rollover residence replacement rule" tax referral. As always, please consult your tax advisor for details.

- **The seller customarily pays for maintenance during the lease-option period.**

Of course, this is negotiable, but to be fair with tenants, the landlord should pay for repairs since the tenant has no knowledge of the property's condition. Incidentally, in California, the seller is required to give the tenant-buyer a written "Seller's Transfer Disclosure Statement" at the time of entering into the lease-option so the prospective buyer is aware of any defects of which the seller is aware.

Creating Lease-Options

As mentioned earlier, most lease-options are created. Very rarely will you see a lease-option advertised in the newspaper or in the local multiple listing service book. Here are the best ways to create lease-options:

- **Look for highly motivated owners.**

Many homeowners whose residences have been listed for sale a long time are lease-option candidates. Also, most owners advertising in the "houses for rent" newspaper want ads will often be thrilled with your lease-option offer. After you inspect the house and like it, that is the time to ask the owner if he or she will lease with an option to buy. Or, you may prefer to run your own classified ad under "houses wanted for rent."

- **Tempt the owner with an attractive lease-option offer.**

Most property owners don't know what a lease-option is and have never considered it. But, when you find a property you would like to own, write up an attractive lease-option offer.

I realize some real estate experts recommend separating the lease and the option into two separate documents, but I prefer the two-page lease-option from Professional Publishing Co., 122 Paul Drive, San Rafael, CA 94903 (phone 800-288-2006 to order). They also have an excellent five-page lease-option, but I find it too complicated to explain to the other party. After reading two or three pages, a client's eyes will glaze over.

The up front option money is the key to convincing the property owner to agree to the lease-option. If you were renting a house to tenants, how much money would you expect to receive from the tenants? Perhaps the first month's rent plus a security deposit. Wouldn't you be surprised if instead I offer you, $2,000 or $3,000 nonrefundable option money plus the first month's rent? The truth is many landlords would be thrilled to lease-option their houses, but nobody ever asked them.

An additional strong lease-option incentive is to offer the owner a year of postdated rent checks so all the landlord need do is deposit one check on the first day of each month. Easy rent collection is such a strong inducement the landlord will have a hard time saying no if you offer both nonrefundable option money and a year of postdated rent checks.

Incidentally, renters who are occupying the premises need not record a memorandum of option, as you should do if you are not living in the lease-option property, to give constructive notice because buyers and lenders are obligated to inquire as to the occupant's rights in the property.

Summary

Lease-options are ideal for most people who buy homes, for sellers, for realty agents, and for investors. However, only homes which must be sold for cash are not good lease-option candidates. By thoroughly understanding the pros and cons of this transaction, you can use lease-options to buy and sell properties with minimal cash.

Make $5,000 by Next Sunday

You don't need money, a job, or good credit to utilize this very creative technique which I have been teaching for years. It's possible to increase your income $1,000 a month in less than one week and make from $5,000 to $10,000 cash besides. Here is how you do it.

This technique works best in areas where properties are not selling, and I recommend the higher the value, the better. Why the higher priced property? Because that is the property that is not selling as fast, and there are less buyers for a $250,000 home than a $40,000 home.

Let me take you through a recent example of how this works. This is an actual example of what one person did. He found a home listed at $250,000 that was not selling to buy as a lease-option. Naturally, if the seller can find an all cash buyer for the home, the person wouldn't entertain this idea, but there are plenty of sellers out there who are having trouble selling in today's market place for their price. In fact, this technique is an excellent way to sell any property or to buy foreclosures as well.

I met a banker during a stopover at an airport last year, and he reported that he was using this technique to sell 9 million dollars worth of bank REO's in Florida. The bank jumped on the idea.

A few years ago, I purchased a home under lease-option. I offered $185,000 over 10 years ago. My offer stated I would provide a $1,000 earnest money deposit, and I offered $800 per month for one year. At the end of the one-year period, I asked the seller to credit me with this $9,600, plus the $1,000, and finance me. This is the normal lease-option whereby all or part of the monthly payment applies to the down payment or purchase price.

The banker in Florida sold his REO's in this manner. The buyer moved in, with no-money-down, paid money for 12 months and was credited with this money as his entire down payment. The bank then financed the buyer for 30 years.

A Different Twist

This technique differs slightly. Instead of offering the seller a one-year lease-option, offer a three to five-year lease-option. It's important to follow these rules:

- **Settle on a set price with the seller, such as $250,000.**

Explain that you have no idea what the property will be worth in three years but that you want to establish a value now. Take the asking price of $250,000 and stay with that. The house may go down in value over the three-year period, stay the same, or go up in value.

- **In exchange for the seller agreeing to sell to you for $250,000 in three years, you will forfeit all monies paid to the seller and not have them allotted to your down payment or purchase price.** This means the seller gets to keep your payments entirely.

- **Payments being made to the seller could be ordinary income to the seller if called rent.**

I suggest you call them "Option Payments." The IRS has ruled that all option payments are tax-free until the option is exercised or rejected. That means that whatever you pay the seller (my man negotiated $1,150 per month) the seller can keep the money tax-free for the three-year period. $1,150 per month to the seller is approximately $1,500 if the person pays taxes. This will help you in negotiating a payment figure. Keep your payments below $1,500 per month regardless of what you pay for the house.

- **It's imperative that you have the right to "sublet" the property.**

This means that you have the right to rent it to somebody else in case you can't live in it. If the seller questions this option, tell the person that you might be transferred or lose your job, and if so, you may need to rent the property to keep payments current. Incidentally, it's far better to sell on a lease-option than it is to rent your home. A renter may not take care of it as well. When you sell, or buy, under a lease-option, the buyer has a tendency to treat the home as a future home and will take care of it accordingly. The person wants the value to go up and will maintain it just as if he or she owned the property.

- **Record the lease-option, a process that costs you perhaps $10 to $15 and only takes a few seconds.**

Once recorded, it is listed on the title report of (A's) property. It lists (A) as the owner, but you (B), have a three-year option to buy the property. It is interesting to note that even though (A) is the legal titleholder, the person really can't do anything with the property over the next three years since you have an option to buy. You (B), don't own the property. You just control it. It's far more important to control than own. This, however, allows you the freedom to sell (A's) property without the person's consent. That is exactly what you are going to do. You can't deliver the title because you are not the legal titleholder, but you can sell on a contract, subject to your lease-option. How?

- **Run an ad in the Sunday's paper advertising (A's) property for sale under the following terms and conditions: $255,000 price, $5,000 down.**

Why $5,000 down? Because you are entitled to make $5,000 by next Sunday. You had to find this property and write an ad. If the seller wants an option deposit of $5,000, change your ad to read $260,000, $10,000 down. Give the owner $5,000, and you keep $5,000. Balance of terms: NO QUALIFYING, NO CREDIT CHECK, NO CLOSING COSTS, NO TAXES, NO INSURANCE, 10% INTEREST ONLY! You can't charge your buyer, whom we'll call (C), taxes and insurance because (A) is still paying them for the next three years.

I suggest you write the ad where lots of people will read it and head it up with a heading that will trigger calls, such as DESPERATE, MUST SELL, FANTASTIC TERMS or something to this effect.

Do you think you'll get a call with these terms? I guarantee the phone will ring off the hook. $255,000, $5,000 down, no qualifying, no closing costs, no credit check, no taxes, no insurance and 10% interest only. Incidentally, this doesn't have to be a $250,000 house. It works on any priced property.

It's important to sell interest only so that the amount owed to (A) is the same as (C) owes (B).

- **Set up an appointment whereby all who call come and look at the house at the same time, such as 2 o'clock Sunday afternoon.**

Take them in order of arrival and show them the property. Be sure and get the name, and phone number, and email (if the person has one) of everyone who shows up. You can use this contact information for future sales.

- **Check out each person who is interested and check credit history in order to pick the person you best feel can afford to buy.**

That may be the third or fourth person who looks at the house. You will sell to them on Contract for Deed or Land Contract as it's sometimes called, subject to your lease-option. That means the person will have to come up with the $250,000 or the specified amount on or before your lease-option comes due. We call this a "balloon" payment.

In three years one of two things happen. One, (C) calls to report that he or she is ready to take title and has the $250,000. You, (B) in this case, contact (A) and report that you are ready to exercise your option. All three of you meet, along with the title company, a realtor if one is involved, the lender, and possibly an attorney. (C) pays the money directly to (A) and (A) deeds the property to (C).

(B) just sits there.

Or, if (C) for whatever reason, can't come up with the $250,000 to meet the balloon, you ask (C) to move. Then report to (A) that you can't exercise your option, thereby giving back the property to (A) You, (B), have no further liability.

Let's see what's happened over the three-year period. You have $5,000 cash in hand. You are paying (A) $1,150 per month, cash which you may or may not have. But you are collecting 10% interest only on $250,000 per year or $25,000 per year. Divide this by 12 months, and you come up with a payment to you of $2,083 per month. You are collecting $2,083 and paying out only $1,150 creating a positive cash flow (on a home you don't own) for almost $1,000 per month. Overall, you've made over $40,000 over the next three years with absolutely no risk, management, or maintenance. The seller gets what he or she wants, you come out very nicely, and your buyer gets his or her home. Everybody wins! You don't even need to go this far. Once you lease-option the home for $1,150 per month, you could turn around and lease-option it to somebody else for $1,350 per month, netting $200 per month, plus whatever option money you get from this person.

Protection Information

You will want to be sure that (A) keeps the payments current during this time frame and just doesn't keep the $1,150 per month. If that happens and the lender forecloses, you could lose or get involved with a lawsuit. I suggest you either get verification that the person is paying the mortgage payment on time, or you stipulate that you will pay the lender directly. Your payment to the lender probably will not pay the mortgage payment in full, so it will be up to (A) to cover this negative.

Also, what if (C) doesn't pay you, yet has a recorded contract? Escrow a Quit Claim Deed deeding the person's interest back to you, (B). Then evict the person and find another buyer.

Why Doesn't "A" Do This?

Because (A) didn't buy my book or think of doing it. Should you tell (A) what you intend doing? No. If (A) finds out later, he shouldn't really care as long as everybody performs. (A) got what was wanted. You got what you wanted (an income and money) and (C) got what was wanted, (A's) house. I suggest you have a real estate attorney draw the lease-option and your attorney draw the Contract Sale, protecting all parties during this three-year period.

Hey–do this three or four times and you can quit your job.

Taming the Alligator

Most experts will tell you that the safest and most conservative investment in today's real estate market place is the buying of a "bread and butter" type single-family home. These are properties that will always be in demand and are estimated to appreciate faster than any other type of real estate investment. In addition, many times they can be bought with little or no money down.

The major problem with single-family homes, however, seems to be one of not knowing how to rent them for enough to cover the mortgage payment. In fact, many experts will tell you up front not to expect a break even or positive cash flow. This for the most part is totally false. Not only can you make that single-family home produce a positive cash flow, but if handled correctly, the positive cash flow can be all tax-free. Let's examine how it could work for you.

I've had several students who have acquired anywhere from 40 to 400 single-family homes for nothing down. One in particular was a gentleman named Ali. While each student may have used different techniques in acquiring the homes, each was faced with the same problem of covering negative cash flow or renting out the house for enough to cover the mortgage payment. All used the same technique, however, to overcome the negative cash flow problem.

> *Why doesn't "A" do this? Because "A" didn't buy my book or think of doing it.*

The homes Ali purchased were all in the $60,000 price range and all had mortgage payments of approximately $550 per month. The average rental charged for these particular properties was only $450 per month, leaving him with a negative cash flow of $100 per month for each home. This meant that he was feeding an "alligator" that consumed right around $10,000 per month. There are few of us who can afford that size of monetary outflow for very long, and Ali was no exception.

How Ali Overcame Negative Cash Flow

To overcome this apparent disadvantage, Ali advertised the homes for lease with option to purchase. That was the only way he would rent a home. You can play with the figures to make them work for you in your particular situation, but this is how Ali made it work for him. He asked for an initial deposit of $2,000 from the prospective tenant, calling this an option or good faith deposit. He explained that this amount would apply to the down payment if the option were exercised and would be given back to the tenant if the tenant chose not to buy. In other words, the tenant, to this point in time, has nothing to lose. The money is applied to the down payment if he buys and given back if he doesn't exercise his option.

In addition, Ali asked the tenant to pay $600 per month instead of $450. The additional $150 per month would also be considered option money. At the end of one year, the $2,000 deposit plus the extra $150 per month, or $1,800 would be the down payment, and Ali agreed to carry the balance of the financing himself using a Contract of Sale method.

If the buyer did not exercise the option, the person did forfeit the extra $1,800 that was paid. However, if this happens, the tenant actually loses nothing since the tax laws allow the tenant to write off this extra amount either as a capital loss or expense on income tax. The tenant/buyer also does not have to qualify for a new loan, nor does the person have any closing costs. The tenant also has the benefit of obtaining financing from the seller at a reasonable interest rate. In addition, the person gets to live in his or her own home for one year before buying. Wouldn't it be nice if we all had that alternative? It certainly would eliminate a lot of wrong purchases.

Turn an Alligator into a Teddy Bear

In this transaction, Ali receives $2,000 in option money up front, and this money is tax-free until the option is exercised or rejected. Multiplied by 100 houses, this amounts to a whopping $200,000 that the seller can use without paying a cent of tax on it. In addition, $150 of the monthly rent on each house qualifies as option money and is also tax-free. If his revenues are $450 plus $150 option money for a total of $600 per house, and the mortgage payment is $550, this gives Ali a $50 overage per home per month—a total of $5,000 on the 100 homes. Since it is option money, it becomes tax-free to Ali. Ali has taken an alligator that was eating him for $10,000 per month and turned it into a teddy bear that is now bringing him $5,000 per month tax-free.

If the tenant does exercise the option to buy, then the seller would pay taxes on the $2,000 as well as the additional amount received each month. But, the person will only have to pay the capital gains rate on that amount. If the tenant decides not to buy and gets the $2,000 refund, Ali turns right around and finds another tenant with $2,000 and moves that person in. In short, Ali always has $200,000 tax-free money to use, unless the tenant exercises the option, in which case it becomes capital gains. How many more homes could you buy using this method? And, if the tenant doesn't exercise the option, do you think the person might leave the house in excellent condition? You bet. The reason is the person thinks like an owner and not as a tenant.

What about Price?

Should you price the house before renting with option to buy or suggest an appraisal be made at the end of the option time? It really depends on whether you want the tenant to buy or not. If you are just using the option technique to overcome negative cash and wish to keep the house, then set your price up front and keep it high. Then, if the tenant exercises the option, at least you get a nice price. If you want the tenant to buy, change your terms to entice the person to buy by making the price attractive or perhaps by giving more credit on the option money. Or, you might consider stating that you expect all cash for the price. This will often discourage the tenant from buying. If you want cash but want the tenant to buy, then provide the person with more credit on the rent payments to entice the person to come up with the cash.

Getting around the Due-on-Sale Clause

Another one of my students, this one from Boston, purchased 35 buildings over a 6-month period, 11 in one weekend. He took a slightly different approach, and I suggest you consider this idea as well. This person buys anything—houses, commercial buildings, shopping centers, or whatever. He finds motivated sellers who are willing to sell for below market value for all cash. For whatever reason these people just want out of their payments.

My student asks them to refinance the building for whatever money the person wants because most of the time it's far easier for the present owner to refinance to market value than it is for the buyer to convince the lender to loan based on appraised valued rather than for what is being paid.

While this technique works on any price, let's use an example of $100,000. The seller is willing to sell for $80,000 but wants cash. The seller refinances to $80,000 and then gives my student (buyer) a 30-year option to buy at this same refinanced amount, or $80,000. For this my student gives the seller $1.00 (that's right–one dollar).

In other words, my student takes over the mortgage payments and agrees to make them. When the loan is paid in full or when he resells in the future or refinances, he exercises his option and takes title. He rents out the properties for enough to make the mortgage payments and, in his case, has a nice positive cash flow besides. He tells the sellers that he had no intention of assuming the loan, and the seller will still remain responsible in case he defaults. He also goes on to say, however, that the probability of this happening is very slim and besides, they have all their money that they want, and the worst thing that could happen is that they get their property back at less than market value. Are there others out there who might do the same thing? Why don't you try it for yourself?

Write Off Your Rent with Lease-Option

I personally wrote off my rent with a lease-option when renting a condominium in Las Vegas several years ago. The units were actually for sale, but the market conditions were unfavorable at that time, so the units were not selling. They were being offered for rent just to provide the owners with some kind of income. The problem with rent, however, is that you can't write it off on your income tax as you can interest on your mortgage. I needed some tax write-offs, so I offered to lease-option the unit with all of my rent being applied to the down payment in one to three years. This meant my rent was actually option money. The IRS ruling is that "all option money is tax free until the option is exercised or rejected." This meant that the owner could receive my money without having to report it as income until the time period elapsed. Of course, if I did not exercise my option, the owner would have to pay taxes on it, but in the meantime the person had the use of the money tax-free. The law also states that if you don't exercise your option you can write off these option deposits on your income tax. So, instead of paying, let's say, $1,000 per month in rent and having nothing to show for it, you get to write off this $12,000 on your taxes. It's quite easy to see that this is definitely a win/win situation for both the owner and the buyer.

This technique could be changed slightly by offering to buy the unit and paying interest only of, say, $1,000 per month. Again, you as the buyer get to write off the interest as an expense. The difference to the seller is that this interest is income to the seller, and the seller pays taxes on it as the money is received. However, if it were rent, the person paid the same taxes, so the seller has nothing to lose. You, the buyer, have everything to gain, however, since you can now write off your rent.

Turn $20 into $5,000 in Two Weeks

I was giving a seminar in Orlando recently when a student of mine approached me to tell me his recent success story. If you've got $20, you might be able to do the same.

He, like a lot of us, has the knowledge to make money, but doesn't have the good credit or money to back up this knowledge. I'm sure you've heard that "it takes money to make money." This is not true. All it takes is knowledge to make money. You can lose your money, but no one can take away your education and experience.

This student knows a bargain when he sees it, but he just doesn't have the credit or money to take advantage of bargains. Such was the case when he attended a recent real estate auction. One house in particular sold very cheap to a cash buyer standing behind him. He wished he could have bid on the property, but, unfortunately, he only had $20 in his possession and no more where that came from.

He turned and asked the new owner what he was going to do with the house. The new buyer reported that he was going to flip it for a profit. In other words, he was going to resell it for more than he paid. My student asked him how much he'd take for a quick sale of perhaps two weeks.

The buyer replied that if he could flip it in two weeks, he'd take a $5,000 cash profit. Whereby my student asked him if he'd take $20 for a two-week option at the price he wanted. He apologized but said that $20 was all he had. The new owner said two weeks wasn't all that long and that he'd give him a two-week option to buy the property.

They signed an agreement on a small piece of paper to that effect, and my student proceeded to advertise this house, at a wholesale price I might add, adding on not only the $5,000 the new owner wanted but an additional $5,000 for himself.

The rest is history as they say. Everybody came out a winner. The man who bought at auction made a quick $5,000, my student got $5,000, and the man who ended up owning the property bought considerably below market.

Remember that you don't need money to make money, only knowledge; plus it's better to control real estate than own it.

Buy a $100,000 Home for $1,000

It is also possible to buy a $500,000 property for $5,000 and even a $1 million property for only $10,000. You can even buy apartment houses, shopping malls, department stores, or whatever with this technique.

We have been taught over the years that when we want to buy real estate, we must contact a conventional lender about borrowing a percentage of the price we are paying. In order for him to agree loaning us money, we must qualify for that loan, pay closing costs, credit checks, pay whatever interest rate they want to charge and generally be agreeable to whatever terms they want. In addition, of course, there is that problem of a large down payment, generally 20 percent of the selling price, plus the good possibility of a negative cash flow if you have tenants.

Well, this technique eliminates all of the above plus gets you a positive cash flow and a sure profit down the road. If you are retiring or thinking of retiring, this could also double your retirement income. Several of my students are using this idea to purchase homes valued up to $1 million and living quite nicely on the rental income.

This Is How It Works

Instead of offering the seller all cash, such as $100,000 for his or her property, these students offer a Letter of Credit, sometimes referred to as an LC, for $100,000. An LC simply states that you are good for the money, and if you don't pay, the institution issuing that Letter of Credit will pay on your behalf. In the meantime, the seller can use that Letter of Credit as cash or pledge and borrow against it. In short, the person is receiving a document that is as good as cash but has to wait to cash it in at face value. The person can, however, borrow the amount of the letter of credit from a bank, paying interest on that money or could use it to trade to others as cash.

Why would a seller take an LC? The person doesn't have to worry about whether you qualify for a loan or not since the individual gets the asking price now. Nor, does the individual have to carry paper and be concerned whether you will perform or not, and the person is assured an immediate closing.

How long does an LC generally last? The time is negotiable. In this case, I'm suggesting you line up one for 3-5 years. You might accomplish your objective in one year, but give yourself some leeway.

What does a Letter of Credit cost? Generally one half to one percent of the amount. This means that you can buy an LC of $100,000 for $500 to $1,000 total. This also means that you can buy and control a $100,000 piece of real estate for $500 to $1,000 and at the same time have no mortgage payments.

What does it take to get an LC? Naturally, banks won't give out a Letter of Credit without some background knowledge of the person requesting such or without some sort of collateral. In other words, to obtain a $100,000 LC, you may need $100,000 in collateral to offer the bank.

A Letter of Credit without Collateral

Can I get a Letter of Credit without collateral? Yes, under the right circumstances. Sometimes you can get the bank to issue such a letter secured by the property that you are buying and nothing else. This is especially true when you are buying below market but can also work if you are in a fast appreciation area. I suggest you attempt to use whatever it is you are buying as total security for the LC. That is why I suggest three to five years initially. The bank has no risk for that time frame since the letter can't be called until the time is up. The property should appreciate enough to cover the $100,000 plus much more over that period, or you can resell before the letter is called.

You End with Free and Clear Property

Think about it. The seller gets a $100,000 LC which can be called in three to five years in exchange for deeding property to you free and clear. Do you think you might be able to rent out the property for a positive cash flow if you have no payments? At the end of the three to five years, sell, paying off the lender, or refinance at the new value, paying off the issuer of the LC. If it doesn't appreciate enough during that time frame, refinance, paying the issuer part of what is due and give the person a note for the balance or ask the individual to take a second on the property. Think about this. The seller gets the price in all cash, not up front, but the person gets something that can be used as cash or pledged to get the cash, so the person wins.

The buyer buys for no-money-down, gets a property free and clear, has a positive cash flow and an eventual profit when the property goes up in value, so the buyer wins.

The lender is fully protected with collateral and knows that the LC will never be called because the buyer intends selling or refinancing before the LC comes due, so the lender wins.

- POSSIBLE PROBLEM: The seller doesn't get money for three to five years, and while the seller can borrow against that LC, the person could complain about loss of interest on the money.

- SOLUTION: Offer to pay the seller interest on money that is coming as an additional benefit for the person taking the LC. I wouldn't suggest a lot, and I only suggest this as a last resort. Make the interest payment less than what you are collecting in rent so you still have a positive cash flow.

Again, a Letter of Credit simply states that you are good for the money and if you don't pay, the issuing institution will make good on that guarantee. When used in real estate, I like three to five years, longer if possible, because that gives ample time for the property to go up in value so that it can be sold or refinanced to cover the $100,000 when due, instead of controlling and owning it for about $1,000. Isn't that the ultimate in leverage?

Final Note on No-Money-Down

The possibilities and opportunities using this technique are endless. First of all, find a seller who is flexible in either price or terms. It really doesn't make much difference which is more important to the person—the price or the cash, but it works best if the seller wants all cash. Naturally, if the seller wants all cash, the person should be willing to discount the selling price. The bigger the discount, the more profit you'll make. The more expensive the property, again the more profit you'll make. For this example, let's say you find a seller who is willing to sell a $100,000 market value home for $80,000 cash. For whatever reason the person needs cash now and is willing to discount to get that cash quickly. At the time of writing this book, based on today's market place, this should be easy.

In fact, if you take the time to look, you will probably find all kinds of sellers willing to discount anywhere from 15% to 30% just to get that required cash. Find a lender who will allow you to borrow 80% of the market value, in this case $100,000, not 80% of the purchase price.

If a lender says, "We will loan 80% of market value or purchase price, whichever is less," use my buddy technique. Have two sales, one with your buddy purchasing at $80,000 and you buying from the partner for $100,000. Use your $100,000, contract to secure an 80 % loan, or $80,000. Schedule a simultaneous closing. In this case, you qualify for the loan and pay your buddy $100,000. The person now has a $20,000 profit which can quickly be refunded back to you after closing as a credit for improvements of some kind.

If you can't qualify yourself, have your buddy qualify. You enter into a contract to buy for $80,000 and sell to your buddy for $100,000. Your partner obtains the loan and then deeds it to you. For this you would pay your partner a fee, such as $1,000 or $2,000. I suggest you get the assistance of a qualified attorney in this case, so your partner doesn't pay taxes on a profit the person really didn't make.

Another alternate would be for the seller to refinance to $80,000, obtaining an assumable loan and sell to you with you taking over the loan. This may or may not work, but as I mentioned earlier, I did have one student use this technique 35 times in one year.

Interest rates are negotiable, and the less exposure the lender has, generally speaking, the lower the interest rate. As an example, if you put up 50% in cash as a down payment, your interest rate should be lower than if you put up 15%. Likewise, if your loan runs for only 15 years instead of 30, you should be entitled to a lower rate of interest since the exposure on a fixed loan is not quite as long with a lender. I normally suggest you get as long a loan as possible, but in this technique I'm going to suggest you only ask for a 15-year loan.

Let's say the going interest rate for a 30-year mortgage is 10%. In all likelihood, you probably can negotiate this rate down to 9% by getting a 15-year loan. You now have a fixed rate loan of $80,000 at 9%. Turn right around and offer it for sale for no-money-down for the market value of $100,000 and 10% interest over 30 years. You act as the lender and carry the financing. That means your buyer won't have to qualify. If you are interested in a lot of cash in 15 years, I suggest you put a 15-year balloon on this financing. If you want a monthly income of close to $900 per month for the rest of your life or for another 15 years, just keep the time fixed at 30 years. If you aren't sure, why not put in a 15-year call with the option of a rollover, at the discretion of the lender, in this case you.

Let's See How It Works

If you obtain a 15-year, 9%, fully amortized loan of $80,000, your payments will be $811.47 per month. On the other hand, you are selling for $100,000, no-money-down, 30-year amortization and 10% interest. The payments you receive on this loan amount to $877.58 per month, meaning that you have just produced for yourself a nice positive cash flow of $66.17 per month with none of the problems connected with owning real estate. Over a 15-year period, that amounts to a total cash return of $11,910.60.

In addition, your 15-year loan will be completely paid off, but your buyer will still owe you a balance on the $100,000, which the person originally agreed to pay. If a balloon is due at that time to you, guess how much you have coming—$81,700. Add this to the $11,910.60 you've already collected, and you now have an overall return of $93,610.60 on a property you purchased for no-money-down, and the seller got all cash. Why is this the case? In the beginning, most of your payments are interest, and you really don't see the loan balance coming down until the last 50% of the loan period. Since the buyer loan to you is for 30 year (not 15 as yours is), that loan won't move much until after the 16th year. And, remember that the person's loan to you is $100,000, while yours is only $80,000.

If you want to use this, and several other like transactions as a retirement income, leave the 30-year loan in place, and you now have a positive cash flow of $877.58 per month coming in for the next 15 years. This increases your yield on this one house to just under $170,000. Do this 6 times this year, and what's your overall return over the next 30 years? **Over one million dollars.** Yet, you purchased every property for no-money-down.

PART V

BONDS: THE GREATEST FINANCING TOOL OF ALL

21

Creative Use of Bonds

Unfortunately, many people understand little about municipal bonds and government securities. Municipal Bonds and U.S. Securities are the same as money. They are equivalent to cash, are fully guaranteed, and insured at full value by the agency issuing them. Suppose you traded $200,000 equity in your home for $600,000 in Municipal Bonds. When these Bonds mature, they have the same value as $600,000 in cash in your bank account. Even though the full value won't be $600,000 for a period of years, you can still trade them as $600,000 or use them as security and borrow up to 92% of the present value of the bonds.

Various types of bonds and securities can be exchanged for cash or real estate; they can be sold, traded, or given away.

While U.S. Government Securities usually mature in 10, 20, 30, and 40 years, most of them can be cashed in much earlier at a discount. And certain types of bonds are tax-free.

During the past ten years, millions of Americans have used their hard-earned cash to purchase over $400 billion in Municipal, State, and Federal Bonds. If they didn't have great value, why would people use good money to buy them?

So, why do people spend their good money to purchase them?

- For retirement to assure their financial security

- For their children (or friends or relatives)

- For their children's (and grandchildren's) education

- To cover unforeseen difficulties in the future (illness, accidents, financial reverses, balloon payments, etc.)

- To take care of mortgages, business investments, and personal commitments

- Endowments to church, school, lodge or favorite charity

- For vacations, cruises, and a life of travel and adventure

Most of us will find that our dreams and needs fit somewhere in that list.

Making Your Dreams Come True

Statistics show that most people will never accumulate enough cash to make those dreams and plans come true. At this point in time, you now have the opportunity to take a portion of your real estate property and turn it into a form of future security that otherwise you may never be able to achieve. The Municipal Bonds or Government Securities that will be provided in these real estate exchange programs will be handled through the offices of some of the nation's leading brokerage firms, such as Merrill Lynch, PaineWebber or E.F. Hutton, and they will be as safe as your state and federal government.

Most important of all, they may provide comfort, pleasure, and security at the very time you and your family will cherish them most.

Zero Coupon Bonds

Get ready to get excited. Get ready to make lots of money because, without a doubt, the greatest creative financing tool of all is Zero Coupon Bonds. There has never been and probably never will be any other financing tool so powerful that it solves just about any situation. If used correctly, there absolutely is no downside to Zero Coupon Bonds. There are only winners.

I've had students acquire sailboats, cars, mortgages, houses, churches, motels and even apartments with bonds. It is also possible for a person to send a child to college for four years for about $10,000 total.

Think of the savings you can create for yourself using bonds with just this reason alone. If used as I teach and suggest, this technique could literally solve all the banking problems that exist and even help reduce the deficit. In fact, I've suggested the use of zero bonds to Washington, but so far my advice has fallen on deaf ears. They haven't even acknowledged receiving this information.

Used with real estate, Zero Coupon Bonds make it possible to sell anything you own and get your price or more, regardless of the economy. Zero Coupon Bonds make it possible for every buyer to buy at his or her value and never have to worry about losing the property to foreclosure. Zero Coupon Bonds allow every lending institution to make loans without any fear of default. In other words, this technique, when used properly, makes it impossible for a lender to make a bad loan. If the borrower, for whatever reason, defaults, the lender ends up making money, not losing it.

If Zero Coupon Bonds have all of these advantages, why aren't they used more? Mostly because people seldom understand how to use them, or they haven't been exposed to the idea. A few banks have seen the advantages and use them, but the majority of lenders aren't willing to try something new and different, regardless of the safety and end results.

Hopefully, enough lenders will read this book and give my suggestions a try. As importantly, I wish someone from the Senate and House Banking Committee would read this and consider giving my ideas a try.

What Kind of Zeros Should I Buy?

There are several types available, but for safety's sake, I recommend just two. Your safest investment, bar none, is a U.S. Treasury Bond. Why? Because it's backed and guaranteed by the United States Government. Your second safest investment is a tax-exempt Municipal Bond. The single most important feature of this type bond is that it is exempt from Federal Income Tax and many times State Income Tax. Tax-free bonds are hard to find, but when they become available, go for them. U.S. Treasury Bonds are available anyplace, anytime. As a matter of fact, banks buy U.S. Treasury Bonds on a regular basis because they know them to be 100% safe, and their money is available immediately if needed.

Despite the fact that instead of loaning out money, banks buy U.S. Treasury Bonds, they express concern when approached about using them in real estate transactions because they are afraid they might violate some banking regulation.

The Difference Between a Treasury and a Zero

Using an example of $100,000, you can put up $100,000 and buy either a U.S. Treasury Bond or a tax-exempt Municipal Bond. The bond issued shows a value of $100,000. The bond pays interest in cash. The cash is reported to Uncle Sam, and if you buy a U.S. Treasury Bond, you will pay taxes on this income. If you purchase a tax-exempt bond, you will have no tax obligation to Uncle Sam and many times you won't have to pay state tax either. In both cases, you put up $100,000 in cash.

How Do Zero Bonds Work?

A Zero Coupon Bond works in this manner. Instead of putting up $100,000 cash and buying a bond that is presently worth $100,000, you put up a small fraction of this amount and buy a bond that will be worth $100,000 sometime in the future. Your cost to buy this bond is dictated by the time it takes to grow to the future value of $100,000. The amount of money invested accrues interest and does not pay it in cash.

Common sense states that the shorter the time the bond is to be held, the more the bond will cost. For example, let's say you wanted your investment to grow to be worth $100,000 in 30 years. Your cost to buy this $100,000 bond will be around $10,000. In other words, that $100,000 will accrue interest each and every year until that $10,000 becomes $100,000. If you want the $100,000 in 10 years, you may have to put up as much as $50,000.

You will have to contact a bond broker if buying tax-exempt

> **Think of using bonds as cash, instead of cash itself.**

bonds and will want to know their cost, but you can get an idea of what the U.S. Treasuries are trading for by reading the *Wall Street Journal.* They are quoted every day under "U.S. Treasury Strips" and are located at the very end of the stock and bond quotes.

Think of using bonds as cash instead of cash itself. If you offer to trade your car to someone for the equity in the person's house or even for another car, you in effect, are offering the car instead of cash, or the car is your cash in this transaction.

The difference with using bonds instead of cash now is that you are offering future cash value, not present cash value. Yes, there is a present cash value now for the bonds, but it is smaller than what they eventually will be worth.

However, if you need the cash now, you can cash them in for the present cash value. A better idea might be to borrow against this cash value. You can borrow up to 90% of that value from the broker that sold you the bonds. By borrowing against these bonds, you will not only have the cash you need but can also keep the bond in place.

Let's now examine some of the ways to use bonds and how to overcome any problems that might come up.

Actual Examples

It is important to remember that all of my examples are actual examples, something that either I have done or one of my students has accomplished. As of this writing, the cost of purchasing bonds is significantly higher than the examples shown. While it used to cost, maybe, 20¢ on the dollar to buy a 10-year bond, it may now cost as much as 50¢ or more. Bond prices fluctuate daily, depending upon the stock market, so don't get hung up on the price schedule I have used. It is more important for you to understand and apply the concept and change the years to fit your transaction. You might have to change your years to 15 to 20 to make it work. The concept is the important thing to understand.

Bonds as Security

Bonds can be offered as security for a note and often are far safer than other types of collateral. In real estate, we are accustomed to offering the seller or lender a note secured by a mortgage or Deed of Trust on real estate. If we default in the terms or conditions of that promissory note, the seller or lender "forecloses" on that security and takes our property away from us. If we borrow money to buy a car, the lender loans us money secured by the automobile. If we default, the lender takes our car away. Bonds offer an excellent alternative as security for a note on just about anything you may purchase.

A Simple Explanation

Imagine buying a dollar for 75¢. If you could find a person or institution that would do this, you'd stand in line. After all, trading 75¢ for one dollar provides a substantial profit, and anyone, anywhere, would take advantage of such an incredible offer.

Then, suppose I offered you one dollar's worth of real estate purchasing power for 75¢. Same offer, except you could only use the purchasing power to buy real estate. If you are a real estate investor, the purchasing power would certainly be useful for increasing the size of your real estate portfolio. Now, suppose, on top of the additional buying power I am offering, I also provided you with a return on your real estate investment that was far above any rate of return you could have imagined, and I showed you how to get the U.S. Treasury to indirectly guarantee the payments to the seller on the seller-held mortgage.

What if I said, "I'll show you how to offer the seller more money if you default than if you pay as agreed." Wouldn't this be a real bonus to the seller? And, in addition, I'll show you why it works just as well when interest rates are high as when they are low.

This may seem incredible to you, but you can use just such a system to buy some of the finest real estate in the U.S. today, and do it using none of your own money. At the same time, you can build a portfolio of U.S. Treasury Bonds timed to mature at whatever age you wish that will pay you enormous sums of money.

Here's How

Like real estate investors, you should ascribe to two fundamental principles. First, buy for no-money-down (meaning you use none of your money), and second, the property must pay for itself. A third principle might be added, and that is to get paid every time you buy.

The first principle is easy. If you use conventional financing, all you have to do is find a seller who will take back a note for part of the purchase price with the property being security for this note. The seller's security would be in the form of a second mortgage or Deed of Trust. Borrow the balance from a lending institution, and you've purchased for no-money-down. And, if you get the seller to take back a note for 40% or $40,000 on a $100,000 purchase and you borrow $70,000, or 70% of value, you can pocket $10,000 at closing.

Where most people fail is when it comes to buying a property that will not pay for itself. With the recent changes in the tax laws, it is essential that you not buy unless the property breaks even at worst. In the past, you could write off any negative cash flow, but that isn't the case now, nor is it what I've been teaching for years. The foolish buyers buy based on appreciation and wait for the property to go up in value, covering the negative in the meantime. But what do you do when the sellers want an extremely high price and you really want the property, but the income is not sufficient to pay a mortgage payment? Let's apply the use of bonds to solve the problem.

I'm sure one of the reasons you like real estate is because the purchased property pays for itself through rental income. Bonds are similar in that they yield interest. Zero Coupon Bonds don't actually pay out cash interest each year, but the interest builds up in the bond and is paid at maturity. If it is a U.S. Treasury Bond, the interest, although not received in cash every year, is still taxed as if you had received it.

The tax-free Zero Bonds also accumulate interest, but this interest is not taxed to you now or at maturity. Then, you have bonds that pay interest each and every year in the form of cash. Depending on the type of bond purchase, this interest could be taxable or tax-free. Almost all of my examples include methods of acquiring or selling real estate using Zero Coupon or U.S. Treasury bonds that accumulate interest. Let's now take an example of how you might use a bond that is paying cash interest every year to buy real estate.

Buying with Bonds

First of all, keep in mind that the price you'll pay for this bond is more than you'd pay for a Zero Bond, but still less than the face value of that bond. Whereas you might pay, for example, 45¢ on the dollar for a Zero Bond, you could pay 75¢ for a bond that pays interest. Let's say you can buy a face value $100,000 bond for $80,000. The interest paid is based upon the face value, not what you paid. So, if the bond you purchase pays 7.25%, the interest is calculated on the $100,000 rather than the $80,000 you paid.

Important: Please verify and document this before you buy and make any offer.

Assuming that this is the case, however, 7.25% of $100,000 is $7,250 per year. Since you only paid $80,000, the $7,250 really gives you an effective interest rate of 9%. More importantly, you can pay the seller-held note with the interest generated by the bond.

Look at it this way. When you ask the seller to take a note for part of the purchase price, the seller will want security for that note. Usually the real estate is the security or collateral, and the rents from the property go to pay the note. But suppose, instead, you take the proceeds from the bank mortgage on the property and use it in two ways. First, you give part of the proceeds to the seller as cash at settlement. Then, you use the balance of the mortgage loan to buy a discounted bond and post the bond as collateral on the seller-held note.

Here is what you have done. You have obtained a bank first mortgage on the property, and the rents from the property will pay the loan. Next, you gave part of the mortgage proceeds to the seller at settlement. With the balance of the funds, you have purchased a bond and posted it as collateral with the seller to secure what ordinarily would have been a second mortgage. But now the lien is on the bond, not the real estate.

The bond now pays interest to you that you turn over to the seller as payments on the seller-held note. If this is done correctly, the real estate will pay off the bank first mortgage, and the interest from the bond will pay off the seller loan only.

Let's see how another has used this technique: Let's say we have a property for sale—$220,000. The seller is hung up on a price of not less than $200,000. The property will only support a $180,000 loan, and that is all the buyer wants to pay.

Problem—How does the buyer buy at his or her price and yet satisfy the seller. The buyer asked about seller financing and was told that the seller would help with financing but wanted $90,000 down and would take back a note secured by a first mortgage for the balance of the purchase price he wanted, in this case $110,000.

To the buyer, this was too much to pay, and it required a down payment, which he didn't want to make (or perhaps have).

After much negotiation, this is what the parties finally agreed upon. The buyer offered the seller $90,000 as a down payment (which, of course, he didn't have) and $7,500 per year for 15 years with an additional $45,000 payable at that time in the form of a balloon payment. Security for this $7,500 per year and $45,000 balloon payment was to be a U.S. Treasury Bond which guaranteed both payments in full.

If the buyer defaulted for any reason, the seller was to receive an additional $45,000 as a penalty. This penalty was also guaranteed by a U.S. Treasury Bond. In short, the buyer offered the seller $90,000 in cash at closing, $7,500 per year for 15 years or $112,500 and $45,000 at the end of the 15-year period, or a total of $247,500.

In order to make this offer work, it was essential that the property provide a mortgage in the amount of $180,000, so that was part of his offer. Then, there was the problem of making $180,000 become more than $180,000 because it had to provide the down payment of $90,000, plus the $7,500 per year in payments and this amounted to $112,500 over a 15-year period, with the $45,000 balloon payment due at the end of the term.

The buyer called his friendly stock or bondbroker and asked him if he had a bond that would provide $7,500 in interest every year and a cash value of at least $45,000 in 15 years. In order to do this, the bond broker had to find a bond that had a face value of $90,000 and paid 8.375% interest, or $7,500 per year.

You might want to do this first before making an offer to be sure that a bond is available that will accomplish your objective. The cost of the bond (at that time and not necessarily now) was $69,300 or 77% of face value. (You'll recall that I stated that the seller was to receive $247,500 over a fifteen-year period.) Let's now see how the buyer came out.

Recap

- Bond paid interest of $7,500 per year

- Interest was used to pay the seller payments

- Bond matured to $90,000 in 15 years

- Difference of $20,700 to buyer at closing (minus closing costs) plus $45,000 in 15 years

- EVERYBODY WINS!

22

Problems and Solutions

My experience has been that whenever you are talking about interest rates, the seller has a tendency to tie it in with the prime bank rate or talk about what interest savings and loans are offering. Instead of telling the seller you will pay 9% or 10% interest, I suggest you tell the seller how much you will pay per month in actual dollars. Try to break it down as I have in this example, showing the amount to be received for this property. If the seller doesn't go for it, and not all sellers will, pass it up or perhaps "sweeten" the balloon by offering more of the $90,000 in bond proceeds at the end. Remember that you still have $45,000 to work with, so you might also present your offer with a "guarantee-the-payment" offer since the bond does just that.

Here is a question I get asked all the time, and I will cover it later in the materials, but I will briefly cover it now. "If the bonds are being purchased from the loan proceeds and these proceeds won't be available until closing, how do I pay for the bonds when I have no money?"

There are two ways to handle this, and I have used both. One, give the seller a receipt for the bonds from your broker. The person will order them at closing and deliver them to the seller in about six weeks. Or, you can obtain a commercial loan to order the bonds when they arrive. Use the mortgage proceeds to pay off the commercial loan, thereby freeing up the bonds to give to the seller at closing. You shouldn't have any problem doing this because the commercial lender is fully secured by the bonds and knows payment will be guaranteed at closing.

In days of high inflation and rapid real estate appreciation, one normally prefers real estate as security for a note. In case of default by the borrower, the lender gets back the property, which has probably appreciated considerably in value. The lender has little risk, if any.

However, when inflation is zero to 5%, as it presently is, and real estate no longer escalates in value as it once did, there can be a danger in taking real estate as security. As a matter of fact, many lenders and sellers have ended up getting properties back at less than what is owed.

In other words, since they can't sell the property for the mortgage balance, a loss results. However, if the lender or seller had taken bonds as security, even though the bonds are not worth that amount now, eventually they will be worth the face value and the lender or seller ends up avoiding a loss.

Will Bonds Work for Everyone?

Bonds, of course, will not work for some people. Some won't trade and others won't owner-finance. If a seller can get the asking price and all cash, the person most certainly won't take bonds. But, if a seller can't get the asking price, all cash, has a tax problem, is a bit greedy, or wants security other than real estate, the person is an excellent candidate to take bonds. If used correctly, bonds are the best and most successful method of selling and acquiring real estate in today's market place. And, the nice part is that no one loses; everyone wins.

Using Bonds to Acquire Real Estate

Let's start with a few examples of how you use bonds to acquire real estate. For illustration purposes, let's use a sales price of $100,000. The property can have an existing mortgage on it or not, but let's say there is a loan already in place for $40,000, leaving a $60,000 equity position. There are several other ideas on how to purchase this property using creative financing, but let's direct our attention in this example to buying it using bonds.

You can buy this property by taking over the first mortgage of $40,000 and asking the seller to carryback a note for the difference of $60,000. This $60,000 note can be secured by a second mortgage against his property, something that you own as a buyer or something totally different, like bonds.

You will need to set the terms and conditions of that note, regardless of the security. Let's say the person will take your note for 10 years at 10% interest. This could be interest only, amortized over 10 years or even amortized over 30 years with a 10-year balloon. If you want to get paid for buying, and I prefer to get paid every time I buy, ask the person to take your note secured by bonds, not property. Now, here's the tricky part.

You offer a note secured by $60,000 face value bonds worth $60,000 in ten years. Your cost (estimated) $20,000. Finance the property with a new first or a second mortgage, totaling $80,000. This will give you $40,000 in cash, rounded off. Take $20,000 and buy the bonds and pocket the difference. You just bought a property for no-money-down, received $20,000 in cash at closing and an additional $20,000 in equity (the difference between what you owe, $80,000 and what the property is worth, $100,000).

The Bad News

You now owe $80,000 on a new first mortgage and $60,000 to the seller secured by bonds. The bonds will handle the balloon payment due in 10 years if those are the terms, but it will be necessary for you to make two payments in the meantime.

Solutions

Make the payments, get an equity partner to make them, or sell the property for no-money-down, take over payments, including the note secured by bonds. Let's review:

Price: $100,000

| Existing Loan: | $ 40,000 |
| Equity: | $ 60,000 |

Offer: $100,000 price, no-money-down, you take over first mortgage of $40,000 and the seller takes back a note for $60,000 secured by 10-year U.S. Treasury Bonds, not property. Payments are on the note, 10% interest only with a balloon payment due in 10 years.

If the seller wants a cash down payment, such as $10,000 down, change your offer to $100,000, with $10,000 down and seller to carryback a note for $50,000 secured by bonds. I like offering the seller some cash. The important thing to remember is that the seller is taking back a note secured by bonds, not real estate.

> *You've just made $34,000 buying a $100,000 house.*

You now have a contract to purchase real estate for $100,000. Take that contract to a lender and ask if the person will give you an 80% loan to value, providing you become the new owner. Get a commitment that the person will do so. Since 80% of $100,000 is $80,000, you will have $80,000 in cash available to you at closing. $40,000 will be needed to pay off the old first mortgage, leaving you $40,000 to use as the cash down payment and to buy the bonds.

Call your friendly stockbroker for a quote on how much it will cost you to buy bonds that will be worth either $50,000 or $60,000 in 10 years. Assuming that your cost is about one-third of what you'll need, that means that you will need about $16,000 to buy a bond that will be worth $50,000 and $20,000 to buy one that will be worth $60,000 in 10 years.

Add this cost to your down payment if you have one and combine it with the $40,000 already owed. If you are putting up $10,000 as a cash down payment and asking the seller to carryback a note for $50,000, you will need $16,000 to buy the bond, $10,000 for the down payment and $40,000 to pay off the old first. This totals $66,000. You borrow $80,000 and walk out of closing with $14,000 in cash and $20,000 in equity, or, you've just made $34,000 buying a $100,000 house. If you can buy with no-money-down, you make an extra $4,000 in cash at closing.

At closing, the stockbroker will be there as well as the seller, buyer, and lender. Whatever cash down payment is needed is given to the seller, money necessary to buy the bond is given to the stockbroker, and you, the buyer, pick up the difference in cash. The stockbroker gives a receipt for the bond and promises delivery in four to six weeks, but the seller is perfectly protected.

If the bond is being used for a note, the bond will come in the buyer's name and be placed in escrow. The escrow agent, which could be the bank, attorney, title company, etc., has instructions that as long as the buyer pays on time, the bond remains in the buyer's name. However, if the buyer defaults for any reason, the bond immediately is transferred to the seller.

If you have a 10-year balloon due, cash in the bond at that time to handle the balloon. Your only concern during this 10-year period is the making of the $80,000 mortgage loan and the interest-only payments to the seller on the bond.

If the seller prefers real estate as collateral instead of your bond, show the person the benefits of taking a bond as security. You could even offer both the bond and a second mortgage on the person's property. This second mortgage would come after you refinance to the $80,000 figure. This could overcome any concern regarding the present cash value of the bond. Try and limit the liability of your note to the bond (and property, if used) so that you avoid the possibility of being sued personally.

If the lender or seller insists upon seeing the bonds before closing, you will have to take a slightly different approach. Now, it will be necessary for you to purchase the bonds before you refinance. This could pose a problem if you have no money. Here is how you handle that problem:

How to Buy Bonds with No Money

- Get a commitment from a lender on the property you are purchasing in which the person agrees to loan you the $80,000 first mortgage. Take that commitment to a short-term lender, in this case a bank, and pledge this commitment for a short-term loan. The person will loan you money based upon the lender's commitment. Take the cash, buy the bond, and pay back the bank with the proceeds at closing.

- Depending upon your particular situation, you may be able to obtain the bonds from the stockbroker using the same commitment as security.

- Borrow against something else that you own for the money.

- Sell something else for the money.

- Borrow from a friend or take in a partner in exchange for the person buying the bond.

- Pay a fee to somebody to do it.

- Ask the seller to deed it to you, giving other security for this short time frame. Now, refinance as the new owner. Pay the seller off.

Making These Deals Work

Three weeks after digesting this bond information, Alan was approached about buying a home that was corporate-owned. The company had transferred its employee and, like many big companies, they guaranteed the employee a certain price for his home if he couldn't sell it. Corporations and companies are not in the real estate-owning business and often are receptive to creative ideas. Such was the case with Alan.

Important: This doesn't have to be a corporate-owned home. It can be any home on the market as long as the equity is sufficient. This technique also works very well with owners who want more for their property than somebody might be willing to pay.

The asking price was $123,000. Alan pointed out that if the company did, in fact, sell for $123,00, which was highly unlikely, and put out this money at 10% interest, also unlikely, they would realize a return of both principal and interest of around $500,000 over a thirty-year period. He offered to trade them $650,000 in U.S. Treasury bonds for the $123,000 home, or $527,000 more than they were asking and $150,000 more than they would get by selling for cash.If somebody is asking $123,000 and you offer $650,000, you will get the person's attention.

The cost of $650,000 30-year U.S. Treasury Bonds was $65,000 at that time. Alan asked for a 65% loan to value, or $80,000 from a lender. He could have obtained a much higher loan but opted for this amount so there wouldn't be a problem with qualifying.

He used $65,000 of these funds to buy the bonds and walked out of closing with $15,000 cash and another $43,000 in equity. I don't know what Alan ended up doing with the property, but he could easily rent it for a positive cash flow, sell it on lease-option or even sell to somebody else for no-money-down, taking back a note for the difference between what his buyer could borrow and the selling price. He also could move in and make it his personal home. Regardless of which direction he took, Alan made a nifty $58,000 and did it using none of his own money.

Overcoming Seller's Concern about Default

The seller could say: "What happens to me if you don't pay on your note to me secured by bonds?" Naturally, the person immediately gets the bonds. The bonds do have a cash value, but the cash value is not what it will be at the time of maturity, so the seller may worry that you will quit paying, wherby the seller would lose interest income that you agreed to pay and that you secured by bonds. Here are a few suggestions to handle this problem:

- Sign personally, guaranteeing the interest

- Offer additional collateral such as a second mortgage on the property or something that you own

- Offer twice the amount of the note in bonds. Instead of giving bonds worth $60,000, offer bonds that will be worth $120,000 (or more). You could make the $120,000 bonds mature in 10 years, or you could just have the $60,000 bond mature in 10 years, or you could have the $60,000 bond mature in 10 years with the other $60,000 bond maturing in 15 to 20 years.

I prefer to trade bonds that equal both the interest and the balloon in 10 years, instead of using the bonds as security. In this case of $60,000 at 10% interest over a 10-year period, you would be paying $60,000 in interest plus the balloon of $60,000 due at that time, or a total of $120,000.

Offer the $120,000 bond in exchange for no note and no payments. The person now has no worries since there is guaranteed payback because of the higher-value bond. The person gives up interest income that is paid monthly but is guaranteed to not lose money. If the person also wants a monthly income, buy tax-exempt municipal bonds and trade those to the individual. Based upon yearly cash value, these can be borrowed against. It is quite possible to get the same income that you might otherwise, but the money is borrowed and the bond security is tax-free; all monies borrowed are tax-free.

23

Benefits of Using Bonds

Realtors benefit in many ways by using bonds. Using bonds creates more opportunities for sales or even doubles sales. The realtor can sell the property to a buyer who purchases with bonds and then re-sell that same property to a cash buyer. This is workable with an investor who is interested in cranking cash and not holding onto real estate. Is this ethical? I firmly believe that it is. The seller may prefer the bond method because of the higher selling price and avoidance of taxes on sale. There is nothing wrong with buying and selling at a profit. I do it all the time. In this case, we are just using the same realtor to accomplish this objective.

The seller also gets the asking price. Bonds can overcome a problem of the seller wanting more than the property is worth. The realtor can suggest that the only way to get this price is by taking bonds.

Negative cash flows can also be eliminated by the use of bonds, thereby, creating more investment sales for the realtor. Instead of borrowing $100,000 and having to make payments on that $100,000, suggest to the seller that the person take less cash and more in bonds for the balance of the price. Now, instead of the buyer having to borrow $100,000 and creating a negative cash flow situation, the person may only have to borrow $50,000 to $75,000, putting the person into a break even or positive cash flow.

Realtors can volunteer to take your commission in tax-free bonds instead of cash; however, ask for more in bonds. If your commission is $10,000, you might ask the seller to buy you $30,000 worth of tax-free bonds for this $10,000 or even agree to take less in commission. Example: Instead of $10,000 cash, I'll take $20,000 in bonds, which you can buy for $5,000. This means that the seller puts $5,000 more in pocket at closing. This $5,000 could be the difference between a sale and a loss of one.

Overcoming Seller's Objections

What if seller or lender says, "I can do the same thing myself. I can take your cash and buy the bonds. Why should I take bonds instead of cash"?

Your reply to this often asked question could be, "Okay, do it using my bonds, thereby, doubling or tripling your overall return." Let's take an actual example of an REO to illustrate how you use this deal.

appraised value: $400,000 – can't sell at this figure
possible loan: $300,000, 75 percent of value

offer: $ 50,000, cash
          $700,000, bonds to mature in twelve years
          $750,000, offer for $400,000 property

The cost to purchase $700,000 worth of 12-year bonds is approximately $150,000. $50,000 cash is required for the down payment, or a total of $200,000 is required to make this transaction work. Borrow $300,000 secured by property; use $200,000 to buy the bonds and for the down payment. Pocket $100,000 cash at closing and make $100,000 in equity besides.

Present cash value of the bond is $150,000. Suggest to the lender, or any taker of the bond, that the person borrow 90% of this present value of $135,000 and use these funds to buy bonds. The person can buy approximately $625,000 worth of 12-year bonds for the $135,000 and now has improved his or her overall return from $750,000 to $1,240,000. The seller has taken something that couldn't be sold and turned it into a money making machine.

Let's examine this example from another standpoint. Suppose the owner or lender of this property was to sell for $400,000, 15 % interest (higher than the going rate) only for 12 years with a balloon of the $400,000 due at that time. The overall return would be $720,000 in interest and $400,000 when the balloon comes due or a total of $1,120,000. This is $120,000 less than what the lender would receive by taking bonds.

Turn Lemons into Lemonade

Lenders and buyers can both benefit from using bonds. These are excellent "additional security" for a suspect or bad loan. You can always insist that the borrower use part of the funds to buy a bond for the face amount of the loan. The lender now has double-value security.

This is an outstanding method of getting rid of an REO (real-estate-owned) or a foreclosure. Many times lenders have foreclosed on something that can't be sold for what was originally owed on that property. I know of one example where a lender loaned money on fourplexes that were valued at $150,000 at the time of the loan. The outstanding loan balance at foreclosure was $125,000; however, the market value of the fourplexes had fallen to $75,000. This meant that the lender was going to absorb a $50,000 loss on each fourplex.

Normally, the lender would sell for the $75,000 and hope to recoup this loss by making better loans in the future. Creative lenders have discovered that by using bonds they can guarantee the recapture of that loss and at the same time perhaps "double" their return. Instead of selling for cash, if they can find a cash buyer, they are taking two, three, or even four times that $75,000 in bonds that can be purchased for $75,000.

Let's use an example of three times $75,000 or $225,000 in 10 years. The person buying the REO borrows $75,000 from either the lender who owns the REO or another lender and instead of giving the $75,000 in cash to the lender, the person uses these funds to buy

$225,000 worth of 10-year bonds. The lender who holds the REO is the best one to initiate this since the person already controls the property. The buyer owes the lender $75,000 secured by a first mortgage or deed of trust on the REO. The lender has a loan due of $5,000 plus an additional $225,000 coming in 10 years. Instead of losing on the sale, the lender now wins with this REO.

A typical commercial lender may state that he or she has to report a sold REO at a loss, or $5,000. The lender still reports a loss by taking bonds but is able to recoup that loss when the bond matures. If the bond happens to be a tax-free bond, all monies over and above the $75,000 become tax free to the lender. Otherwise, the money received over and above the $75,000 will be taxed at capital gains.

The lender has turned lemons into lemonade.

Borrow Against Cash Value

The lender can use the cash value of this $225,000 bond every year and can borrow up to 92% of the $75,000 the first year and 92% every year thereafter of the cash value at that time. This means that the lender can sell for $225,000 worth of bonds and still get almost all cash to use for other loans. This definitely is a win/win situation for both parties, those who accept the REO and the lender.

Seller Benefits

An obvious benefit to the seller is that the person gets the asking price or more when taking bonds. The seller can borrow against present value of bonds at less interest than the bond is paying, write off the interest expense, and at the same time never have to make a payment on this money. This can be repeated year after year until the bond matures to face value. At that time, the bond can be cashed in to pay off the loan or loans.

The basis for tax reporting is the value of the bond when taken, not its future value. Example: Property sells for $100,000 with the seller taking all or part of the selling price in bonds. The reported sales price will be the value of the bond the day of closing. If the buyer paid $35,000 for this $100,000 bond, that will be the reported sales price with capital gains being reported on the growth of the bond as it grows in value. If the bond is a tax-exempt one, all monies over and above the $35,000 will be tax free to the seller.

Bonds can also be broken up and used in several increments. You might use $5,000 to purchase property in Florida, $10,000 to buy something in California, etc. Mortgages and Deeds of Trust generally are not acceptable as trading material outside of the state in which they were written.

Risk-Free Security

If bonds are used, the seller has risk-free security. If the economy falls apart or the value of the property goes down, the seller eventually receives money. Bonds are a must for business sales.

Borrow Against Bonds

If the seller is interested in a monthly income, bonds provide a unique opportunity. Normally, a buyer would pay a seller payments of $5,000 per year interest. This interest payment is reportable to Uncle Sam, and the seller pays taxes based upon personal tax brackets. If the seller takes bonds for equity, the person can borrow against the present value of these bonds, still obtaining the $5,000 per year required. But now the money is borrowed money, which means that the seller obtains the same money but pays no taxes. There will be an interest charge to the seller for the use of this money which can be written off by the seller. Since the present value is always more than what is borrowed and because that present value bond pays more interest than it costs to borrow the money, no payments on the borrowed money are required.

Buyers Benefit from Using Bonds

The buyer buys at his or her price or less. Because the bond can be purchased at a reduced amount of money, the buyer can safely offer the seller more than what is being asked and at the same time buy the property for less than the person wants to pay.

Example: The buyer can offer the seller $100,000 in bonds which can be purchased for $35,000 cash. The buyer's actual purchase price is 35,000. The seller eventually gets the desired price and the buyer buys at the desired value. This results in a true win/win.

The buyer can actually get paid every time a property or item is bought. Using the above example of a $100,000 purchase price, if the property value is $100,000, the buyer can obtain a 70% loan or higher, or $70,000. Use the $35,000 to buy the bonds, and the other $35,000 can be kept by the buyer "tax deferred."

Discounting

Bonds are an excellent method for discounting existing mortgages and at the same time an excellent method for a lender to use to eliminate a bad loan or a foreclosure. The buyer offers the lender $400,000 in bonds for an existing loan balance of $200,000. The cost of purchasing these $400,000 worth of bonds is only $100,000. The buyer refinances the property for enough to buy the bonds, or more, reducing mortgage balance from $200,000 to $100,000.

Bonds Reap Many Rewards

Bonds are an excellent way for a buyer to handle an upcoming "balloon" payment. If you have a balloon payment coming due in 7 years for $100,000, buy bonds that will mature to be worth $100,000 in a 7-year period or buy bonds that will have a cash value of $100,000 at that time. Cash in the bond or bonds to handle the balloon or borrow against the cash value at that time to pay off the balloon.

Save Interest

Buyers can save a tremendous amount of interest on a mortgage by using bonds. Example: If you have a 30-year mortgage, buy a bond that will mature to be what your mortgage balance will be in 15 to 20 years. This bond might be purchased for as little as 20¢ on the dollar, or $20,000 for a $100,000 future value. Cash in the bond at that time, thereby eliminating several thousand dollars in interest.

Get Back Entire Mortgage with Bonds

The buyer can actually get back all mortgage money by buying a bond that will mature when the mortgage is paid in full. Example:

A $100,000 mortgage to be paid off in 30 years. At the time you take out the mortgage, buy a bond that will mature to be worth $100,000 in 30 years. The day you pay off your mortgage in full, cash in the bond and get back your $100,000. If you make it a tax-free bond, all monies received are tax-free to the buyer.

Two Forms of Collateral

Bonds can be used as an incentive for a lender to make you a loan. Take part of the borrowed funds and buy a bond that equals what you are borrowing from the lender. Again, because it is a Zero Coupon Bond, you will be buying this future value at a fraction of that value. Now the lender has two forms of collateral, your property and the bond. If you default, the lender gets both the property and your bond.

- Bonds, as additional collateral, are an excellent incentive for a lender to loan you 100% of value or even more because of this additional collateral.

- Bonds are great for eliminating negative cash flow.

Example: Instead of giving the seller a note for $50,000 with interest only payments of $5,000 per year for 10 years and then a balloon of $50,000 at the time, offer the seller a bond for $100,000 due in 10 years in exchange for eliminating that interest payment. The seller still gets the $100,000 but now doesn't have to worry about the buyer performing or having to go through foreclosure if the person doesn't perform. If the seller insists on payments, suggest that the seller borrow $5,000 against the bond each year. The seller still gets the payments, but now instead of having to pay taxes on this income, the person can write off the interest of borrowing the money.

Use Bonds to Buy REO's

REO's (real-estate-owned) come about because some lenders have made loans that just didn't work out, and they end up having to foreclose and take title to the property.

Bonds provide an excellent alternative to (1) help you build your real estate portfolio and (2) help out those lenders who have properties they want to sell. Offer the lender more money than the appraisal.

Combine Paper and Bonds

Let's take another actual example: MAI appraisal on REO—$495,000. The lender will take less if it's a cash offer. The buyer offers lender "paper" (notes secured by mortgages on something else or even one you create on something you own), totaling $140,000, and $1,250,000 in bonds due to mature in 15 years. This totals $1,390,000. In other words, we are offering $1,390,000 for a $495,000 REO. Do you think we might get their attention?

In this case, the buyer purchased U.S. Treasury Bonds that matured to a value of $1,250,000 in 15 years. The purchase price for the bonds was $250,000. That meant that the buyer was able to purchase the home for $250,000 cash and $140,000 in the form of paper or a total of $390,000.

Again, the bonds have no payments. The lender shouldn't be concerned about this since you are offering three times the actual value of the property.

Using the appraisal of $495,000, it was easy to obtain a new first mortgage of $360,000. The buyer used $250,000 of this to acquire the bonds. Since the buyer only needed $250,000 to buy the bonds and the person was actually borrowing $360,000, the person walked out of closing with $110,000 in pocket. This is becoming so much fun—let's do it again.

Buy Back Paper at Closing

Consider using these "extra" funds to *buy back* the paper at a discount. Are the $360,000 mortgage payments too high? Turn right around and *sell* for no-money-down and let *your* buyer assume these payments. Take your $135,000 equity in bonds or just be satisfied with the $110,000 in cash. This is also an excellent way to get rid of paper at no discount or use the equity in your home by creating paper against it.

24

Other Uses for Bonds

Bonds are flexible and easy to use as well as being financially lucrative. Another creative way to use bonds is to use them to purchase rental property. Instead of offering a seller your note for all or part of the down payment secured by either your real estate or the seller's, consider offering the seller bonds as security for your note.

This is an extremely good approach when the seller is afraid of getting the sold property back or having to foreclose. Using bonds eliminates foreclosure and guarantees the seller no loss of money, except possible interest. This method is almost a necessity when one is buying or selling a business. I strongly recommend that you never sell your business and take back a note secured only by the business. A majority of businesses fail and just because the former owner was a success, doesn't mean you will be successful, too.

My 60K Deal

I recently helped a student of mine purchase a rental home using this approach. The seller was willing to sell for $60,000, $10,000 down and a note for the balance of the purchase price, or $50,000. The problem was that the seller didn't want the house back in case of default. I suggested we use bonds as collateral for the note, rather than the property itself. In this manner, if the buyer couldn't perform, at least the seller ended up with the bonds and wasn't out money. We made the offer 10% interest only, or $6,000 per year, for 10 years, with the $50,000 due in full in 10 years. The note was to be secured by bonds that matured to $50,000 in 10 years. These bonds could be purchased at that time for $15,000.

The buyer now has a contract indicating a purchase price of $60,000, which he took to a lender and asked for an 80% loan to value, or $48,000. It will work even better if you can borrow 90 to 95% of value.

Out of $48,000, the buyer took $15,000 to buy the bonds and $10,000 to give to the seller as the down payment. This left $23,000 cash at closing for the buyer.

You Just Made $35,000 Buying a $60,000 Rental

The buyer now owes a $48,000 first mortgage and a $50,000 second one secured by bonds. The buyer has two payments, one on the first mortgage and another of $5,000 interest only on the second. The first is no problem since the property can be rented out for enough to handle that, but what about the second?

My suggestion: Take the $23,000 and invest it in CD's or the money market and use this, plus interest, to handle the negative. You never have to pay the balloon because the bonds mature to handle it. Think about it. You have now just purchased a $60,000 home and made $23,000 in cash at closing, and have an equity position of another $12,000 or a total of $35,000 on a $60,000 property.

Using Bonds to Buy or Sell a Business

Anytime you are asked to take a note in lieu of cash, I strongly recommend that you only take that note if it is fully secured. When buying real estate, we think in terms of securing that note by recording a mortgage against a piece of real estate. This could be something the buyer or the seller owns. If the maker of that note does not perform according to the terms and conditions of that note, the holder forecloses on that security and takes it from the maker.

The security for the note doesn't have to be real estate. It could be stocks, equipment, furniture, or bonds. If buying or selling a business, I strongly recommend that you not endanger your home when buying a business. As we have pointed out, most businesses fail, and I've had several students end up losing their home because they used equity to buy a business.

Never Use Your House Equity to Buy a Business

The seller, on the other hand, doesn't want to take the buyer's note secured by the business that is being sold. A business is a personal thing, and who's to say that the buyer won't run that business into the ground, leaving the seller with a worthless business, plus the chance of losing equipment and other assets.

Bonds offer an outstanding alternative that allows both the seller and buyer to win while offering protection against a loss. This is exactly what happened to a student of mine who wished to purchase a motel. The seller was flexible on how the property was sold, but he was also concerned about what would happen if the buyer couldn't perform.

Here is a situation where an agreeable seller is willing to help with the financing, but something else is needed, something satisfactory to the seller as security for the note. The idea of receiving a nice monthly income for several years appealed to him, but the idea of his getting back his motel didn't. We solved it with bonds. Here is how it worked:

Sales Price	$850,000
Less: Existing First Mortgage	$150,000
Subtotal	$700,000

The seller agrees to take $100,000 down, plus a note and mortgage for $600,000 secured by bonds. The buyer then obtains a new first mortgage based on the selling price of $850,000, or $700,000, leaving this position:

New first mortgage	$700,000
Minus old mortgage	$150,000
Cash available at closing	$550,000

Minus cost of 15-year bonds	$125,000
Minus closing costs (est.)	$25,000
Minus down payment	$100,000
Cash to Buyer at Closing	$300,000

How's that for a no-money-down deal?

Seller Benefits

- The seller now feels comfortable taking a note for $600,000 because no money will be lost, even if the buyer defaults on payments. Yes, the seller does have to wait 15 years to collect in full, but that is a small price to pay for total security.

- The seller can use this note secured by bonds as collateral for a loan, trade it at full face value to buy something else, or even cash them out before maturity. Even though the bonds will not bring face value for 15 years, they do have a daily reduced value that can be captured if need be. Call your stockbroker for a daily quote. And, if you are hung up on getting cash when selling, consider taking two or three times your equity in bonds and selling at the present rate. You've now got your cash.

- The seller receives monthly payments on note secured by bonds.

- The seller gets the desired price and, more importantly, gets peace of mind.

Buyer Benefits

- The buyer is able to purchase something that otherwise couldn't be bought.

- The buyer gets $300,000 in cash at closing (not a bad day's work).

- This cash can be used for renovation, negative cash flows, or whatever.

- If a problem occurs, the buyer can always trade the motel for something else or perhaps sell it for no-money-down and walk away with $300,000.

Possible Problem

The seller wants to be paid off before the bonds mature to full face value.

Possible Solutions

- Sell before that time, allowing your buyer to handle that problem.

- Refinance to handle it or just for enough to handle the difference between present value of the bonds.

- Find somebody else to make the payment for you in exchange for making the person a partner.

- Offer more bonds as collateral, but reduce the amount of your cash balloon payment. Purchase enough bonds to adequately cover the balloon.

Use Bonds to Sell

Having trouble selling? How about offering buyers bonds as an incentive to buy. Do you realize that you can purchase a tax-free Municipal Bond at a fraction of the maturity value? For example, you can purchase a $100,000 tax-free bond that will mature at that face value in 30 years for about 4%, or $4,000. They cost slightly more if you make the years 25, 20, or 15, but it still is a good deal.

This program will allow the homebuyer to not only build equity in the purchase but also to earn the full purchase price back in cash, tax-free upon maturity of the bond.

Bonds of this nature should be rated A or above. They are perfectly liquid and not tied to the home but are the sole property of the buyer.

These Zero Coupon Bonds gain value more slowly than traditional Municipal Bonds but are instant cash any time you wish. Think about it. You can literally buy a home, write off the interest over a 30-year period, and when you finally get it paid in full, you have the full purchase price back because the bonds mature.

If you are eager to sell, this is an excellent method of getting that buyer by adding this incentive. You can either raise the price to cover the cost of bonds or just include it at the seller's expense. If you are the buyer, you get back your purchase price in full without giving up everything to do it.

How about this for an ad?

Buy My Property, Get Back Your Purchase Price — Tax-Free!

That's right! Whatever the purchase price of your home, you'll get it back TAX-FREE! And, even better, when your bond matures, you won't have to pay taxes on that amount. It's all yours to use as a trust fund for your children, fun money for a vacation, or even as retirement security. In addition, you don't have to wait until the bond matures to cash in on it. From the day it's issued to you, it's completely liquid and accessible.

Realtors: Does this give you any ideas to improve sales? In fact, how about this for a Money-Back-Program.

Money-Back Program

- Whatever the purchase price, you will get it back tax-free.

- If you sell your home, the bond stays with you.

- The bond matures in 30 years.

- If you desire to sell before the bond matures: a) The value of the bond before maturity is determined by the market at the time of sale. b) If the homeowner decides to sell the bond in fifteen years (to use for education or anything at all) the approximate value of a $70,000 bond would be $16,299. (This is an estimate.)

- At maturity, the bond will be worth the original cost of the home or greater.

- A reputable stock brokerage firm will issue the bonds.

- When sold at maturity, these bonds are tax-free because they are municipal bonds. In the event the bonds are sold prior to maturity, there may be some tax due if market value is greater than the face value of the bond. The difference between face value and market value will be taxed as capital gains.

- Call back. There is the possibility that the municipality might call the bonds back prior to maturity. If they do so, the bond will be bought at face value at the time for call plus a premium. This is a rarity, but it could happen.

My Suggestion

Stay away from bonds that can be called back.

How to Buy a Home for $1.00

Many lenders have a different set of rules when it comes to financing, depending on whether a person is buying the property or just refinancing as the owner. If it's easier for you to refinance than qualify as a new buyer, consider this idea.

Ask the seller to deed the property to you for the purchase price of $1.00 plus existing financing. I strongly recommend that you set up some safeguards to protect the owner, such as an escrow arrangement or perhaps a note and mortgage on something you own equaling the seller's equity. If you don't own anything, consider using a partner's property or something else.

Record the deed, which makes you the legal titleholder. Now, approach a lender about refinancing your property. Let's take an actual example which one of my readers used. His name is Bill.

Purchase Price:	$165,000
Existing Loan Balance:	$16,000
Equity:	$149,000

Offer $165,000 with $59,000 cash down and a note for $90,000 secured by Treasury Bonds. This, coupled with the $16,000 yet owed, totals $165,000.

Bill purchased $90,000 worth of Treasury Bonds from his stockbroker for $30,000. These bonds were to mature at $90,000 in ten years. The seller agreed to take this note at 10% interest only, with a "balloon" due in ten years.

Bill refinanced as owner at 80% of value, or $132,000. The end result was as follows:

$ 16,000 to pay off first
$ 59,000 down payment to seller
$ 30,000 to buy bonds
$105,000 cash needed to conclude transaction

Seller Nets $59,000–Buyer Nets $60,000

Since Bill (buyer) was borrowing $132,000 and all he needed was $105,000, he walked out of closing with $27,000 cash in his pocket, plus he still had $33,000 in equity (difference between $132,000 and $165,000). Bill's total profit on one purchase with no- money-down was a nifty $60,000.

How's that for win/win? The seller received $59,000 in cash, and Bill got $60,000 in cash and equity.

Problem

Bill now has payments on the first mortgage of $132,000, plus $9,000 per year (interest at 10% on bonds), resulting in a negative cash flow.

Solutions

Use the $27,000 to cover the negative for a period of time, or do as Bill did. He gave away 50% ownership in exchange for his new partner making the negative. His partner received a nice tax deduction, plus 50% of the equity of $33,000, not the cash received at closing.

The $90,000 note comes due in full in 10 years, but Bill will have no trouble handling that since the bonds mature to $90,000 at that time and can be cashed in (tax free, too), and OOPS—sorry! But that totals the balloon.

Offer the Seller Twice the Equity

An offshoot of the Bill approach might be to offer the seller twice the equity in bonds with no payments. Instead of the seller netting $180,000 ($90,000 in simple interest every year, plus $90,000 when the balloon comes due) the seller actually nets $300,000 but waits 10 years to receive it. Let's see how it works:

Purchase Price:	$165,000
Existing Loan Balance:	-$16,000
Equity:	$149,000 (rounded to $150,000)

Offer: $165,000, no-money-down, with the seller to receive $300,000 worth of Treasury Bonds that mature to $300,000 in ten years. In exchange for this, there will be no periodic payments of either interest or principal. Since you are offering twice the equity, you are entitled to this concession.

While the cost of bonds fluctuates daily, your cost should be in the $100,000 area for $300,000 worth of ten-year bonds.

Finance the property to 80% of value, or $132,000. This will leave you in this position:

$ 16,000	to pay off first mortgage
$100,000	to purchase bonds
$116,000	cash needed to conclude transaction

Buyer Nets $49,000 at Closing

You are borrowing $132,000 so that means you net at closing just $16,000 in cash and $33,000 in equity or a total of $49,000. This still isn't bad for a no-money-down purchase. Now, you have eliminated the $9,000 interest payment, which should put you into a break-even or positive cash flow situation or, at best, make your negative so small that the $16,000 can be used to handle it for several years.

Another option would be for you to offer the tenant a percentage ownership in exchange for the person making the mortgage payment. The person gets the benefit of future appreciation plus interest, taxes, and insurance deductions as well as getting into the property for no-money-down, no closing costs, and no qualifying.

Or—you could turn around and sell the property subject to the loan of $132,000 and walk away with the $16,000 in cash or take a note for the difference (secured by bonds, of course) for your equity.

25

Build Cash Flow

We have talked about using bonds in lieu of real estate as security for a note. Again, the problem is one of having to make two payments. You could borrow more than needed and set that money aside to cover the negative cash flow problem, or you could consider the alternative of offering more bonds than equity. Let's assume the seller is willing to take your note for $50,000 secured by bonds and expects 10% interest, paid yearly on that note. The bonds to handle the balloon are due in ten years.

Over a 10-year period, you will pay $15,000 for the bonds and $50,000 in interest, or a total of $65,000. The seller received $50,000 in interest and bonds that mature at $50,000, or a total of $100,000 in the 10-year period. The person has to pay income tax on the $50,000 in interest.

Offer Bonds and Pay No Interest

Instead of offering $50,000 in bonds and paying interest, try $100,000 in bonds and pay no interest. Couple this with another idea in this book about buying tax-free bonds. If you buy tax-free bonds totaling $100,000, the seller no longer has to report the interest income and pay capital gains on the other $50,000, but rather the seller gets $100,000 tax-free. If the person is in the 50% tax bracket, the savings is $25,000 on the interest income and $10,000 on the capital gains portion, or the person saves $35,000 in taxes.

The buyer, on the other hand, eliminates the $5,000 per year interest payments, which probably put the person into a negative position to begin with and now the buyer can live very comfortably knowing that payments can be made. Even with a $60,000 house, such as the example I used earlier, it works. In that case, the offer was $10,000 cash and a note for $50,000. In this example, you are now offering $10,000 cash and a note for $100,000 for a $60,000 property. We finance the property to 80%, or $48,000, use $30,000 to buy the bonds, $10,000 for the down payment and walk out of closing with $8,000 in cash and $12,000 in equity or a total of $20,000. We also have no negative.

Use Bonds to Create a Positive Cash Flow

You can use bonds to create a positive cash flow if you combine it with this technique: "Buy a Created Second Mortgage with Bonds." Only do it with a slightly different twist. This is another actual example. Perhaps the idea will work for you.

Again, the seller in this case needs a tax write-off, so the person "created" a second mortgage on owned property for $500,000, 12% interest paid quarterly, with the entire sum due in 12 years. This technique allowed the person to write-off the interest payments on personal income tax. The seller did not borrow money but created the illusion of borrowed money.

For illustrative purposes, let's refer to the seller in this example as the owner. The owner gives this note to an investor who in turn gives a $750,000 note back to the seller secured by a 12-year bond that matures at $750,000 in 12 years. There are no payments with this note. In 12 years, when the "created" note for $500,000 comes due, the $750,000 worth of bonds matures and $500,000 is used to pay off the note with $250,000 in cash going to the owner.

Recap

- The owner creates a note secured by a mortgage on his or

her property for $500,000—the note to have interest of 12%, with a balloon of $500,000 due in 12 years.

- The owner receives a $750,000 note from the investor secured by 12-year bonds.

- There are no payments on the bond note.

- The bonds mature in 12 years at $750,000. $500,000 is used to pay off the "created" note, and the other $250,000 belongs to the owner.

- The owner benefits because of interest deduction—improved financial statement—and the person can "pledge" the note and bonds for borrowing.

The Investor

- Gives $750,000 note secured by 12-year bonds. No payments.

- Receives the owner's note and mortgage.

- Borrows approximately $180,000 from cash flow of interest payments.

- The investor keeps spread in payments, resulting in positive cash flow.

  Example: $5,000 per month interest income, $3,000 per month to bank to pay back the $180,000 loan, leaving the investor with a positive cash flow of $2,000 per month on something that is not even owned.

Investor Nets $788,000

In 12 years, the mortgage of $500,000 comes due. The investor receives a bonus of $500,000.

Overall the investor receives $2,000 per month for 12 years or $288,000 and an additional $500,000 or $788,000. The $180,000 loan is paid back in full from the interest payments.

How to Write an Offer

Price: $515,000 (actual example)
Down payment: $150,000

Balance of purchase price as follows: At closing the Buyer(s) shall deliver to the seller U.S. Treasury Bonds (Insured A or better Municipal Tax Free Bonds) in the face amount of $500,000 with a maturity date of 2/17/2012.

This offer is subject to the property and buyer qualifying for a new $400,000 loan under terms and conditions acceptable to the buyer.

Note that the contract calls for the real price.

Note that even though I'm offering $650,000, $150,000 in cash and $500,000 in future face-value bonds, my contract calls for the real price of $515,000.

While the seller is receiving $650,000 overall, and the contract calls for a sales price of $515,000, as far as the IRS is concerned, the real sales price is none of the above. The actual sales price for tax purposes is the $150,000, plus the cost of the bonds.

If the bonds cost $130,000 at time of acquisition, the sales price is $280,000. The seller reports that as the selling price and the buyer, even though the person has financed the property to $400,000, has a basis of the same amount, $280,000.

When the buyer sells, all monies received over and above the $280,000 will be taxable. If the buyer were to turn around and immediately resell for no-money-down, take-over loan of $400,000, there would be a gain of $120,000. However, if reselling on a wrap-around, it's possible to defer this gain. Check with your accountant for more information in this regard.

If the bonds are U.S. Treasury Bonds that are taxable as far as Uncle Sam is concerned, the seller will report the interest income each year on personal tax returns, even though the person is not receiving it in cash.

If the bonds are tax-free, all monies over and above the cost when taken are tax-free to the seller. My experience has been that most conventional lenders prefer the U.S. Treasury Bonds, while most sellers prefer the tax-free variety. Why? Because most lenders don't have the same tax concerns that an individual might have.

What if the seller has more in the property than the selling price of $280,000? Can the person take a loss on income tax? The answer is yes; a loss can be taken. The seller can actually sell at a profit and yet report a loss. Bonds are definitely win/win for both buyer and seller.

26 _____

Using Bonds to Buy or Sell

Remember there are three kinds of bonds available: Corporate Bonds, U.S. Government Bonds, and Municipal Bonds. All can be used in the buying and selling of real estate, but I caution you on using Corporate Bonds. Before you use them, be sure and have them checked out by your stockbroker. Whereas they may appear to be better because of the interest return, they could be "callable" bonds which means that they can be called before maturity. You are 100% safe using U.S. Treasury or Municipal Bonds.

You want to buy these "fully insured and guaranteed" bonds at a discount. Be sure and keep them in increments of $100,000 or less. The government and municipalities insure bonds up to that amount. If you wish $500,000 in bonds, obtain them in $100,000 amounts, or less. Keep in mind that you don't need any money to buy these bonds. You are going to use the real estate that you are acquiring or perhaps something that you own as collateral to borrow the necessary funds to buy the bonds.

U.S. Government Bonds and Corporate Bonds are taxable as far as the U.S. Government is concerned. In many instances, Municipal Bonds are exempt from federal and state income tax. With that in mind, let's see how we might use them to buy or sell property.

An Example

For example, let's use $70,000 as a selling price.

- Offer the seller the entire equity in bonds instead of cash. This probably won't work since the seller has to wait for money.

- You could offer the seller the entire equity in tax-free bonds. This is more attractive but still unlikely to work because the seller has to wait to get money.

- You can offer the seller a note for the equity and secure it with bonds rather than the person's property. This allows you to borrow against the property equity to come up with the money to buy the bonds and put cash in your pocket. You now have two payments, one on the note secured by bonds and the other on the new first mortgage.

- You can trade the seller bonds in lieu of cash for the equity. I already mentioned that this probably wouldn't work, so why am I suggesting it now? If you take this route, I suggest you offer the seller *more* than the equity in bonds, or if you will, raise the price above what the person is willing to take.

Bob of Denver was most successful with this method. The seller was willing to sell for $50,000. The property had an appraised value of $70,000 and there was an existing mortgage of $23,000 in place. He could have used my "buddy" system to buy the property, whereby his buddy purchased at $50,000 and in turn sold to him for $70,000 with Bob financing to $56,000 (80% of $70,000). In this case, Bob could have walked out of closing with $6,000 cash.

Instead, Bob offered the seller $47,000 in tax-free bonds and offered to take over the mortgage. There was no cash involved in this transaction for the seller. He was to get bonds only, but his selling price was now $70,000, not $50,000. And, the $46,000 was tax-free to the seller, over and above the present value of purchasing the bonds. If the seller needed some cash, he could borrow against the cash value of the bonds.

Bob refinanced the home to $56,000, paid off the old first, took $13,750 to buy the bonds and walked out of closing, not with $6,000 in cash, but $19,250 in cash and an additional $14,000 in equity.

- Bob could have offered the seller some cash and the balance in bonds. For example, he could have offered $10,000 cash and $37,000 in bonds. I have found that if you offer the seller some cash, you have a better chance of the person taking the bonds. The important thing to remember is that you must be able to borrow more than it will cost you to buy the bonds and come up with the down payment.

Bonds as Additional Collateral

- You can use bonds as "additional collateral" for a loan.

If a lender is involved, you might take part of the loan proceeds and buy bonds, which can be given to the lender as additional collateral for the person making the loan. You can also entice a seller to take bonds by offering the person as additional collateral both bonds and a second mortgage on the person's house or yours.

- Consider using bonds to buy mortgages at a discount.

A student of mine is doing this very successfully. For example, he finds a person with a $50,000 mortgage. He offers to trade $100,000 (twice the amount of mortgage) tax-free bonds in exchange for the $50,000 mortgage. The owner of the mortgage doubles the expected return, and it is tax-free. My student buys the bonds at less than the mortgage balance, pledging the mortgage as security to obtain the money to buy the bonds. Let's say it takes $30,000 to buy 10-year bonds. He pledges the $50,000 mortgage at a bank and borrows the $30,000 necessary to buy the bonds. The payments on the mortgage make his payment to the bank and he ends up netting some $20,000 down the road.

Extra Idea: Trade the mortgage at its full face value of $50,000 as a down payment to buy real estate, financing the property to come up with enough to pay back the bank.

Another student of mine, Bill, combined bonds with my MLS Discount Technique, which is near the end of this book. He went to the courthouse and researched records for properties that had owner financing or more than one mortgage, one of which was privately financed.

In his search, he found where a builder had sold one of his homes and taken back a 20-year note and mortgage for $150,000. It still had 19 years to go, and so was very new. Because of the length left on the mortgage and the newness of it, the most he could sell it for at a discount was $85,000. This meant he stood to take a $65,000 loss if he sold it for cash. Bill saw this as an opportunity.

Bill offered to *exchange* $450,000 worth of tax-free 30-year bonds for the mortgage. This meant that the builder would have to wait an additional 10 years to get his money, but he eliminated any possibility of buyer default and foreclosure, and he stood to make much more money, tax-free in addition, by taking the bonds rather than monthly payment. Cost of the bonds at that time–$50,000.

Bill didn't have the $50,000 to buy the bonds, so he obtained a $50,000 second mortgage on his home. (If you don't own anything, use one of my other methods to come up with the short-term loan.) Bill now controlled a $150,000 mortgage for $40,000. He should keep this for cash flow, trade it, or sell it at a discount for the $85,000 offered the builder. Whereas the builder would have realized a $65,000 loss, Bill actually made a profit of $35,000 by selling it for $85,000. How's this for win/win?

If you run into realtors who refuse to cooperate or question the legality of using bonds, ask them to check the Civil Rights Act 1968, Title VIII, which states that it is illegal for a real estate person to discriminate in "terms or conditions of financing." This would include bonds.

Keep It Simple

Try not to make the technique of using bonds too complicated. It really is quite simple and straightforward. What you are doing is offering the seller something other than cash in exchange for the person's equity or as security for a note. You think nothing of trading a seller your car or boat as part or all of the down payment. In this case, you are trading the person bonds.

In the "Creation of Wealth Formula," you create a note secured by something that you own and use this note as a down payment to buy other real estate. All you are doing is substituting bonds in place of something else that you might own as collateral for a note. The problem with the "Creation of Wealth Formula" is that you have to own something to make it work. With bonds, you don't need to own anything because you are going to finance the seller's house to obtain the funds to buy the bonds.

You Can Offer the Seller *More* with Bonds

The nice part about bonds is that, because of the extreme discount in purchasing, you can offer the seller more for property than the person might expect. In addition, you as buyer, can buy the property for your price. Both sides win. And, you can safely offer the seller a tax-free profit by using bonds.

A student called me not too long ago with this idea. He eliminated a negative cash flow problem by offering the tenants tax-free bonds which would return all their rent to them tax-free in the future.

Here's How He Did It

His tenants were paying $800 per month, and he needed $1,000 per month to come out ahead. He called the tenants in and told them that if they would sign a three-year lease and pay him $1,000 per month instead of the $800 per month, they were presently paying, he would give them a tax-free bond for $36,000, which would return all of their rent *tax-free.* He gave them a 16-year bond, but that is a small price to pay to get back $36,000 tax-free in 15 years.

In the meantime the tenants could write-off the rent as an expense and look forward to some additional retirement, college funds, or just play funds in 15 years.

I asked him where he was going to get the money to buy the bonds, and he replied that the cash flow above his outgo was sufficient to buy the bonds. What a great idea!

Another Example

Another student of mine used this method to eliminate a negative cash flow. She had an opportunity to buy a property for $63,500, no-money-down and seller financing at 12% for 15 years. While the terms weren't good, she found that she couldn't rent the house for the $761.12 necessary to pay the mortgage payments. She multiplied her monthly payment times the number of years of her loan and found that she was going to pay the seller $127,000 in principal and interest over the 15-year period.

She called a stockbroker to find out what it would cost to buy a $63,500 bond that would be worth $63,500 in 15 years, tax-free. She then changed her offer to the seller. She offered a bond for $63,500 due in 15 years and a note for $63,500 to be paid monthly over a 15-year period, but the total to be received by the seller was to be the same $127,000.

Since the bond covered half of the amount owed, all she had to do was pay the other half, which amounted to just $408.33 per month. In other words, she cut her payments from $762.12 to $408.33 by using bonds. Where did she get the money to buy the bonds? She used credit cards, but you could take out a new first mortgage on the property for enough to buy the bonds with the seller subordinating his or her $63,500 note to this new loan.

How Jeff Made $1.9 Million with Bonds

Jeff made my day with this exciting story. He found an apartment complex that had an appraised value of $3.5 million and a loan value of $2.8 million, or 80% of value. He was able to purchase the property with this offer:

- Price: $3.5 million

- Cash down: $400,000 (which he didn't have)

- Bonds: $2.5 million in tax-free bonds due in 15 years and another $7 million in tax-free bonds due in 30 years. He actually paid, $9.9 million, $400,000 in cash and $9.5 million in bonds.

- Cost of Bonds: $500,000

- Cash Needed: $400,000 for down payment and $500,000 to buy bonds.

- Loan Obtained: $2.8 million. He took $900,000 of this for the down payment and to buy the bonds and walked out of closing with $1.9 million in CASH and another $700,000 in equity. Not bad for a no-money-down purchase.

My Suggestion: If the lender is at all uncomfortable with this loan, even though the value is there, consider taking $500,000 of the $2.8 million and buying an additional sum of bonds equal to what you give the seller. Now, the lender has $2.8 million loaned but has as security a $3.5 million apartment complex, and $9.5 million in bonds. His security—13 million.

Everybody Gets Paid This Time

One of my students, Jim, was very successful in just four weeks buying one house using bonds. I thank him for this example:

- Value and Price: $425,000

- Cash Down Payment Requirement: $85,000

- New First Mortgage Available: $340,000

Jim was buying this property but had another buyer who wanted to buy it from him under these terms: no-money-down and be paid $20,000 in cash for buying. Jim's offer was $85,000 cash down (which he didn't have) and $700,000 in Zero Coupon Bonds due to mature in 15 years, tax-free. The cost of the bonds --$190,000. The total cash needed by Jim to close--$275,00 ($85,000 down payment and $190,000 to buy the bonds).

Once Jim had entered into the contract to buy for $425,000 (which included $700,000 in bonds due to mature in 15 years), he immediately entered into a contract to sell to his friend for the same price of $425,000, subject to his friend obtaining a $340,000 first mortgage. (This is an offshoot of the buddy system).

Jim took a note and mortgage secured by something that his friend owned for the down payment. This allowed his friend to buy from him for no-money-down. The lenders want the buyer to have something invested in the property, but it doesn't always have to be cash. In this case, Jim's buyer had $85,000 in equity in something that he owned at risk, so the lender felt comfortable. There were two closings, one between Jim and the original seller, and the other between Jim (now the seller) and his friend. They happened minutes apart and were done in escrow. The same title company handled closings.

The lender was comfortable because all borrowed funds went to the seller, in this case, Jim. It wasn't a case of the buyer walking out of closing with cash. After closing, Jim gave his friend $20,000 in cash from the $340,000 that he received and forgave the note and mortgage which his friend had used as the down payment. The transaction produced this end result.

- Seller: Received $85,000 cash and bonds for $700,000

- Jim: Received $55,000 cash (difference between $275,000 which he needed to buy the bonds and the down payment, minus the $20,000 he gave his friend).

- Second Buyer: Received $20,000 cash and $85,000 in equity.

Jim didn't need any money, a job, or good credit to make this transaction work. Anybody reading this can do it. Why don't you give it a try?

27

Everyone Wins

While using bonds to buy and sell properties can easily create a win/win situation, always keep in mind a few rules when working with bonds, especially when using bonds to acquire real estate. Whether using them as security for a note or trading them in lieu of cash, there are certain things you must investigate first. The number one concern is how much money can be borrowed against the property you are buying because this money will provide you with the down payment, purchase of bonds, and cash in your pocket. So, first of all, find out how much you can borrow against the value of the property.

Let's say you are paying $515,000 for a property, the seller doesn't need all cash, and the person is interested in taking part of the purchase price in the form of bonds.

In this actual example a $400,000 loan was available based upon the $515,000 value. The seller needed $150,000 cash but was flexible on the balance. A check was made with a local stockbroker, and it was learned that $500,000 worth of bonds could be purchased for $130,000 at that time, with maturity in 11 years.

Since a loan was available for $400,000 and all the money that was required was $280,000, $130,000 to buy the bonds and $150,000 for the down payment, the buyer was able to walk out of closing with $120,000 cash. In addition, there was another $115,000 in equity, the difference between the $515,000 value and the $400,000 loan, so the buyer actually made $235,000 buying the property.

Always Have a Plan for the Payment

Then, there are these concerns: "How am I going to pay back the loan on the property?" and "How do I qualify and prove a down payment?" All of this is very important. Getting cash at closing helps, but I strongly recommend that you avoid buying just because you get paid.

Have a plan to handle the payment problem, even if it is a year or two away because of the cash received. Either you pay it yourself, share in the payments with somebody else through equity participation, or have someone else pay it. Perhaps reselling for no-money-down to somebody else would work.

Why would a person want to buy something that has a negative? Tax benefits—number one, but terms and equity are more important. The buyer immediately picks up $115,000 in equity and doesn't have the hassle of going through a new loan situation and qualifying. I have gone both ways, but I always know what I'm going to do before I buy.

You also will have to qualify to borrow the money. Again, use my buddy system and pay someone to help, give away partial ownership in exchange for a partner's financial statement, or sell before closing. If you have to prove a down payment, even though you don't need one, check my proof of down payment section for ideas.

Cut Mortgage Payments with Bonds

You also win when you can cut mortgage payments with bonds. This can be done when you initially set your loan or anytime during that loan period. To make the formula work, multiply your monthly mortgage payment times 12 months times the number of years left on your mortgage. Let's say, for example, that you took out a 30-year loan 15 years ago and it still has another 15 years to go. Your interest rate at that time was 8%, and your mortgage payment is $734 per month. Interestingly enough, on a 30-year $100,000 loan at 8%, your loan balance after 15 years will still be $76,800. Why? Because in the beginning almost all of your mortgage payment is interest. You don't really start retiring your debt until you are halfway through your mortgage.

Using our formula, multiply $734 times 12 months times 15 years, and you'll see that you will pay the lender an additional $132,120 over the next 15-year period.

Offer the lender a $150,000 tax-free bond due to mature in 15 years. This gets the lender more than would normally be received from you, and, at the same time, the person can borrow against that cash value every year. Your cost in buying the bond – $37,500. That means you have just saved $39,300 on your mortgage, $37,500 subtracted from $76,800.

Here's another way you might cut your mortgage payment. I had a young disabled student who lived with his mother who was on welfare. His father had recently died, taking away any income they had, so his mother couldn't afford the $300 per month mortgage payment.

Yet, they had lots of equity in their property. Apparently there was no way they could use this equity or refinance because they couldn't make even the $300 mortgage payment, much less qualify for any new financing.

The young man approached the existing lender with this unique approach. He asked the lender if refinancing and a loan for more money were possible if the United States Government guaranteed the loan. The lender, of course, was interested in what my student had to say.

He then asked the lender to rewrite the loan for eight years and loan more money. In exchange, he offered to give the lender U.S. Treasury Bonds totaling the principal portion of the loan, due to mature to the loan amount in eight years.

In exchange for this guarantee, he asked the lender if he would drop the payment to interest only, or $80 per month. Put yourself in the place of a lender. He gets a first mortgage on a property that is worth more than the mortgage, plus a U.S. Treasury Bond guaranteeing complete repayment of the loan in eight years.

In short, the lender had absolutely no risk. If the borrower defaulted, he not only got the property, which he could sell, but U.S.

Treasury Bonds as well which paid off the loan in full when they matured. His mother, on welfare, could afford the $80 per month, so they had no problem.

My disabled student used part of the new financing to come up with money to buy the bonds and still had cash left over to spend on other things. To top it off, my student asked me, after telling me his story, "Did I do it right?" I kept congratulating him as I was busy writing down his story so you could have the benefit of reading it.

Lenders Benefit from Taking Bonds

For example, let's say that a lender has foreclosed on a property and now has it as one of its REO's. Let's also assume that the lender has $100,000 in that property. In other words, the lender has to sell for $100,000 to recoup all monies.

Common sense says that if somebody will pay him $100,000 all cash, the person will take it. More than likely, however, the property is not worth $100,000, and even if it is, nobody will pay all cash.

If the lender sells for anything less than the value of the property, the difference is reported as a loss. If the lender (or any seller for that matter) sells for $70,000 all cash, the lender has a taxable loss of $30,000.

The person can, however, report a loss and still manage profit in the end by using bonds. As a matter of fact, the lender can actually get 20% or more interest on the investment by taking bonds instead of cash. More than likely, a buyer will want to pay no more than $50,000 all cash for this property, but let's be nice and say a buyer will pay $70,000, or 70% of value. Here's how it works out:

- Property Value to Lender: $100,000

- Offer: $ 70,000

If the lender were to sell for $70,000 all cash and loan it out again at an interest rate of 10% for 10 years, the lender would have $70,000 coming in interest over that 10-year period and still have the $70,000 in principal (rounded off, of course). This totals $140,000.

If, however, the lender were to agree to take bonds that will have a $150,000 value in 10 years and also agree to loan the buyer $50,000 secured by a first mortgage on the property, the end result is quite different. (Incidentally, the $50,000 which the lender agrees to give to the buyer is the money used to buy the bonds, meaning that the buyer is buying for no-money-down. It also means that the buyer will not have a negative cash flow situation because the mortgage is only $50,000.)

Using the same 10-year period, let's say the lender agrees to loan the buyer $50,000 at 10% interest with a balloon at the end of the term. Remember that the buyer's only payment is on the $50,000, not the bond since the lender is agreeing to take that in full settlement of his or her equity.

The Lender Receives:

Bond at end of 10 years	$150,000
10 percent on $50,000	$50,000
Principal repayment	$50,000
Overall Return to Lender	$250,000

In other words, the lender receives $110,000 more in cash over a 10-year period taking bonds as opposed to selling for $70,000 all cash.

Let's put in another way. Suppose the lender were to sell for $70,000 and loan out the proceeds at 20% for the next 10 years. This means the person could collect $140,000 in interest and the $70,000 original amount, for a total of $210,000. This is still less than the $250,000 the lender receives by taking bonds.

What if the lender sold for $100,000 and loaned the proceeds out at 10% interest? The lender's return would be $200,000 over the 10-year period, still less than the $250,000. As a matter of fact, that lender would have to loan the money out at 15% interest for the next 15 years to equal what will be received by taking bonds.

At the current time, a person can borrow money at less interest than 15%. Do bonds make sense to a lender (or seller who wants to carry the financing)? Explain it in this fashion, and I think you'll find far more lenders willing to listen.

Sam Seller
10 Main Street
Anywhere, U.S.A.

Dear Mr. Seller:

I am interested in purchasing your property located at
_____. I would like to offer you Municipal Bonds or
Government Securities for part of your purchase price, and I invite
you to read my enclosed flyer with a brief explanation of what
these bonds and securities are all about.

For your information, I buy these Bonds or Securities at a discount.
Just as IRA's and various retirement programs are purchased for
their long-range benefits, I purchase these Bonds at a discount now,
so that you will someday, in the future, come into a great deal of money.

Municipal Zero Bonds, when they are available, are usually TAX-
FREE! Can you imagine you or your children someday receiving a
vast amount of money and not having to pay taxes? The interest
rates may vary, but at maturity the Bonds are always paid off at their
full value. Interest payments are not made during the maturing period.
The interest accumulates and is compounded till the final maturity
date. That is why they build up to such a large amount.

Bonds are rated by the firms Standard and Poor or Moody. Most
investors favor bonds rated A, AA or AAA. It would be Bonds
within these top ratings that I would give you, and they would be
issued through one of the major brokerage firms, such as Merrill
Lynch, E.F. Hutton, etc.

I want to emphasize that these bonds are not for everyone. They are
designed to be cashed in at maturity but can be cashed in earlier
than the maturity date at some discount. However, even though
they are not worth the face value as cash now, they can be used at
full face value as cash. And, a big plus, YOU CAN BORROW UP
TO 92% OF THE PRESENT CASH VALUE OF THE BONDS.

In other words, you can borrow against them now, immediately
obtaining some cash, trade them anywhere in the world at the full

face value for real estate, use them as gifts, for estate planning, college education, etc.

You might say to me: "I can take the cash and do the same thing myself." Yes, you can. But that means that somebody is going to offer you all cash (and your price), and even if this did happen, I doubt seriously that you will spend this cash on a long-range retirement or investment program. Who of us has the necessary wisdom or the means to plan so far ahead? So, if you do not get the necessary cash (or the wisdom), I provide a rare opportunity for the sale of your property to be used as a vehicle that will someday provide you, your family, or someone of your choosing a life of comfort and security.

THINK ABOUT THIS! You can actually sell your property for MORE THAN IT'S WORTH and at the same time get that money TAX-FREE! And, the Bonds that you receive are good anywhere, anyplace. You often will find that a property owner in a distant state will not exchange for your property in another state or take mortgages or Deeds of Trust in that state, but he might take your Bonds because they are not tied to any location. In addition, no longer do you have to concern yourself with depressions, falling real estate markets and buyers defaulting on their payments making it necessary for you to foreclose--getting your property back in *whatever* condition. You can rest easy at night knowing that your security is backed 100% by your government against any type of loss.

So, whether you use the Bonds to pyramid your investment portfolio, grant them to your alma mater, keep them for a secure retirement or place them in a family estate, you are getting more than double your equity in flexible, transferable, exchangeable securities that are backed by the integrity of your local, state, or national government.

If this idea appeals to you at all, I will be most happy to sit down and discuss it further at your office, my office or even at your stockbroker's office. Thanks for your time, and have a very nice, profitable, positive day.

Sincerely,

28

Try One of These Ideas

Since there are many creative ways to buy and sell real estate, property, or whatever it is you want to sell, use the method that fits best into your financial planning.

For illustrative purposes, let's first assume that you have a $100,000 property that is free and clear. You refinance your home to 75% of value, or $75,000. Then you purchase a bond that will have a cash value of $100,000 in 4 years. This should cost you about $75,000, or the amount you refinance your home.

Check to see what it would cost to buy such an insurance policy or bond and refinance accordingly. Offer to sell it to a buyer for little or no-money-down and interest payments of 9% per year or $9,000 on $100,000. Either ask for a balloon due in 4 years or give the property to the buyer free and clear when the bond matures to $100,000. Or, continue with the buyer at interest only and have a nice little retirement income.

Alternative

As an alternative, offer no interest payments or you do it as the buyer. You obtain a $75,000 first mortgage, giving the seller a bond instead of cash. The problem now is that you as the buyer probably can't afford to make an interest payment to the seller and make the mortgage payment. You will either have to get the person to waive the interest payment or ask that the person refinance and do it as I first suggested.

Another Idea

You can refinance your home to $75,000, but instead of buying bonds with a maturity date of 4 years, make the maturity date 7 to 15 years. The $75,000 will now buy a bond that could be worth $150,000 to $200,000 in that time frame. Write off the interest on your mortgage payment, and when the bond matures, cash in the tax-free dollars and pay off your loan, keeping the balance tax-free for yourself. You could even borrow less than the $75,000 or not spend the entire $75,000, keeping the difference up front. You still end up paying off your mortgage in 7 to 15 years, and you still end up with cash at the end. Only now, you get cash both up front and at the end.

Or, you could sell on a lease-option or small down payment on a wrap or even rent out your property. Have a property that's appraised at $100,000, but you can't sell it? Are you a buyer who wants to buy at 75% of value, but the seller won't sell for less than his price? This idea might work for you.

A True Story

REO (real estate owned) used in this context, means properties that lenders have taken back via foreclosure or other means. Lenders are in the loaning business, not the owning business, so most of the time they are very motivated to sell their REO'S, and are willing to listen to creative offers. One of my students is buying properties from lenders using bonds. You might try the same approach in your area.

Here Is How It Works:

Asking Price from Lender: $100,000
Offer: $100,000
Terms: $20,000 down payment, and 15-year U.S. Treasury Bonds: $100,000

In other words, the buyer is offering $20,000 in cash (which he doesn't have) and $100,000 in U.S. Treasury Bonds (which he doesn't own). His offer is subject to the lender giving him an 80% loan to value or $80,000. Lenders like 80% loans when they receive a 20% "cash" down payment.

Buyer Needs

$20,000 for the down payment and $27,500 to purchase the 15-year Treasury Bonds (that was the cost of the bond at the time the offer was accepted). His total investment: $47,500. The lender loaned the buyer $80,000. The bonds were purchased at closing, and the down payment was made from the loan proceeds. My student walked out of closing with $32,500 IN CASH!

If you do this, the lender may want verification of the $20,000 down payment before closing. If this is the case, it will be necessary for you to have those funds on hand or borrow them for a short period of time. You might even consider offering somebody with $20,000 a fee for the use of money or perhaps a partnership. If you can't qualify for a new loan yourself, a partner could do it for you.

Suggestion

You could buy a second $100,000 bond using $27,500 from the $32,500. This will allow you to either get back the $100,000 loan if paid off in 15 years or allow you to pay off the mortgage in 15 years and get extra cash besides.

Another Possibility

Borrow 65% of the value, or $65,000. There are lenders who will loan 65% of value without you having to qualify. You still walk out of closing with cash. Now, rent out the property for a positive cash flow or turn around and sell on a lease-option.

Buying Free and Clear Properties

Another student of mine is using this method to acquire free and clear properties and get paid at the same time. The more motivated the seller is, the easier it is to do, and the more the property value, the more you stand to make doing it. Let's keep it simple once more and stay with a $100,000 value.

Offer

Offer 1 1/2 times the seller's asking price in 15-year U.S. Treasury Bonds. The cost at this writing was $35,000 for a $150,000 15-year bond. It could be more or less, so be sure and check with your bond broker.

Again, ask only for a 65% loan to value, or $65,000. There are many lending institutions who will loan 65% of the value, in this case $100,000, without you having to qualify. This means that you will receive $65,000 from the loan proceeds. $35,000 will be needed to buy the bond, and you can pocket the balance of $30,000.

You have now just purchased a $100,000 property, made $35,000 in equity and $30,000 in cash or a total of $65,000 on a $100,000 property. In addition, because the loan is only 65% of the value, you can easily rent it out for a positive cash flow. If the loan payment is higher than the rent, take part of the $30,000 in cash that you receive and escrow it to cover the negative.

Keep the property and sell when the reserve runs out or turn right around and sell now on a lease-option for $100,000. I suggest you give the buyer credit for most or all of the monthly payments toward the down payment. In that manner, you will have a positive cash flow and a motivated buyer because the person is buying for no-money-down and is getting the down payment through monthly payments. Ask the buyer to obtain a new loan in two or three years, taking you out of your present position.

Why Would a Seller Do This?

In this example, the seller is not getting any cash up front nor is the person receiving payments on the money. The seller is being asked to wait 15 years to get money. Naturally, if the seller could come up with a $100,000 cash buyer now, the person probably wouldn't consider such an offer, but if the seller can't sell for cash now, doesn't need the cash now, or has a property that has gone down in value (and there are many of those now across the United States), and yet insists upon a specified asking price, the seller could be a prime suspect.

In addition, the seller can pledge this bond policy and use it as cash to buy something else or borrow against the cash value of the policy during the 15-year period.

Use Bonds as Additional Security

Example:

- Apartment complex Tampa, Florida

- Price: $600,000

- Existing First Mortgage $ 213,000

- Existing Second Mortgage: $100,000

- Down payment: $100,000

- Seller to Carry Second Mortgage: $187,000 at 10% interest only for 10 years

- No Payments

- New Loan: $750,000

- Security: First mortgage on property, plus a $1-million dollar bond due in 26 years.

To Review

There is a first mortgage balance of $213,000 and a second of $100,000 which must be paid off with new financing. The seller is asking for a $100,000 down payment in the form of cash and will carry back a note secured by a second mortgage on the property for $187,000, 10% interest only for ten years with no payments. That means the entire $187,000, plus interest, is due in 10 years. The property has a huge cash flow and enough income to support a $750,000 loan, but the buyer can't borrow this much because the person was only paying $600,000.

The buyer offered the lender a $1-million-dollar 16-year face-value bond, plus a first mortgage on the property for a loan of $750,000. This gave the lender $1.6 million in collateral for a $750,000 loan and a guarantee that the loan will be paid off in 16 years because the bond matures to pay it off at that time.

Cost of Bond (at that time)	$243,000
Loans and Down Payment Payoff	$413,000
Cash Needed	$656,000
Borrow	$750,000
Cash to Buyer	$ 94,000

This is a case where the buyer used a bond as additional collateral in order to borrow more than the individual was paying for the property. The bond matures to $1 million in 16 years, paying off the mortgage, leaving an overage of about $250,000 which the buyer also gets. The lender is fully secured. If buyer defaults, the lender gets the property back PLUS a $1-million-dollar bond. As a matter of fact, that is the best thing that could happen to the lender. Certainly, the buyer has motivation to see to it that it doesn't.

29

Tax Implications

Before we begin exploring the tax ramifications of using discounted bonds, please be advised that I AM NOT ENGAGED IN RENDERING LEGAL, ACCOUNTING, OR OTHER PROFESSIONAL ADVICE. I can only tell you what I have been able to find out on my own. I strongly recommend that you seek your own personal legal and professional advice before proceeding. The following information, however., has been verified by both my CPA and the IRS, and has been researched in the IRS tax code.

You can buy bonds at face value that pay an interest rate. Some bonds have interest that is taxable, and other bonds are 100% tax-free. In this case, it's easy to decide your tax consequences.

Some of the bonds we discussed are not face-value bonds, but are discounted or Zero Coupon Bonds. In this case, the interest accrues each year and builds to the eventual face value of the bond. Some bonds are tax-free, while others are not. In the case where your bond is tax-free, both the interest and the face value of the bond are tax-free and do not have to be reported.

If your bond is not a tax-free bond but was bought at discount with the interest accruing to bring it to face value, the IRS takes the position that you are receiving this income each year even though you aren't getting it in cash and you pay taxes accordingly.

You can defer the yearly payment of taxes on this income by buying the bonds through a Pension Retirement Corporation or similar entity, but you will pay taxes on this interest eventually.

Any balloon notes secured by tax-free bonds are 100% TAX-FREE when they come due. So, instead of paying capital gains on this amount, if you are the taker of the note secured by bonds, your gain is tax-free. This is important to know.

If you offer *more* than the seller wants, the amount equal to the equity in the property is considered the basis, but all monies received above this, again as long as the bonds are tax-free, are tax-free to the seller.

For review, let's take an example of a sales price of $100,000. If the seller's basis in the property (what the person paid for the improvements, less depreciation) is $40,000, the $60,000 received over and above the $40,000 will be taxed either as ordinary income or long-term capital gains. If it is your home, as long as you purchase something equal or more in value to what you are selling, you will defer the payment of taxes. If it is an investment, property taxes are due that year unless you include it in an exchange.

The seller can actually eliminate the paying of any tax by taking tax-free bonds instead of cash. Let's say the seller takes $200,000 in tax-free bonds which can be purchased by the buyer for $40,000, instead of $100,00 cash. The selling price will be the cost of the bonds the day they were purchased, or $40,000, meaning that the seller sold for exactly what he or she paid. As long as the bond is a tax-free bond, all monies over and above will be tax-free to the seller. If the bond is one that pays interest that is reportable to the IRS, the seller will pay taxes but they are paid as the seller collects the interest.

In other words, a person can now spread taxes over a period of time instead of having to pay them all at one time. And, in most cases, a person can shelter this small amount if it is spread out over a number of years, but will not be able to if the taxes are paid in one lump sum. This could also be a way to keep your real estate taxes down. Some states tax you according to what you pay for a piece of property. By using bonds purchased at a fraction of the real value, you might be able to keep those taxes at the same level.

If you attempt to pay off an existing mortgage by trading bonds in lieu of cash, such as $420,000 worth of tax-free bonds due to mature to $420,000 in 14 years in exchange for a lender "forgiving" or showing paid-in-full a mortgage balance of (perhaps) $185,000, this is the case. If the property is your own home, you are obligated to pay taxes on the difference between the mortgage balance of $185,000 and your cost of purchasing the $420,000 worth of bonds. This gain is treated as ordinary income, just as it would be if you paid off your mortgage with cash at a discount.

Example: If the cost of purchasing $420,000 of tax-free bonds is $100,000, your ordinary income would be $85,000. If the discount comes on a mortgage on rental or business property, it is merely a reduction of basis and not taxed at that time. Example: If your base property with the $185,000 mortgage is $300,000 and you pay off the $185,000 with $100,000 worth of actual value bonds that will mature to $420,000 in 14 years, you have just reduced your basis from $300,000 to $215,000. You would pay capital gains on this portion when you sell.

What does it mean for the lender? The rule is the same whether it be a hard money-lender or an individual. You are offering $420,000 worth of bonds for an existing $185,000 mortgage balance. The basis in these bonds remains at $185,000 as far as the lender is concerned. If the lender sells the bonds at a lower figure, the person has a taxable loss. If the lender keeps the bonds, all monies received above the $185,000 are tax-free.

If you think about it, the use of tax-free bonds to discount a mortgage is a win/win for both the lender and the owner, unless it's your own home. If it's your home, it still might behoove you to do it if your tax situation is such that it won't hurt you.

Interesting Point

You can borrow up to 70% of the present value of the bonds from your stock brokerage firm. That means you can take bonds and still get some cash. Your interest expense may or may not be a deduction in this case. Check with your accountant.

For those of you interested, this information can be verified in the IRS tax code under sections 108, 1012 and 1017.

Sample Letter

DEAR MR LENDER:

With the recent negative publicity given lending institutions in general and the need by these lending institutions to make what are called "ultra-conservative no-risk loans," I feel I can offer just such a loan opportunity to you. My concept and idea could revolutionize the lending industry so that it would be virtually impossible for an institution to make a bad loan or one that necessitated foreclosure. I urge you not only to listen to my proposal but to consider it with all your loan requests in the future.

Your main concern in the past has been the capability and responsibility of the buyer plus the value of the security for the loan. While a person borrowing the money might have excellent credit and an income to qualify for such a loan in the beginning, many things could happen during the course of that loan to change both the credit rating of the borrower and the security involved. Donald Trump is just one example of this. The economy is another. As long as the value of the security, such as real estate, is holding in value or going up and the borrower is maintaining the status he had when obtaining the loan, you have no worry. Past experience has shown that this is the exception rather than the rule in today's present economic conditions.

You are now "forced," by law to only lend 80% of the purchase price or market value, whichever is less, and the borrower must make enough money on his own to support the payments, even if it is an income property. Wouldn't it be nice *never* to have your loan at risk or have to worry about the value of the security going down in value? Wouldn't it be nice to know that even if the borrower took bankruptcy or lost his job and couldn't pay his loan payment that you'd never lose money? To me , this is the panacea of all loans. Does this possibility exit? Yes, it does and you can do it, as other lending institutions have recently discovered and are doing themselves.

What is your *safest investment*, bar none, in the United States? U.S. Treasury Bonds or notes, of course. Why—because they are backed and guaranteed by the United States Government. What better guarantee can you have? If this is true, why not use them each and every time as "additional security" when you make a loan. By using U.S. Treasury Bonds as additional security, or even as total security, you eliminate risk *forever.* I'm sure if I came into your institution and asked to borrow money secured by such an instrument, you'd bend over backward to make the loan. And, why not? You can't lose! I'm going to suggest you incorporate just such a vehicle in my loan request and perhaps in all others from now on. Value and price of the other security, as well as the credibility of the borrower, take a back seat compared to what I'm about to offer. Even if the borrower didn't qualify up to your standards or the property didn't measure up to what you'd like it to be, you can't lose because you are literally guaranteed complete repayment of the loan!

I realize this is something brand new to both you and your institution, and as such it's quite easy to be negative and just say "no" without first studying the proposal and investigating it. I CHALLENGE YOU to find something in this proposal that won't work to your benefit. No longer will you be looking at "suspect" 70% to 80% loans but rather loans of 40% to 50% of overall security with NO THREAT OF LOSS! As I said before, other lending institutions are doing it. Why not you?

I would like a _____ year loan with the following security: I will give you a first mortgage (deed of trust or whatever) on _____ which has a market or appraised value of _____. As additional security for this loan, I will put up a U.S. Treasury Bond with a Face Value of _____ and a maturity date of _____. This bond does not have a "cash value" of the "face value" until maturity but is *guaranteed* to be worth that value at the end of the maturity day. The bond can be cashed in at any time, at less than the maturity value, of course, pledged, traded or kept at your discretion. It can also be used for income purposes because it is possible to borrow against the cash value every year. The bond literally guarantees that you can't lose money. If I were to default, for whatever reason, you would not only get my security but the full value of the bond as well. It is easy to see that your loan is just (percentage) of the overall value of both my security and the bond.

BEST NEWS OF ALL! Even though the bond doesn't have a present cash value of the full face value, you may be able to show it on your balance sheet at FULL FACE VALUE, improving your "statement" immediately. Please check with your accountant for verification, but this was told to me by a reliable source by his banker.

The bond can be in my name or the name of (your lending institution). Either way it should be placed in escrow. When the bond matures, part of the proceeds will pay off the loan with the balance coming to me. Although my loan may be amortized over _____ years, the bond actually pays it off in _____ years.

Escrow instructions should call for the bond to remain in escrow as long as I am current with my loan requirements. However, if I default for any reason, the escrow instructions should indicate that the bond is forfeited in full and becomes the property of your institution. It is obvious that your percentage loan is far less than the security involved, so it behooves me to always be current with my payments. Otherwise you get the property back, plus the U.S. Treasury Bonds. Your security is unbelievable. I urge you to seriously consider this loan proposal, and I look forward to a favorable reply as soon as possible.

Thank you for your consideration.

Sincerely,

30

A Final Note about Bonds

Most lenders cannot recoup what they have lost by foreclosure. Nobody will pay them what they feel they have coming. Example: The property was worth $500,000 when the lender made a loan of $400,000. Eventually the lender foreclosed and now has the property back. It is presently worth $300,000. To sell for $300,000 would mean the lender has to accept a loss, yet nobody will pay them the $400,000 they need to break even. Also, they want a down payment of 20% to 30% of what they are selling for, and many won't even loan on their foreclosures.

I suggest you *ask them* to loan you the entire amount, in this case $300,000 or $400,000. This is dictated by what the property will support in the way of payments. Let's say it will support a loan of just $250,000, but the bank wants $400,000. Ask the foreclosure bank to loan you the $250,000 in cash. Take this cash and buy a bond that will be worth $1 million in 15 years. (Don't take my figures as accurate— just concern yourself with the concept. You obtain current quotes yourself.)

You can offer to trade them this $1-million-dollar bond for the property free and clear, forgiving the $250,000 loan. This is your best bet, of course, but they might not go along. I suggest you try this first, however.

You could also offer them this bond as "additional collateral" for the $250,000 loan with this loan being paid in full at maturity with an additional $150,000 due in the form of a balloon payment at that time. Remember, you have $1 million to work with and only $250,000 (rounded off) that is needed, so you could sweeten the pot up to another $750,000.

If the foreclosure bank will not loan on the property, consider offering to trade them bonds for their property. In this case, it will be necessary for you to borrow the $250,000 from another lending institution and buy bonds sufficient to give them $1 million, or whatever, in the 15-year time frame.

Or, you in turn give them the $250,000 with the promise that they will "lend it back to you" for this time frame and you give $1 million in bonds as security. Again, there will be no interest payment on the loan. While they do not get a payment, they, in fact, get something that can be pledged, borrowed against or traded and once again, shown on their balance sheet. Also, 20% interest on $250,000 is $50,000 per year. This times 15 years adds up to $750,000. Twenty percent is more than they can get any place, yet that, in fact, is what you are offering them.

Don't get hung up on the 15-year time frame. This can be 10-30 years depending on the numbers and what you can negotiate.

Presenting Your Loan Request

You are going to ask the lender to loan you money secured by both the bonds and the real estate. The lender gets a first mortgage as well as the bond as security. I suggest you obtain a maximum loan that the property and/or you can support. Part of the proceeds are to be used to acquire the property with the balance going to buy the bond.

I suggest the maturity date of the bond be as long as you can negotiate, preferably the length of the loan negotiated, such as 30 years. You might get a better response, however, if you made the maturity of the bond less than the maturity of the loan, such as 15 or 20 years. In this case, negotiate a 30-year amortization with a 15 or

20-year balloon. With this additional security you should be able to borrow more than you are paying for the property.

Again, all of this is conditioned on your being able to afford the payments or the property being able to do so with your help. I call your attention to the property recently acquired in Tampa whereby my student borrowed $750,000 on an apartment complex for which he only paid $600,000. A lender should not object to loaning you more money than you are paying provided you use part of the funds to buy security that will justify such a loan. In this case, the buyer gave the lender a $1-million-dollar bond as well as a first on the property, using part of the proceeds to buy the bond.

If the figures work out correctly, it might even be possible that you could ask the lender to loan you money secured totally by bonds. You, as the borrower, would have to prove to the lender that you could pay the interest on the loan but the bonds would guarantee the principal portion of the loan.

As an example, you might buy a 10-year U.S. Treasury Bonds for $400 per thousand or $400,000 for $1 million. Ask the lender to loan you $500,000, of which $400,000 would go to buy the bonds, leaving you with $100,000 to do whatever. The $1-million-dollar bond would be security for this loan, but in addition, I suggest you pay interest on the $500,000.

When the bond matures, it pays off the principal portion of the loan, but you recoup the interest with the excess. In this instance, you get $100,000 up front, write off the interest as an expense, and recoup it when the bond matures. At worst, if you default, the lender waits till the bond matures and pockets the $1 million. Over a 10-year period, if you paid no payments, which, of course, would not happen, the worst that could happen to the lender is that the person would realize 10% interest on the loan. This is figured as follows: 10% interest on $500,000 each year is $50,000. $50,000 times 10 years equals $500,000. This, plus the $500,000 borrowed equals $1 million.

The purchase price should not come into play since the security offered far exceeds the loan request. Try and keep it to a 40% or 50% loan to value. By doing this you shouldn't have to worry about good credit or qualifying. If you are dealing with a bank who likes loans of no more than five to seven years and the security is "other than real estate," such as equipment, etc., you will have to adjust according to the cost of bond purchase. Naturally, the cost will be much higher on a short-term loan than on a longer loan.

Why Should Sellers Take Bonds?

It is common knowledge in today's market place that real estate is not selling for what it once did. In some areas, values have actually gone down, not up. Yet, some sellers are unwilling to take *less* for their property than they think it's worth, or perhaps some "can't afford to sell" because of capital gains taxes they have to pay on their profit. So, we have two types of sellers, those who can't, or won't sell, because their value is down, and those who can't or won't sell because they must pay taxes on their profits. Bonds offer an excellent alternative for both types of sellers.

Let's first tackle the seller who doesn't want to "take a loss on his sale." Appeal to the person's greed! Offer more than the person is asking.

How much more? That depends on what you can borrow. This amount of money will dictate your offer. If the person needs some cash, take this from the loan proceeds, add what you'd like to take yourself, and the balance can be used to buy bonds. The longer you can get the seller to wait, the more bonds you can offer. You can also offer some bonds with 7-year maturity, 10-year maturity and even 15 or 20 years. In other words, divide them up. Sure, the seller waits to get cash but at least the person gets it. And if done correctly, the person can not only write off a loss if it is an investment property but can recoup it tax-free if the bonds are tax-free bonds.

The second type of seller cannot afford to sell because of the taxes attached to profit. Both of you can also win in this case. The IRS has ruled that the seller's selling price, for tax purposes, is the amount of cash received, loan forgiveness, and cash value of the bond the day it was taken out. As an example, if you give the person a $1-million-dollar tax-free bond that you only paid $250,000 for, the selling price would be $250,000, plus any other cash and debt relief the person might get. The seller could literally sell for more than was orginally paid yet report a loss on income tax. On the other hand, your basis would be the same and when you sell, you would be looking at a profit. This, of course, could be handled by you taking tax-free bonds when you sell.

How to Make It Impossible to Ever Make a Bad Loan

All lenders, whether private or conventional, listen up! Attention: United States Senate and House Banking Committees! This idea can solve all banking problems, now and in the future. This can eliminate any lender from *ever* making a bad loan. At the same time it will pump millions into the government that can be used for other programs, including cutting the deficit.

Why not insist that part of the loan proceeds be used to buy a U.S. Treasury Bond guaranteeing complete repayment of the principal over the life of the loan. Or, instead of a cash down payment, have that borrower use that money to buy a bond equaling the amount of the loan. The lender might even take some of the money to buy the bond, charging it off as insurance. Let's see how that could work.

The buyer/borrower borrows a total of $100,000 to be paid back over a 30-year time frame. In this unstable financial climate, many lenders, including owners who owner-finance, are "scared to death" that the buyer will default, and they (the lender) will end up having to foreclose and take back the property and probably a loss as well.

This is why most lenders *insist* on the buyer having some investment in the property or loan. The feeling has been that if the buyer has money invested, the person will be less likely to default. Unfortunately, this hasn't solved the problem, and foreclosures are at an all-time high. Is there any way to end the probability of foreclosure and eliminate *all* risk? YES!

A U.S. Treasury Bond is purchased that will equal the amount of the loan at the end of the 30-year period. If the loan is for 20 or 25 years, a bond should be purchased that will be worth that amount when the loan is paid off. If there is a "balloon" payment due in 10 years, buy a bond that will equal the amount due at that time. A lender *cannot* lose, only *win*. In fact, a lender is better off money wise if the buyer does default because not only does the lender get the property back, but it can be resold. The person is also *insured* no loss of principal because the bond automatically becomes the property of the lender.

As an incentive to the borrower, I suggest that if the borrower performs as agreed (something the lender worries about) and pays off the loan in full, the borrower gets the bond. If the borrower of the $100,000 knows that he or she will get back $100,000 once the loan is paid in full, I can assure you the person will do everything within reason to make sure there is no foreclosure. The person also knows that even if the property goes down in value, no loss occurs. In short, if the buyer performs as agreed, both the lender and borrower win. If the buyer defaults, the lender wins. The lender wins regardless of what happens.

Think what this could do to pump up the real estate market. Sellers would have an easier time selling regardless of market conditions. What if the borrower doesn't fit the criteria of the lender, has suspect credit, or doesn't have the required down payment or even qualify based on job income? Who cares? A bond would eliminate all risk for everybody.

In fact, every purchase could be a no-money-down purchase. 100% loans could become commonplace, making qualifying, as we presently know it, obsolete. A buyer could still put up a down payment, cutting payments. In this case, the size of the bond and cost would be reduced accordingly. Instead of the government guaranteeing or insuring the top percentage of any loan such as in VA and FHA, the entire loan is now--100% guaranteed.

31

Creative Ways to Become a Millionaire

This is a story, a true story, not one made up or wished to come true, but one that actually happened. It's also a story about faith, trust, and attitude. It's not a story without trials, tribulations, and problems, but rather it's a story of the real world and the people in it.

This is a story about *millionaires* and about those who became millionaires in one day. It's also a story about how people react when faced with a situation of becoming a millionaire. Not everyone can accept making one million in a lifetime, let alone in one day. There are those who said it couldn't be done and even after it happened, there are those that still can't accept or comprehend what happened. Then again, there are those who finally are convinced it could happen but refuse to take that step to make it happen for them.

The nice part about this story is that you don't need money to do it, you don't need a job, nor do you need good credit. In fact, anybody reading this material who wants to become financially independent can do so because I'm going to take you step by step and show you how to do it.

Become a Millionaire in One Day

Three people, one being myself, each walked out of closing with 1 million in cash. Another acquired over 1 million in equity with no-money-down and no negative cash flow and others have equity positions of almost 1 million. And, the realtors made almost $300,000 in commissions.

There are three things necessary for you to become successful in whatever it is that you want to do or become:

1. **Desire.** You have to want to become successful. If you don't have that desire, regardless of the other two points, you just won't make it.

2. **Belief.** You can desire success, but if you don't believe you can be successful, you won't reach your goal.

As an example, you can desire to be a good tennis player, but if you don't think you can be good at tennis, you won't reach your desire. On the other hand, if you believe you can be a good tennis player, but you'd rather watch television, and the desire just isn't there, you again will fail.

3. **Plan.** You have to have a plan to accomplish your goals and desires. Many of us have belief and desire, but we fail in knowing what to do with our beliefs and desires.

While this next example is simplistic, it shows the impor-tance of planning. For illustrative purposes, let's say that you believe you want pizza for dinner. You even desire pizza for dinner, but unless you actually put forth a plan and implement that plan, you won't have pizza. You either have to make the pizza, buy a pizza, or have someone prepare it for you or bring it to you, or I can assure you that you won't have pizza for dinner.

I am hereby assuming that you have both belief and desire to be successful but are lacking in a plan—a way to get what you want from life. I will, therefore, provide you with the plan, from A to Z.

Copy and follow it. If you do, you can be financially independent, and you, too, can become a millionaire in one day.

Are you ready for the challenge?

Make a Million Dollars with Fourplexes

The object in this next illustration is not to buy and keep real estate but to make a million in one day, so we don't look for the same opportunities we might look for otherwise. We look for "in-and-out" situations. But what do I mean by in-and-out?

My definition of an in-and-out purchase is one where you buy at one figure and sell at another price. It works best if you can buy real estate collectively and resell individually.

Let's take an actual example of thirty-five fourplexes for sale for three million dollars. It could have been thirty-five houses, duplexes, condos, or whatever. Common sense dictates that if you are buying thirty-five units at one time, you are entitled to a discount over what you'd pay individually if you purchased just one fourplex. The same concept applies if you are buying two cars or even two suits instead of just one.

So—look for opportunities where you can buy collectively rather than individually.

Secondly, be sure when you buy collectively that you can subdivide and resell individually. Check the zoning to be sure that what you want to do is not a violation of the law of that area. If you are purchasing an apartment complex with the intention of converting the units to condominiums, be sure that you can do so without any violation of local law. I'll cover that more in detail later.

The majority of us have no idea as to value, so before making an offer, it's important to know the present value as well as the values of each fourplex on resale. It's also important to know if they can be sold individually as bought, or will they have to be subdivided and have separate titles issued. I prefer to step in and resell immediately, but many times, if that is the case, the present owner could have done the same thing. If units need to be divided or need titles issues, much time, effort, and money will have to be spent.

If a realtor presents the property to me, I ask the realtor to provide me with comparables of similar properties in the area plus advise me as to what individual financing is available. In other words, will these units that I might pay $84,000 each sell for $150,000 or more? My criteria is about 50%, no more than 60% of what they can be resold for. The purchase price will be dictated by what financing is available on resale. New individual loans will probably be available for 75% to 90%, depending on if owner occupied or if investor financed. You cut your options if the lender will only loan owner occupied, especially when you are buying fourplexes. With condominiums, it's quite different.

Lenders probably will want an appraisal before committing to a loan commitment on resale. It may be necessary for you to talk with an appraiser ahead of time to get an idea of value. If the fourplexes are identical, the realtor's job is much easier. If they are different in layout, you will need individual appraisals. Rather than risk the money in the beginning, I ask for windshield appraisals, which keeps the cost down but still gives me an idea of value. In addition, try and get the appraiser to wait for fees until after closing.

In this example, the appraiser advised that the units would indeed resell for $150,000 or a gross of $5,250,000. This also meant that there was a gross profit to be made of $2,250,000, certainly enough to pursue further. Be sure you have your individual financing in place before proceeding. I prefer to make it as easy as possible on resale, so I am agreeable to taking back a second mortgage or Deed of Trust for all or part of what the buyer can't borrow. Many lenders allow sellers to do this, provid-ing the buyer qualifies for a loan. 75% of $150,000 is $112,500, indicating a gross profit cash wise of $28,500, the difference between the $84,000 paid and the $112,500 new loan.

A Million in Hand

After subtracting closing costs, commissions, etc., maybe this will be cut to $15,000, but $15,000 times thirty-five amounts to $525,000 plus you have a second mortgage on each unit for an additional $590,625. You've just made yourself a million dollars and yet sold every unit for no-money-down. If you can get even $5,000 from the buyers as a down payment, you've increased your cash tremendously. Do you think you can sell a fourplex for no-money-down?

Want all cash? Sell your second mortgage or trade them as cash for something else.

If using a realtor to resell them, the realtor will more than likely cut his or her commission as well since the person gets thirty-five sales. Here is a case whereby a realtor actually sells something for no-money-down, yet gets a cash commission. That in itself is something most realtors don't believe can happen.

Try for a Simultaneous Closing

The object is to close without using your money. To accomplish this type closing, try and get all loans to close the same day. A Title Company will be most happy to work with you since they stand to get paid on thirty-six closing, not just one. Try for a four to six-month escrow period, longer if possible. This will give you the time to sell the individual units before closing. Even if you don't sell them all, sell enough to come up with the three million to pay off the seller. Selling for no-money-down should mean quick sales, eliminating you from worrying about selling. Don't be greedy! It's much easier to sell for little or no-money-down rather than $37,500 down. Once you've sold enough to cover your purchase price, you can sell for all cash to the rest of your buyers.

Review

You should buy collectively at about 50% to 60% of what the units will sell for individually. Be sure you know what the units will resell for before buying and be sure you have your individual financing in place before closing. If nothing else, get a commitment from a lender to make these loans beforehand. You can always take this commitment to a short-term lender to buy the project. The lender will loan based on the commitment, not you. Your credit and financial situation are secondary.

Make a Million Dollars Using Trees

A good friend and partner of mine by the name of Dan called me one evening to state that another student of mine did him in.I asked Dan what happened. He said, "Do you remem-ber that duplex I own?"

I replied, "Yes." He said, "Well, I sold it and took a $1,500 cash down payment and am carrying the financing. Your student asked if I would take a $1,500 note instead of cash for just one day for the down payment. I replied that I would and, when I returned the next day to pick up the $1,500, he had it all right, but the walnut tree in the back yard was gone! Your student sold the walnut tree for $1,500 and that was his down payment."

The Money Tree

Another student of mine reported that he had a better story. He found a farmer who had several hundred acres but some of the acreage was useless to him because it was loaded with walnut trees, and he didn't know what to do with that section of ground. My student offered to buy that acreage from him and because the owner thought the land was useless, my student was able to negotiate a very low price. After buying the land, my student proceeded to sell the walnut trees off the acreage for more money than he paid for the land plus the trees.

It is interesting to note that when trees are removed, the ground turns into what? That's right, farm ground. My student then sold this very same ground back for more money back to the original owner.

Making Money on Japanese Trees

If you're intrigued by this idea, consider looking for similar opportunities or even growing trees of your own. If you are going to grow trees, however, grow trees that mature very rapidly.

I had two students become millionaires in the Philadelphia area by finding property that had paulownia trees. Paulownia are Asiatic trees of the figwort family with large, heart-shaped leaves and large, erect clusters of violet flowers. I am told that they are much like bushes and grow very rapidly. This Japanese tree, I am told, is the only tree the Japanese use for their woodcarvings. Since there is a big shortage of these trees, their value is extremely high compared with other trees, and the trees aren't all that prevalent in Japan.

My two students were in the tree-removing business and were asked to remove trees for a client. While there, they noticed that the back part of his property was loaded with paulownia trees. My students stated that they would remove the trees the client wanted to be removed, free of charge, if the owner gave them the trees in the back. The owner had no idea what the trees were and, in fact, was disgusted with them because he couldn't use the land in the rear, so he readily agreed. My students removed the trees and sold them for over *one million in cash*.

Make a Million Dollars Using Water Rights

A few years ago I was in Denver giving a creative financing seminar when one of my students shared this experience with the class. Four thousand acres were for sale in Southpark, Colorado. Southpark is an area in between Colorado Springs and Breckenridge. There was no improvement on the land, and at the time it wasn't being used for anything. The asking price for the 4,000 acres was 2.5 million, all cash, no terms. My student offered 1.8 million cash even though he had no money.

It's very important to include a Weasel Clause with any offer you make when buying real estate; however, in this case you don't want to include a clause which could tip off the seller as to what you intend doing. You might make it "subject to" your attorney's approval, an appraisal, soil test, a partner approval, or even financing.

It's also very important to ask for everything that goes with your real estate purchase. Many times I've asked for the car in the garage, the furniture, etc., even though it may not have any interest to me. It could later be a very valuable negotiating tool. I also suggest you ask for everything that goes with land. You might include a paragraph such as this:

> All oil, gas, water and mineral rights and leases thereto, for subject property owned by seller shall be transferred to buyer at close of escrow.

Colorado Water Rights

In Colorado there is something that is more valuable than the land itself—that something is water rights. So, by including the above paragraph, my student was able to obtain the water rights with his purchase. Give yourself as long as possible before a closing date is set.

Once he had the property under contract, he controlled that property, even though he didn't yet own it. He then visited the city of Thornton, Colorado, and offered to sell all water rights to that city, except for just enough to operate the 4,000 acres. His asking price was 1.8 million. Interestingly enough, that was his purchase price.

The water rights proved to be worth 1.8 million, and the city of Thornton quickly jumped at the opportunity. He arranged a simultaneous closing so that the city of Thornton could provide him with the necessary cash to give to the seller. Instead of the funds coming from a lender to give to the seller, in this case, the funds came from the city of Thornton. My student walked out of closing with 4,000 acres free and clear, no mortgage payment ever! He now has the land rented for $9,000 per month. He just made 1.8 million buying and reselling part of what he purchased. Not bad for a day's work

I repeated that story in a seminar I was giving December 1982 in Denver, and in March of 1993 a student called to thank me for making him a millionaire. He did the same thing. You know what's so irritating to me—I lived in Colorado for nine years. Why didn't I do it?

Make Money with Vacant Schools

A major roadblock to being successful in real estate invest-ing is lack of creativity. Most tend to see things as they are and few have enough imagination to know what to do when opportunity strikes. If I were to ask you how much you'd pay for a 50,000 square foot building, all brick, on a 3-acre tract of ground, what would you say? You'd probably say, "What do I do with a 50,000 square foot vacant building?" And, yet, the profit potential of such a building is unlimited.

Let Your Imagination Do the Walking

I don't look to invest in motels or hotels as a motel or hotel, but rather I look at these opportunities as possible mini-warehouses, nursing homes, or efficiency apartments. A vacant school offers all sorts of opportunities if you'll just let your imagination do the walking.

The story I'm going to tell you about took place in the Kansas City area. A former student of mine, John, approached me about buying a 50,000 square foot, all brick grade school that had been vacant for almost four years. I asked the same question that many of you reading this are thinking: "What do I want with a vacant school?"

John replied that the school was in excellent condition, and the classrooms were large enough to inexpensively make the building into apartments or condominiums. He explained that the heating and air conditioning could be installed, using the type commonly found in motels, and the existing gym could be rented to a health group or other group who might need a large, open space for some sort of physical activity or equipment.

There was ample parking around the school and enough room to build fourplexes on the already commercially zoned playground. The school was built in sections so part of it could easily be turned into office space or office condos. The location was ideal, as most schools locations are, since it was close to downtown and in a very nice neighborhood. John reported that in his opinion, a duplicate structure would easily cost $750,000 or more.

I questioned John as to how one buys a school. He said that we would need to first contact the school board and indicate an interest in purchasing the building. To comply with the law, they would, in turn, advertise that the school would be going up for bids on a specific date. That, of course, meant that several others might show up and bid on the school.

I asked John if he had any idea as to how much we should bid, and he told me that the school board had a minimum bid amount fixed of $100,000. Anyway you slice it $100,000 for a 50,000 square foot commercial building on 3-acres of ground is dirt cheap, as long as you have a use for the building, and we did.

The Postal Connection

During this same period of time, the United States Post Office officials were advertising in the newspaper for a site, which just happened to be exactly where the school was located. Since the present post office was only four blocks away, we now thought in terms of turning the school quickly for a profit instead of developing it into condos or apartments. Our only concern was would the post office officials turn up and bid to buy the school? They, too, would find out that the minimum bid was $100,000. If they thought that no one else would be there, they would bid $100,000, so we changed our bid to $100,001 to give us a $1 edge.

As it turned out, our fears were for naught inasmuch as no post office official showed up to bid. They did find out about it the next day and called about bidding but by that time we were the successful bidders and our only problem was one of coming up with the $100,000 cash to buy. However, since we now controlled the only area of ground that the post office officials wanted, they had to end up calling us about buying the school.

To make a long story short, after much negotiation, we ended up offering to sell the school (which we did not yet own) to the post office officials for $250,000 cash. The post office officials paid our price.

Having a contract to sell to the post office made it very easy to borrow the necessary funds to buy the school. I went to my friendly banker and showed him my offer to pay $100,000 and the offer from the post office to pay us $250,000 and asked if he would advance me $100,000 to buy the school. This is about as risk-free as you can get. I borrowed the funds, paid cash for the school, and we waited patiently for the post office officials to pay us $250,000. This transaction was not one of those $1 million dollar profit deals, but $150,000 isn't all that bad for a no-money-down purchase.

I strongly recommend you look at the possibility of buying vacant schools. Again, they might make an excellent apartment complex, condo, or office possibility. Small church organizations that have their own school facilities are also excellent possibilities as purchasers. If nothing else, $200,000 for 3 acres of commercial ground is pretty inexpensive.

Use the Seller's Property to Buy

Several years ago I taught a seminar in Colorado Springs, Colorado. When lunchtime arrive, a gentleman asked me if he could buy my lunch and tell me his story. He stated that he had only lived in the Springs for one year, yet was able to purchase two businesses, an apartment complex, an office building and his own house in that period of time, and he started with just $16.00. Needless to say, I was interested in listening to his story.

He started by telling me that he had graduated from college one year earlier as an optometrist and at that time had never worked a day in his life, except for summer vacations. Further-more, he had no checking account and upon graduation had only $16.00 in his pocket.

The university offered suggestions as to where he might locate, and he decided on Colorado Springs, even though he had never been there before. Since he only had $16.00, he couldn't afford to drive home, so he headed directly for the Springs. On the way, he made up his mind that he never wanted to work for anyone, so he decided to immediately purchase his own business. The fact that he was fresh out of college, had no money, no credit, and no job history didn't seem to enter his mind.

After arriving in town, he drove around Colorado Springs and introduced himself to all the optometrists, always asking if they would be interested in selling. He finally found one who said yes, but he wanted a $25,000 cash down payment.

My student didn't feel that would be a problem since his future was in front of him.He felt he could borrow the necessary down payment from any bank in the area. He soon discovered his problem, however, when he visited several banks and each asked the same questions: Are you a banking customer? Do you live in town? Do you have any collateral? What is your job history? And, of course, how are you going to pay us back? Since he had never worked a day in his life and had no collateral, each banker turned him down.

He went back to the selling optometrist and asked him to reconsider and sell to him for no-money-down. The seller responded with "I want a $25,000 cash down payment." My student finally determined that the only way he could buy was to come up with $25,000 and the only way he could get the $25,000 from the bank was to provide the bank with collateral.

Since he had no collateral, he came up with the idea of using the seller's property as collateral. The only thing the seller had was equipment, so he asked the seller if he would consider giving him the equipment in exchange for the cash down payment, with the balance of the purchase price being secured by the business.

The seller quickly said yes. Now, my student had collateral which he could offer the bank for the $25,000 loan. However, in this case, the equipment only had a book value of $3,000, so the bank refused to lend him $25,000.

Instead of rolling over and playing dead, the buyer called a leasing company and asked if they would buy his very expensive equipment and lease it back to him. That's the business the leasing company was in, so all they did was ask him what the value of the equipment was. He replied $30,000. After all, it was worth $30,000 to him.

The leasing company doesn't inspect the equipment or take it out since they know you need it to operate. All they did was take out a blue book and ask the buyer what he could afford in the way of a payment. Naturally, he could afford anything!

By making a long story short, the leasing company agreed to the loan. At closing, they were there with $30,000, and the seller was there with a title to the equipment. The title went to the leasing company and $25,000 went to the seller, leaving the buyer with $5,000 in cash with which to start his business and find a home. My student stated that he now owned two businesses, an apartment complex, an office building, and his own home and he accomplished it all by using the equipment to get started.

More on Selling the Seller's Property

I was offered a Bible college, seventeen houses, and a sixteen-unit apartment complex at a purchase price of $2,350,000. The terms were $500,000 down and the seller was to carry the balance of $1,850,000 secured by the properties. I offered the seller's price of $2,350,000 and the $500,000 down payment but asked for the seller to give me the seventeen houses free and clear for the down payment. I stated that the worst that could happen to him was that he sold all seventeen houses and only had the Bible college and apartment complex left, so he couldn't lose. Again, he bought this and signed a purchase agreement.

Once the contract was signed, I controlled the seventeen houses and had every right to sell them subject to my taking title. If I could sell them before closing, I intended using these houses as security for a short-term loan at a bank. They were to sell in the $600,000 range, which would allow me enough to pay a realtor and other holding costs.

At closing, I owed the seller $1,850,000 and had title to the Bible college and the sixteen apartment complex. I really had no use for the Bible College, even thought it would have made a great office condo, additional facility for the university, or some other use.

My real interest was the apartment complex. My intentions were to sell the Bible College for no-money-down, $1,850,000 price and end up with the apartment complex free and clear. Sure, it would be tied into the mortgage balance of 1.8 million, but the purchaser of the Bible College would be making the payments, and I would end up with all the income on the 16-unit apartment complex and no mortgage payment. Not bad for a no-money-down transaction and the seller getting his cash.

How to Use Land to Buy or Sell

We've talked about using water rights, trees, equipment, furniture, cars, houses, and fourplexes for the down payment. Now, let's consider using land as the down payment. The important thing to remember is that you want to see something the seller owns to secure your down payment. That down payment can come from selling that security or offering it as collateral to the lending institution to borrow the down payment until what was taken as collateral sells.

When Everyone Wins

I knew a woman who had a lot appraised at $7,000. Desperate for cash, she reduced her asking price to $4,000, in cash. Unfor-tunately, no one was willing to pay her asking price, even though the price was below market value. I suggested we raise the price and lower the terms. I said, "Let's advertise the lot for $7.000, no-money-down, or perhaps a $500 or $1000 down payment if the market so dictated."

She said that amount wouldn't help. She needed $4,000 in cash. I assured her that she had nothing to worry about because we could sell the note and mortgage to an investor for $4,000 in cash. There are many investors who will buy a mortgage or Deed of Trust at a discount.

The seller received her $4,000 in cash. She won! The investor purchased a $7,000 mortgage for $4,000 cash secured by the property, so the investor won!. The buyer of the lot purchased for no-money-down and will make payments to the investor who purchased the note and mortgage, so the buyer won! In fact, everyone won!

A Similar Story

I told that story one weekend and a student of mine rushed up to me to saying that I had just showed her how to sell everything she owned. She said that she, too, had land, but she was going to sell it using a slightly different approach. Instead of raising the price and lowering the terms, she indicated that she would give the buyer something to use as a down payment.

For illustrative purposes, let's say she had 50 acres of land, and she wanted $5,000 in cash as a down payment and was willing to carry the balance in the form of a note and mortgage. No one was willing to come up with the down payment. She said that she was going to advertise the property for sale but would give the buyer five acres free and clear for the $5,000 down payment which would allow the buyer to sell or use this five acres as collateral for the down payment money.

This transaction would not only eliminate a negative cash flow (an alligator) but would put her into a positive cash flow because she would now be receiving payments on her land. She wrote me six months later to report that she had successfully used this technique to sell everything she owned.

When buying or selling, feel free to ask the seller to give you something for the down payment, or as a seller, offer to give part of what you own in exchange for the down payment.

Make $500,000 with No Money

Let's piggy back a little on asking the seller to give you some-thing for the down payment. I assisted a man who wanted to purchase 88 fourplexes. His intention was to buy all 88 and resell each individually, making a profit of $500,000 in twelve months. That is exactly what he did.

His problem was one of coming up with the necessary down payment of $100,000. I suggested we ask the seller to give us fourplexes in exchange for the down payment. We first determined how many fourplexes we would need to create the $100,000 down payment and found that it would be necessary to sell two of them before closing to come up with the cash. Or, we could pledge the two as collateral to a bank and borrow the $100,000, telling the banker that we would pay off the $100,000 loan as the fourplexes sold.

The fourplexes were owned by a banker, and he immediately asked these questions, "Why should I do this? I'm giving you the collateral to come up with the down payment."

My response was simple: "What is the worst thing that could happen to you? You've sold 2 fourplexes for cash and only have 86 left. The best thing that could happen is that you've sold all 88." He bought this argument and my student made a $500,000 profit in one year.

Let's Do It Again

You don't have to think millions when doing these transactions, although it's much more fun when you do. You can make money on a smaller scale if the right opportunity presents itself.

Again, this example uses fourplexes, but this time there were only three fourplexes with which to work. My purchase price was $180,000 for all three. I asked my broker how much I could resell the three fourplexes for, and he responded with $75,000 each, or $225,000 total.

I tied up the three fourplexes with a promissory note for $1,000 due at closing and promptly resold all three fourplexes before taking title for $75,000 each, only this time to owner occupants. You may wonder how my broker could show the units without the seller finding out. If you are a real estate agent and stand to make a $20,000 commission or nothing at all, you find ways to get the people in. The client could be the appraiser, the lender, the insurance official, or a partner. You get the picture.

Again, all closings were set for the same day, however, in case it didn't happen, I had made arrangements to borrow the necessary funds to close on my purchase, using the resale contracts as security for the short-term loan.

The bank quickly agreed to the funding to take over the existing loan balances of $124,000 or $56,000. I told the banker I'd pay him off with the proceeds as the loans closed. In this case, I only made $45,000 gross but that was still not a bad deal for a no-money-down purchase and no risk.

Ending Thoughts

One thing I've noticed while traveling across the United States giving seminars is that many people just don't know how to handle failure, and, in fact, many people are afraid to try for fear of failure.

I know that everyone won't and can't make it to the top. However, keep in mind, that trying and failing is much better than not trying at all. Do you realize that a successful person fails more times than an unsuccessful person? Why?

Because those who are successful keep trying. On the other hand, a lot of us know more about losing than we do about winning. One of the most difficult times I have is when I am talking with a person who has really tried and hasn't yet made it.

The Fire

First, remember that failure is always relative to perspective. There is an old Norwegian tale about a fisherman who with his two sons went out for daily fishing fun. The catch was good, but by midafternoon a sudden storm blotted out the shoreline, leaving the men groping for the direction of home.

Meanwhile, at home, a fire broke out in the kitchen of their rustic cottage. Before it could be extinguished, the fire had destroyed the family's earthly possessions.

After a while, the father and sons were able to row safely ashore. The man's wife was waiting to tell him the tragic news of the fire. "Karl, fire has destroyed everything," she tearfully said. "We have nothing left."

But Karl was unmoved by the news. "Didn't you hear me, Karl?" she asked. "The house is gone!"

"Yes, I hear you," he replied. "But a few hours ago we were lost at sea. For hours I thought we would perish. Then, something happened; I saw a dim yellow glow in the distance. It grew larger and larger. We turned our boat toward the light. The same blaze which destroyed our home was the light which saved our lives."

When Failure Turns Sweet

Little commentary is needed on the lesson of the fire story. Failure is often success when seen from a different point of view. History is full of these teachings. Columbus, looking for a new route to India, failed in his intended mission but unintentionally opened a new world.

In 1872, a severe hot spell in California shriveled a farmer's entire grape crop. He sent his dried-up grapes to a grocer who advertised them as Peruvian Delicacies. They sold at a good price, and we've been eating raisins ever since.

Failure is largely determined by your point of view. It is almost impossible to think of anything, no matter how bad, which doesn't have some good in it, if you only look for it.

Failure Is Relative to Our Use of It

No one can evaluate the place of an event in life. Whether it is good or bad depends on how the circumstances are used. In John Wooden's biography there are a couple of meaningful lines: "Things turn out best for those who make the best of the way things turn out."

Over a hundred years ago in Tuscumbia, Alabama, a 19-month-old child was deprived of seeing and hearing. The child soon became mute. Yet, 24 years later, this child graduated cum laude from Radcliffe College. Helen Keller's closed eyes have opened the eyes of millions. There are times when the blind can lead the blind. Helen Keller did. Nothing is good or bad within itself. Value has some relationship to every event. The worst can be made to serve the best purposes if we know how to utilize it.

Failure Is Relative to Time

Did you ever consider the fact that people seldom know when a good day falls upon them? Wallace Hamilton tells an old story about a Chinese landowner who had a large estate. One day wild horses wandered onto his property. The horses were worth a fortune. The neighbors gathered to congratulate him on his good luck. The man stoically remarked, "How do you know I am lucky?"

Later the man's son was trying to break one of the horses. The boy was thrown and broke his leg. The neighbors tried to console the man on his misfortune. He asked again, "How do you know I have been unfortunate?"

A while later, when the king declared war, the landowner's son was exempted from military duty because of his broken leg. The neighbors came in to say how fortunate the man was. He asked the same question, "How do you know I am fortunate?"

How do we really know when we have had a good day? All of us have looked back on some happy experience that seemed good at the time, but later realized that those experiences turned out to be less than happy ones. We have had bad days, but far down the road we have been compelled to say, "It seemed terrible at the time, but as I look back, it was the best thing that ever happened to me."

Time turns a lot of failures into successes. The fact is you never really know when, or if, you have failed.

I recall a short time ago when a good friend of mine pleaded with me to help him buy a very expensive home. He wanted me to assist him with financing and making payments. I refused, and he was depressed and felt like a failure because of his inability to get me to help him.

Later, he called to thank me for not helping because he had found a home he could afford without my help, which was much better for his family.

A New Measure for Success

We need new standards by which to measure success. Genuine success is not climbing to the top of the heap and staying there. I know a lot of people who have arrived, but they aren't very happy. Success is doing what you can, with what you have, where you are.

People who succeed can look back on life and not be ashamed of what they see. No one who can do that is a failure.

Dear Abby

I recall reading a letter addressed to Dear Abby sometime ago, and I'd like to share that with you just as she printed it in her column:

"I'm forty years old, have a wonderful husband and a 14-year-old son. I have an inoperable brain tumor the size of a baseball. I've been through six weeks of radiation treatment, but I have absolutely no complaints.

The tumor has been a blessing because of the relationships it has mended, and for making individuals face their mortality seriously."

The woman then went on to ask Abby if she'd print the following, which she read daily and stated that it had helped her tremendously. I first heard this poem about ten years ago and every time I start feeling sorry for myself or come close to considering myself a failure, I, too, take out this poem and read it.

Today, upon a bus, I saw a lovely girl with golden hair.

She seemed so gay, I envied her and wished that I were
     half as fair.

I watched her as she rose to leave—I saw her hobble
     down the isle.

She had one leg and wore a crutch—but as she passed—a
     smile.

Oh God, forgive me when I whine. I have two legs, the
     world is mine.

Later on I bought some sweets; the boy that sold them
     had such charm.

I thought I'd stop and talk awhile—if I were late, it would
     do no harm.

As we talked, he said, "Thank you, sir—you've been so
     very kind.

It's nice to talk with folks like you, because you see, I'm
     blind."

Oh God, forgive me when I whine. I'm blessed indeed,
     the world is mine.

Later walking down the street I met a boy with eyes of
     blue.

But he stood and watched the others play—it seemed he
     knew not what to do.

I looked and then I said, "Why don't you join the others,
     dear?"

He looked straight ahead without a word and then I knew,
     he could not hear.

Oh God, forgive me when I whine. I have two ears and
     the world is mine.

Two legs to take me where I go,

Two eyes to see the sun set glow,

Two ears to hear all I should know,

Oh God, forgive us as we whine. We're blessed and the
     world is mine.

I can think of no better way to end. I hope I've touched each one of you in some way and that each of you becomes the success you want to become. Just remember: "Yesterday is a cancelled check, tomorrow a promissory note, but today is golden opportunity."